The Orderly Entrepreneur

D0729553

Anthropology of Policy

Cris Shore and Susan Wright, editors

The Orderly Entrepreneur

Youth, Education, and Governance in Rwanda

Catherine A. Honeyman

Stanford University Press
Stanford, California

Stanford University Press
Stanford, California

© 2016 by the Board of Trustees of the Leland Stanford Junior University. All rights reserved.

No part of this book may be reproduced or transmitted in any form or by any means, electronic or mechanical, including photocopying and recording, or in any information storage or retrieval system without the prior written permission of Stanford University Press.

Printed in the United States of America on acid-free, archival-quality paper

Library of Congress Cataloging-in-Publication Data

Names: Honeyman, Catherine A., author.

Title: The orderly entrepreneur : youth, education, and governance in Rwanda / Catherine A. Honeyman.

Other titles: Anthropology of policy (Stanford, Calif.)

Description: Stanford, California : Stanford University Press, 2016. |

Series: Anthropology of policy | Includes bibliographical references and index.

Identifiers: LCCN 2016001494 (print) | LCCN 2016007831 (ebook) | ISBN 9780804797979 (cloth : alk. paper) | ISBN 9780804799850 (pbk. : alk. paper) | ISBN 9780804799867 (e-book)

Subjects: LCSH: Entrepreneurship—Study and teaching (Secondary)—Rwanda. | Education, Secondary—Curricula—Rwanda. | Education and state—Rwanda. | Economic development—Rwanda.

Classification: LCC HB615 .H66 2016 (print) | LCC HB615 (ebook) | DDC 658.4/21071267571—dc23 LC record available at http://lccn.loc.gov/2016001494

Designed by Bruce Lundquist

Typeset by Newgen in 10.5/15 Brill

To Gitta and Don, who left before they could read this: I would have liked to tell you these stories, as you so often told me yours. And to Naim and Elena, who arrived in the middle of it all, and who will surely be writing their own stories soon.

Contents

Figures and Tables

Figures

Tables

Preface

AFTER SUNSET, WHEN KIGALI comes alive with all of the people returning home from work, there is always a group of women waiting in the shadows at the major intersection closest to my home. Standing outside the shops, they search for clients among the people and vehicles that fill the streets.

But before you jump to the wrong conclusion, I should clarify—these women have quite an innocent occupation. They sell fruit: pineapples with juice dripping down their sides, neatly tied bags of passion fruit and tree tomatoes, shiny green imported apples, golden-skinned finger bananas.

Except that, these days, these products are rarely visible at the intersection.

Linger in the crowd with me for a few minutes when the local police are around, and this is what you will see: with empty hands, these women run to each car that pulls up, asking if the occupants would like to buy their fruit. If they find a potential client, they dash back through a worn-looking door, tucked back in the shadows beside the more-established shops. A few moments later, they emerge again, running with fruit in hand, hoping to make their sale before the buyer loses interest and drives on. Along the way, these women often glance over their shoulders for the police.

This is not how it used to be. At one time, the side of the road at this intersection was crowded with women carrying their merchandise in wide baskets atop their heads and in woven bags slung over each arm. Near them, you could always find a young man or two selling sweets and biscuits from a cardboard box. Needed to clean the dust off your shoes before venturing into town? Someone was always carrying around packages of tissues for 100 francs each.

Once a characteristic image of street life just about anywhere on the African continent, this sort of scene has almost disappeared in Rwanda. Street businesses have been tidied up and brought into the formal market, and they are required to have a fixed and formal place of business. Prepared foods must be properly labeled and inspected for consumer safety; motorcycle taxi drivers must belong to a cooperative, wear numbered uniforms, and provide helmets; all businesses must register, obtain a license, and become part of the tax system.

These are all sensible regulations, arguably modeled on the way things work in many developed economies. And in Rwanda, they are enforced with increasing effectiveness each year. This is Rwanda's contemporary aesthetic of entrepreneurship, of national progress: clean streets, orderly businesses, everything registered and known—an orderly and regulated form of self-reliance from the broadest policies down to the tiniest details.

In Rwanda, in other words, the streetside "lemonade stand" wouldn't be considered an iconic and positive image of the youthful entrepreneur—it would be disorderly conduct, plain and simple. And yet the Rwandan government is in favor of youth entrepreneurship. Highly in favor, in fact. Rwanda is the site of one of the most extensive efforts to promote youth entrepreneurship in the world—since 2009, all secondary school students have been required to take a six-year course in entrepreneurship, with equal weight as their other principal academic subjects. And just like their other subjects, this course is examinable on the high-stakes national examinations that are popularly seen as determining access to university—and therefore to "good" jobs.

Youth entrepreneurship promotion in Rwanda, however, can sometimes seem like a contradiction in terms. Efforts toward self-reliance meet regulations that present significant barriers to small business start-ups. At the same time, rote learning in schools with an emphasis on examinations often seems incompatible with independent problem solving. Cultivating entrepreneurial creativity may, in other words, conflict in real ways with the simultaneous emphasis on introducing controls to regulate an orderly process of development, and with the widespread perception that school is more about acquiring credentials than capabilities.

And yet this delicate, tension-filled balance of creativity, credentials, and controls is in fact just what the Rwandan government hopes to achieve as it works to harness the population's entrepreneurial initiative in service of national development. And Rwanda is not alone. A number of former developmental states with strong traditions of state regulation and strategic economic planning—such as China, Singapore, South Korea, and Taiwan—are pursuing goals essentially along the same lines. Like Rwanda, these states are all involved in attempts to transform their educational systems in order to promote qualities like creativity, independent problem solving, and entrepreneurial initiative while still retaining a strong state role in a regulated process of economic growth.

Since Rwanda has explicitly adopted Singapore as a role model, this similarity is no coincidence. In an age when these very states play such a key role in the world economy, a consideration of the economic and social ideals that are being produced in countries as distant as Rwanda and Singapore is both timely and globally relevant. In this book, I argue that Rwanda's experience with entrepreneurship education provides insight into a "post-developmental" approach to governance that is rising on the world stage, promoting an ethos of regulated self-reliance and envisioning the ideal citizen as a sort of orderly entrepreneur.

The purpose of this study is neither to praise nor to critique the post-developmental style of governance. My objective is to bring together a set of ideas that will make it possible to discuss what is happening in such disparate parts of the world, countries that—while they will likely never share a single form of government—nonetheless may be developing a recognizably similar style of governance. I also seek to make available my observations of the underlying processes at work in the cultivation of the orderly entrepreneur in one particular context among Rwanda's youth studying in or near the country's capital, Kigali. For young people, not surprisingly, have their own perspectives on the policies that are intended to shape them into orderly entrepreneurs, and it is their interpretations and reinterpretations that will help determine the eventual significance of these governmental strategies.

As a dual Rwandan-American citizen, business owner, friend and advocate for young people in my Kigali neighborhood, and as a mother, I also hope for the best possible future for Rwanda's youth. May this book provide insight into their abilities, their aspirations, and the challenges they face, in order to inform continual refinement of the policies intended to support their efforts.

Acknowledgments

THIS BOOK HAS COME into being thanks to the willingness of a significant number of Rwandan policy makers and NGO staff, curriculum developers and teachers, and—especially—young Rwandans, to share their ideas and experiences with me. I am particularly grateful to the graduates in this study for welcoming me into their homes, to the students and teachers in this study for allowing me to sit week after week in their classrooms, and to the staff at the former National Curriculum Development Centre for giving me the opportunity to understand firsthand how they do their work. Everyone featured in the following pages has been given a pseudonym to protect their privacy, so I cannot name their names here but to all those of you who took the time to have real and often challenging conversations with me: thank you.

I also owe a great debt of thanks to Flora Mutimukeye, my research assistant, who very capably accompanied me through more than half of this long research process. She has been extraordinarily patient with me and with this project. Much more than just providing translation and doing some of the difficult repetitive work involved in research, I relied on her to help me get to know the students in this study and to help me understand their perspectives. Any errors I have committed in the process of conducting this research or interpreting its results, however, are my mistakes alone and not hers.

To my professors and classmates at the University of Wisconsin–Madison: thank you for the good books, difficult ideas, and helpful advice. Professors Amy Stambach, Stacey Lee, Nancy Kendall, Anne Miner, and Jeremy Foltz deserve particular acknowledgment for guiding me in the preparation of the doctoral dissertation that became this book. There are also a number of other teachers, from university and before, whom I would like to acknowledge here for the many ways in which they contributed to my own learning and to my understanding of what it means to educate the next generation: Mary Gooze, Leyla

Sanyer, Carina Voly, Jody Spiwak, Gail Gregory, Brian Root, Cynthia Ellestad, Eleanor Sapiro-Mitten, Swanee Hunt, Fernando Reimers, Erin Murphy-Graham, and Daniel Pekarsky.

My appreciation also goes to the Scott Kloeck-Jenson international research grant for helping me fund the first steps of this research, and the two programs—the UW University Fellowship and the Jacob K. Javits Fellowship—that supported my graduate studies. Finally, I thank the editors of the Anthropology of Policy series Susan Wright and Cris Shore, as well as Michelle Lipinski at Stanford University Press, for believing in the value of this book and for helping me refine it.

I was privileged to have a small group of friends in Rwanda offer to read and comment on this manuscript before publication. Thank you to Sofia Cozzolino, Michael Kalisa, Jessica Massie, Isabelle Umugwaneza, Rayshawn Whitford, and, of course, Flora Mutimuyeke. Your detailed and often passionately argued suggestions have helped me more than you may know.

To my parents, my first and last readers, my support throughout: thank you for teaching me to write by allowing me to "edit" your papers, and thank you for giving so much time and thoughtfulness to help me edit mine. To Neil, my partner in all things: without you I would never have begun this very long journey, much less have been able to persevere up to the end. Thank you for the well-timed chocolate and child care, for the seriousness and the laughter, and for the good company every step of the way. And to Naim and Elena: thank you, among other joys, for the excuse to take a walk and gain a little perspective, with our frequent visits to the kinds of farms that continue to sustain the livelihoods of so many Rwandans today.

The Orderly Entrepreneur

Part I
Envisioning the Orderly Entrepreneur

Figure 1   A clean Kigali streetscape

Source: Photo credit Odessa Cozzolino.

Chapter 1

Creativity, Credentials, and Controls

A FEW MILES OUTSIDE of central Kigali, our car rolled through a rural town featuring the same cluster of businesses that one can find just about anywhere in Rwanda: tiny shops selling dry goods, a few places to get a cup of tea or fresh milk, and a group of youngish men waiting around for customers to ride on their bicycle taxis. Only the buildings painted with advertisements for a telephone company (bright yellow) and a popular kind of beer (bright blue) added variety to the otherwise dusty brown of all the buildings.

Past the trading center, my research assistant Flora and I continued along a rutted dirt road to a public school, where a few hundred students in uniform were leaving their classrooms to go home for the day. A small group of students remained, occupying the school canteen while they enjoyed a cup of sweet milky tea and square *mandazi* doughnuts.

These students were members of the first nationwide cohort to study the new course in entrepreneurship implemented by the Rwandan government in 2009, and they would soon graduate from Rwanda's nine-year basic education cycle. Like their classmates, they had kindly agreed to participate in a focus-group discussion for this research. Our conversation began with the students talking about their families and their hopes for the future. For several minutes, they spoke passionately about the problem of youth unemployment and how it would affect them. "Who do you think is responsible for solving this problem?" we asked.

One student raised her hand: "It's each one of us, personally. Maybe you don't sit at home, [but instead] you go sell something [. . .] Create a job for yourself, selling. Or maybe go outside, because there are many people in the countryside that want things, for example cloth. You could go and bring things to sell even in the countryside, not just stay in the city."

"Me, I think that people could make an association," her classmate added. "Let's say, groups of, like, ten people, to look for the kind of work they'll do together."

Nodding, another classmate continued: "Don't refuse any job, do what you find. Don't underestimate the value of a job, [be willing to] use your arms."

These students had apparently learned their entrepreneurship lessons well. A consensus seemed to be developing among the group: the responsibility for solving Rwanda's problems of youth unemployment falls on the individual; all the country needs are more entrepreneurial citizens who understand the value of hard work and take the initiative to create their own jobs.

Checking that we had understood their perspective, we asked one more time: "So—if you had to choose between, for example, the government, the wealthy, employers, or the population in general—who is most responsible for solving the problem of unemployment?"

To our surprise, four other students spoke up simultaneously, apparently directly contradicting their classmates' earlier remarks. "It's the government!" they exclaimed.

"Why the government? Let me hear each one of you," Flora probed.

"Because it's the government that makes the laws," one student began. "They make it so that people come to a common understanding, and then that's how [unemployment] can end [. . .] You see, the authorities, when they tell the population to do this and that—if they say to go make associations, then people will do it. But if they don't say anything, then they aren't giving you the right to do it. There could be a time that you create something without permission, and then it fails; you see that they have refused to allow you to do it. And then there are those taxes, too, and everything. But if they established a regulation to say that 'such-and-such group will do this'—for example, weave people's hair—then people will say, 'let's do that,' and then they would get together to do it. In that case, poverty could be defeated and there would be work available."

Her friend added, "But that all depends on the understanding of the people [. . .] If they don't agree, the government can't do anything—because then even if the government made a law, the population wouldn't follow [. . .] But if people understand and agree, then the population will join together. And then the government can make a law, and the people will get together and look for a kind of work to do in order to develop and advance."

Again, other students in the group nodded in agreement. A new consensus had apparently been reached: solving unemployment in Rwanda depends not only on entrepreneurial initiative but also on government regulation and a population willing to be regulated.[1]

. . .

Self-reliant yet strongly state-regulated—this particular approach to entrepreneurship and national development is a recurring theme in Rwanda today. In government offices and in policy meetings, on radio and in the newspapers, in the classrooms of every secondary school, and in towns and cities around the country, this same idea is disseminated, discussed, encouraged, and enacted. To understand the outlook for youth livelihoods and even personal identity in contemporary Rwanda, one must first explore this intriguing paradox: in Rwanda, calls for greater entrepreneurial self-reliance and creativity jostle elbow-to-elbow with expectations of increased governmental regulation and controls. What that paradox looks like in practice—and whether it is viable in the long term—is the question at the heart of this book.

Regulated Self Reliance and the Orderly Entrepreneur

In much of the world, Rwanda is best known for its complex and emotionally fraught history; but what is happening in Rwanda today is no less significant. The first generation of children born after the 1994 Genocide against the Tutsi is just now reaching maturity, hoping to take up their adult roles in Rwandan society and economy. Rwanda's postgenocide government is also forging an increasingly confident and independent path, characterized by its own emerging philosophy of business-friendly yet strongly state-regulated social and economic development. Even as some Western countries continue to debate the reasons for their recent economic crises, Rwanda has confidently settled on a strategy for twenty-first-century economic growth that draws on the recent experiences of a number of East and Southeast Asian regimes. Combining a strong-state "developmental" approach with certain entrepreneurial ideals learned from free-market neoliberalism, these countries are pursuing a new form of governance that is quickly rising to prominence on the global scene.

Conventionally, developmental and neoliberal approaches to governance have been framed as contradictory (Fishlow, 1994). Neoliberalism emphasizes free-market mechanisms and individual responsibility, and characterizes government as an obstacle to growth. In contrast, developmental states privilege state-centered economic intervention and planned development, with strong confidence in the guiding power of state regulations. Despite these apparent contradictions, however, a number of governments are experimenting with a combination of these two approaches, in what might be called a neoliberal-developmental (Liow, 2011) or post-developmental form of governance (Baildon, 2009; Ismail, Shaw, & Ooi, 2009; Ong, 2006).[2] Regardless of the particular label one favors, a number of states with dramatic recent histories of economic growth—including Singapore, South Korea, China, Taiwan, and now Rwanda—seem to be converging on a style of governance that places an ethos of regulated self-reliance at its core.

The following pages explore how this rising style of governance takes shape in practice, as it is re-created in new contexts, and as it is interpreted and re-interpreted by policy makers and citizens alike. Using Rwanda as a case study, I examine the internal tensions of the post-developmental state through an investigation of one iconic policy initiative—the Rwandan government's decision that a course in entrepreneurship should be required learning during all six years of secondary school. This policy, I argue, exemplifies how transformations in economies and governments are often deeply intertwined with learning processes—both within and outside school walls.

In late 2007, the Rwandan government published a new national policy document, the Economic Development and Poverty Reduction Strategy (EDPRS) for 2008–2012. Among hundreds of recommendations, the EDPRS document called for the secondary school curriculum to be revised in order to include entrepreneurship as a major topic of instruction (Rwanda, 2007). As a result, when today's Rwandan secondary school students graduate, they have spent nearly five hundred hours learning about entrepreneurship over the course of six years of required classes. During that time, they have learned about entrepreneurial qualities such as initiative and creativity, and they have been introduced to the basics of business planning. They have studied various forms of commerce, basic commercial law, and accounting methods. Yet they also graduate into an economic context in which many formerly common microscale enterprises are now illegal or discouraged, in which some rural forms of entrepreneurship are channeled into specific mandated activities, and in which government oversight of business registration and taxpaying is increasingly far-reaching and effective.

On the one hand, this policy of entrepreneurship education suggests that young Rwandans should be self-reliant; creatively and resourcefully finding their own ways to make a living and move ahead. On the other hand, the same policy—along with Rwanda's extensive regulatory regime—insists that this very entrepreneurial resourcefulness must be orderly, regulated, and to some extent strategized and planned from above. Today's Rwandan secondary students, in short, are expected to become a generation of orderly entrepreneurs.

Development's Next "Top Model": The Post-Developmental State?

Changes are afoot on the global political and economic scene. Following the 2007–2008 global financial crisis, a flood of commentators and analysts began asking—regarding the economic systems that seemed responsible for the collapse—"If not this, then what?" For the first time in years, free-market principles that had become largely taken-for-granted truths in much of the world began to be questioned in mainstream public conversation. If the United States was ever considered the global model to follow, that no longer seemed to be the case—eyes everywhere began to turn in search of other options. "Whether new political and economic policies will emerge from this [financial] crisis, and what forms they may take," an issue of the journal *Development Dialogue* began, "are among the most important political and social questions of our times" (Brand & Sekler, 2009, p. 5). It was as if a new competition had suddenly opened up in the field of international development, in search of the next "top model" (see Birdsall, 2011, fig. 2). A transformation in the dominant approach toward economic management and governance, in other words, began to seem truly possible— potentially on a world scale.

Many commentators have suggested that countries with a stronger state role in the economy—such as China and Singapore—came out of the financial crisis in a new position of prominence and prestige, poised to become models for developing countries like Rwanda (Birdsall & Fukuyama, 2011a, 2011b; Callick, 2008; Chen, 2011).[3] And indeed, prior to the crisis Singapore in particular was already enjoying a rising reputation for its effective management of economic growth.[4] For eight consecutive years, the World Bank (WB, 2015) has listed Singapore as the easiest place to do business in the world. The World Bank Group also launched the "Singapore Hub" think tank to "leverage Singapore's expertise and the WBG's global development knowledge and operational experience for the benefit of developing countries" (WB & Singapore, 2010). Also reflecting the international interest in Singapore's approach to governance and development,

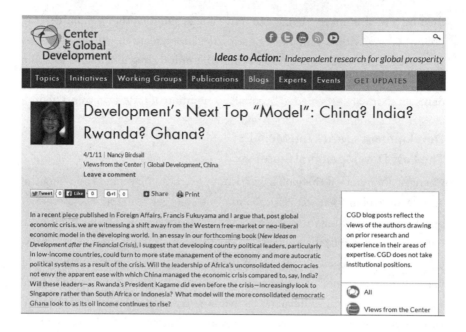

Figure 2   A commentator discussing new models for international development on the rise

Source: Courtesy of the Center for Global Development (www.cgdev.org).

the Singapore Cooperation Enterprise—Singapore's answer to bilateral development agencies—was set up not as a donor organization but as a consulting firm, intended to "respond effectively to the many foreign requests to tap into Singapore's development experience" (SCE, 2011).

As a model, reference to present-day Singapore calls attention to its simultaneously business-friendly policies and effective regulation, economic development with strategic state involvement in certain sectors, a combination of individual responsibility and social welfare policies, and maintenance of order and orderliness—albeit through far-reaching social regulations that are sometimes labeled "authoritarian." Advocates for the "Singapore model" characterize the government's approach as that of a benevolent strong state. Singapore's style of governance, they argue, has led to "one of the highest standards of living in Asia [. . .], benefited the vast majority of citizens, and given them full opportunities to develop their human potential" (Teo, 2008).

Singapore's economic success in the latter half of the twentieth century—like that of Botswana, China, Indonesia, Japan, Malaysia, South Korea, Taiwan, and Thailand—has been ascribed to its "developmental" state characteristics (Johnson, 1982). In all these states, "power, autonomy, and capacity" were sufficiently centrally concentrated to allow the government to "shape, pursue, and encourage the achievement of explicit developmental objectives," in the process deliberately determining the conditions of economic growth (Leftwich, 1995, p. 401). Guidance, regulation, and control were central features of the developmental approach to governance.

From an anthropological perspective, and following Foucault's (1991) writings on governmentality, the developmental state's emphasis on regulation and controls could be considered the enactment of a particular political rationality—an underlying form of reasoning that specifies, in numerous subtle ways, the appropriate goals for governance and the means for achieving them. Conventionally, government is thought of in terms of legal and administrative structures. But the practice of governing also involves complex and often unstated personal and social understandings: our assumptions about what it means to govern others and ourselves (Dean, 2010). Each particular governmental rationality is linked to technologies of power   programs, techniques, documents, and procedures— that structure the range of choices available and that promulgate governmental assumptions down to the level of citizens' very conception of themselves (Bröckling, Krasmann, & Lemke, 2011; Dean, 2010; Foucault, 1991; Lemke, 2002; Rose & Miller, 1992; Shore & Wright, 1997; Shore, Wright, & Peró, 2011).

Developmental state technologies of power, in combination, produced citizens who not only were highly regulated but also, more particularly, were *willing* to abide by regulations as part of their participation in the nation's development (Liow, 2011; McVeigh, 1998; Moon, 2005; Ooi & Limin, 2002; Sung, 2006). This shaping of citizen identity in developmental states was partially accomplished by harnessing citizen participation in highly structured and examination-centered formal education systems in which educational processes and credentials were explicitly tailored to meet the needs of national development programs (Ismail et al., 2009; McVeigh, 1998; Sung, 2006; Trocki, 2006). In this respect, education systems in developmental states acted as disciplinary technologies (Foucault, 1975), establishing and reinforcing norms at the same time as sorting individuals into hierarchies of worth in relation to government plans.

Yet citizens' acceptance of these highly stratified educational systems, just as their acceptance of strong state regulation in general, depended on the ability of the developmental state to guarantee a correspondence between educational credentials and economic opportunities (Sung, 2006; Trocki, 2006). Developmental states earned citizens' willingness to be regulated by promising certain tangible benefits: an effective and ongoing process of economic development and the guarantee that those who followed the rules would be awarded jobs and social roles in a continuous process of upward economic mobility from generation to generation.

Formerly developmental states like Singapore have more recently, however, been backing away from such guarantees for large segments of their populations as they move in a more neoliberal direction (Ong, 2006). In place of predictable economic roles and stable long-term employment, Singapore has joined the global shift toward part-time, outsourced, and temporary occupations demanding continual "reskilling," as workers have been expected to transform themselves and their capacities to fit into different positions in a rapidly changing economic context. In parallel, there are new demands for a different and more flexible role for school credentials, transforming curricular offerings in a more "practical" and "modular" direction to equip students with the versatile skills needed to find or create their own livelihoods in an unpredictable economy, as well as to become drivers of constant innovation for economic growth (Bash & Green, 1995; Hoppers, 2009; Noakes, 1997; UNESCO, 1999; UNESCO & International Labour Organization, ILO, 2002).

The developmental state promise of a guaranteed role in an expanding economy no longer seems suited to the modern age. Singapore and other states in the region have responded to global economic transformations by shifting toward a hybrid post-developmental model that increasingly emphasizes neoliberal ideas of the need for enterprising self-reliance (Baildon, 2009, p. 60). The "enterprising individual" takes responsibility for his or her own life decisions and uses personal initiative to struggle and advance (Heelas, 1991). In an uncertain economic environment, which may often result in rapid obsolescence of skills and long periods of unemployment, entrepreneurial self-reliance requires significant creative abilities. Individuals must be ready to innovate new technologies or quickly adapt to them, they must be resourceful in resource-constrained situations, and they often must create opportunities from whatever materials or resources are at hand (Baker & Nelson, 2005). They cannot, above all, rely on the state to guarantee their own social and economic position—they must create a useful role for themselves.

But the replacement of disciplinary technologies by neoliberal ones is not complete under post-developmental approaches to governance. In particular, post-developmental regimes may want to continue to pursue strong social and economic regulation in certain spheres. At the same time, their very emphasis on individual responsibility and technologies of the self may seem more like state-centered social engineering than laissez-faire. The speech delivered by Singapore's Prime Minister Goh Chok Tong on the occasion of the 1997 educational policy reform called Thinking Schools, Learning Nation illustrates how this sort of limbo between developmental and neoliberal approaches influences the educational realm:

We will bring about a mindset change among Singaporeans. We must get away from the idea that it is only the people at the top who should be thinking, and the job of everyone else is to do as told. Instead we want to bring about a spirit of innovation, of learning by doing, of everyone each at his own level all the time asking how he can do his job better. With such an approach of always looking out for improvement, always asking what is the purpose of our job and whether there is a better way to accomplish that purpose, we will achieve our ambition of national excellence [. . .] Such a national attitude is a must for Singapore to sustain its prosperity. (Tong, 1997)

However much these goals—creativity, innovation, initiative, flexibility, self-reliance in an environment of constant change—reflect a neoliberal rationality, in post-developmental states like Singapore they are nonetheless framed as state-centered development programs, centrally mandated and focused on economic survival for the nation.

Under the post-developmental political rationality, it is the government that determines the nation's educational needs and mandates the best approaches to accomplish that transformation. Yet post-developmental states avoid promising a predictable correspondence between educational credentials and a guaranteed position in a steadily growing economy—instead emphasizing citizens' responsibilities for creating those conditions for themselves. Post-developmental regimes, in short, want to have it both ways: to retain their autonomy in guiding and regulating their societies and economies while simultaneously reducing their responsibility for guaranteeing each citizen a place in that system.

Rwanda as a Post-Developmental State

Rwandan President Paul Kagame has often cited Singapore as his development ideal, remarking that "Singapore's rapid socioeconomic transformation" provides "an inspiration for Rwanda" (Kagame meets for talks, 2008). Rwanda is one of the many countries that have become "clients" of the Singapore Cooperation Enterprise, and Singaporean companies and consultants have been involved in Rwandan sectors as disparate as urban planning, vocational education, and information and communications technology. Although Rwandan policy makers recognize that Singapore's reality is different from their own, its whole approach to governance and economic growth—a hybrid post-developmental approach with developmental roots and select neoliberal sensibilities—has become part of the public imagination about Rwanda's hoped-for future (see, for example, Karinganire, 2013, fig. 3).

Unlike Singapore and the other post-developmental "Asian Tigers," however, Rwanda is not building on a conventional developmental state past. To what extent, then, does it make sense to label Rwanda as *post*-developmental"?

In some ways, Rwanda's history does reflect certain developmental characteristics. Commenting on Rwanda's history can be difficult, since many of

Figure 3 Rwanda and Singapore are often linked in the media

Source: Courtesy of the Rwanda Focus, Focus Media Ltd., Kigali, Rwanda.

the published interpretations of the 1994 Genocide against the Tutsi, as well as of Rwanda's deeper history, have been strongly contested in Rwanda (Dallaire, 2004; Des Forges, 1999; Gourevitch, 1999; Mamdani, 2001; Newbury, 2009, 2011; Prunier, 1995; Straus & Waldorf, 2011; Uvin, 1998; Vansina, 2004). Yet one aspect of Rwanda's history that is largely agreed on within the country is the entrenched nature of values such as obedience, hierarchy, and respect for authority (MINALOC, 2001, 2004).[5] Although the value placed on obedience has never been simplistic or universal in Rwanda (Mulindahabi, 2015; Waldorf, 2007), Rwanda's precolonial history was characterized by the development of an increasingly effective and encompassing hierarchy of authority (Newbury, 2009). Respect for hierarchical authority, coupled with a high level of effective state power, was a major feature in Rwanda's ability to successfully institute development plans in the postindependence area (Uvin, 1998)—and many have argued that these Rwandan characteristics played a strong role in making the genocide itself possible (Prunier, 1995; Straus, 2006). Pregenocide Rwanda, in other words, reflected a number of characteristics of the developmental state, including centrally concentrated power, a high degree of autonomy for state leadership, and the institutional capacity to pursue specific development objectives (Leftwich, 1995, p. 401).

The postgenocide Rwandan government has pursued a number of strategies to address what it calls a historical "culture of passive obedience" (MINALOC, 2004, p. 11). These include extensive decentralization of government structures, the requirement that local government authorities be held publicly accountable to performance contracts (*imihigo*), and the annual live-broadcast National Dialogue (*Umushyikirano*), in which ordinary Rwandans question government leaders in person and via telephone, text message, and social media. Yet it is not a simple thing to change such entrenched disciplinary technologies of power and subjectivity. A number of researchers have pointed out ways that these characteristics continue to appear in contemporary Rwanda (Booth & Golooba-Mutebi, 2012; Campioni & Noack, 2012; Chemouni, 2014; Friedman, 2012; C. Huggins, 2013; Jones, de Oliveira, & Verhoeven, 2013; Purdéková, 2011, 2013; Reyntjens, 2013; Sommers, 2012; Straus & Waldorf, 2011; Sundberg, 2014).

Rwanda thus shares some historically rooted similarities with classical developmental states, but in an important sense Rwanda today is post-developmental by choice, not just as a result of a particular historical path. The massive civil and institutional destruction left in the wake of the 1994 genocide has allowed

Rwanda's governing regime to fundamentally reimagine the state in a hybrid neoliberal-developmental form, explicitly citing Singapore as the chosen model to follow. Like Singapore, the Rwandan government is interested in promoting a creative and entrepreneurial population while playing a strong developmental and regulatory role in Rwandan society and economy. Many of these "strong-state" policies have received significant international praise—such as Rwanda's far-reaching anticorruption measures, the strict cleanliness of its public spaces, the enforcement of environmental regulations and environmentally friendly public practices, the country's high level of organization in fields such as public health, and the development of a business registration and taxation system that will allow the government to become more independent from foreign aid (see, for example, Crisafulli & Redmond, 2012; Kayizzi-Mugerwa, 2000; Kinzer, 2008; Unsworth & Uvin, 2002; van Hoyweghen, 2000). Rwanda's effort to promote the private sector also appears to be paying off, given that the World Bank (2015) now lists Rwanda as the third best place to do business in sub-Saharan Africa, despite the fact that Rwanda has had a mere two decades to recover from the trauma of the 1994 genocide. Yet just like Singapore, even while Rwanda is widely praised for its strong and effective governance, it draws criticism for not conforming to Western democratic norms.

The post-developmental state, it seems, has become a traveling rationality of governance, available for interpretation and appropriation by Rwanda and other states around the world. Rwanda's attempt to promote post-developmental goals through a policy of entrepreneurship education hints at some of the internal tensions and contradictions that may be involved in trying to emulate this form of governance. Entrepreneurship education in Rwanda could, on the one hand, be seen as a quintessentially neoliberal project, involving an explicit attempt to cultivate the neoliberal ideal of the self-sufficient citizen who drives economic progress through entrepreneurial innovation and initiative, creating his or her own job and in the process creating employment for others. On the other hand, while a strict neoliberal perspective would expect these qualities to effervesce in a largely spontaneous way once barriers are removed, the Rwandan government is instead promoting them through what is essentially a well-intentioned social engineering project, using schools to manufacture changes in the attitudes and behaviors of young people. And the new curriculum exists as part of a policy ensemble that heavily emphasizes the importance of orderliness, centralized strategic planning, and regulation in business activities—all signals of the developmental state with strong central authority.

Entrepreneurship education in a post-developmental state thus results in quite a distinctive vision of the ideal entrepreneur. Just as in the rest of the world, entrepreneurship in Rwanda is envisioned as a creative and growth-oriented activity. But whereas the neoliberal iconic view of entrepreneurship suggests images of an improvising, bootstrapping, opportunistic, unpredictable, and even counterculture entrepreneurial pioneer, in Rwanda's post-developmental state, the ideal enterprise seems to be given a radically different emphasis: registered, organized, attractive, aesthetic, clean, and—in some settings—even conforming (see Table 1).[6]

Neither image of the ideal entrepreneur is necessarily right or wrong. Although both portraits evoke positive connotations and conceive of entrepreneurship as a creative and growth-oriented endeavor, one suggests that entrepreneurship by nature involves some disorderly aspects, while the other insists on orderly conduct from start to finish. Rwanda's entrepreneurship policies are thus tasked with simultaneously promoting both creativity and controls.

Each of these objectives for entrepreneurship education in Rwanda implies a different role for formal schooling. But they must also coexist with a third perspective of schools—a holdover from Rwanda's precolonial and colonial disciplinary state—as rewarding excellence in conformity to strict examination standards. This third competing educational goal, the awarding of credentials, has emerged as a catalyst for radical reinterpretation of Rwanda's entrepreneurship education policy. In a sense, curriculum developers, teachers, and students alike have "resisted" the policy simply by placing it within their default frame

Table 1   Comparing entrepreneurship ideals

Neoliberal entrepreneurship	Post-developmental entrepreneurship
· Creative, growth oriented	· Creative, growth oriented
· Improvising, bootstrapping	· Registered, visible, known
· Opportunistic, working around the rules	· Law abiding, tax paying
· Lone pioneer, charismatic	· Organized, grouped
· Burgeoning, unpredictable, organic	· Attractive, aesthetic, tidy, groomed
· Counterculture, unusual, fresh	· Clean and correct, conforming?
May be disorderly	Must be orderly

of reference for schooling: as a sorting mechanism primarily involving testing, credentials, and the resulting structured opportunities for individual social mobility. From this frame of reference, entrepreneurship education in Rwanda's schools is not primarily about cultivating the qualities of creativity, initiative, and problem solving, or even about instilling an attitude of law-abiding obedience. Instead, it is a matter of producing testable bits of information for examinations that could be used as currency in Rwanda's marketplace for credentials and formal employment.

Through the lens of Rwanda's entrepreneurship education policy, the post-developmental state is revealed as a precarious balancing act: attempting to cultivate creative self-reliance while still maintaining control over an orderly process of national development, all the while requiring a fundamental transformation in school culture that goes against teachers' and students' long-ingrained habits. As the post-developmental state attempts to juggle the triad of creativity, credentials, and controls, what will it take to keep all three balls in the air?

Observing Policy in Practice

Kigali, Rwanda's capital city, has an unusual natural topography. To get a sense of its striking beauty, you might turn to the extensive maps and models that have been put together for the Kigali Conceptual Master Plan, with their skyscrapers and gardens, planned housing, and highways contouring the hills (Oz, 2007, fig. 4). But that is only one way of appreciating the scene.

You would understand even more about the significance of this beautiful landscape in person, taking in the sight of some of Rwanda's "thousand hills" from the air, or moving closer to see the interconnecting patterns made by fields, banana groves, and roofs apparently stacked one atop another all along Kigali's slopes. You might also want to speak to and observe people of all kinds as they toil up Kigali's mountains on foot, freewheel down them on bicycle taxis, cruise around the bends in cars and minibuses, drive their cows out to pasture in what open grassland can still be found, farm their plots in the marshes, or as they simply enjoy the scenery of the city's ever-growing blanket of lights, draped each evening over Kigali's rolling hills and valleys.

A similar range of perspectives is available with any effort to study and understand the significance of a given government policy. To examine Rwanda's entrepreneurship education policy, you might read the major policy documents,

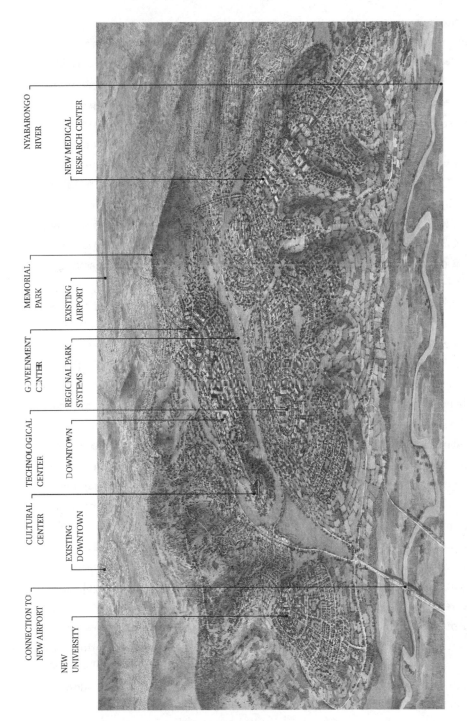

CONNECTION TO
NEW AIRPORT

NEW
UNIVERSITY

CULTURAL
CENTER

EXISTING
DOWNTOWN

TECHNOLOGICAL
CENTER

DOWNTOWN

GOVERNMENT
CENTER

REGIONAL PARK
SYSTEMS

MEMORIAL
PARK

EXISTING
AIRPORT

NYABARONGO
RIVER

NEW MEDICAL
RESEARCH CENTER

Figure 4   Urban design plans for Kigali

Source: Courtesy of OZ Architecture.

identify the problem the policy is apparently intended to solve, and investigate how effective it is in achieving that purpose. This is an accepted approach to policy analysis, and useful in its own way, but like a city model plan, it yields only a sort of schematic map of what might be going on. There is much more to be learned and understood by examining Rwanda's entrepreneurship education policy not simply as a rationalistic solution to specific social and economic problems but as an example of how changes in approaches to governance are produced and mediated in everyday life, by people in specific social situations.

The research presented in this book approaches policy as a social practice in all its complexity (Sutton & Levinson, 2001). An important assumption here is that a policy is *not* "made" once and for all and then implemented uniformly (Walford, 2003). Rwanda's policy has been shaped over time, multidirection-ally, through social interaction in various institutional and structural settings. There are policy makers at many levels—including other governments and international organizations, the government employees who write out the de-tails of official policy, the implementing teachers, and the target population of students themselves—and they all influence the form and significance of what is ostensibly a uniform national education policy.

Fundamentally, this is a work of anthropology: a close study of the ways peo-ple interpret the world around them, as well as the meanings they give to their own actions and reactions. An anthropological approach emphasizes the "social and cultural processes of interpretation, contestation, adaptation, compromise, and sometimes resistance" that shape all aspects of the policy process—from formulation to implementation and all of the sometimes messy steps that inter-vene before, during, and after (Hamann & Rosen, 2011, p. 465). An anthropologi-cal approach to policy research, in other words, begins by "asking not 'How does policy affect people?' but 'How do people engage with policy and what do *they* make of it?'" (Shore et al., 2011, p. 8). Anthropological studies of policy have shed a great deal of light on the nature of contemporary governance, and on neoliberal power in particular (Shore & Wright, 1997; Shore et al., 2011). Attention has been turning, however, to the question of what comes next (Hyatt, 2011). Research-ers working in traditionally neoliberal countries have talked of a transformation toward a law-and-order or security state that features a heightened emphasis on both state control and self-policing (Giroux, 2006; Hyatt, 2011). Here, I address the flip side of the coin: the transformation of traditionally disciplinary and de-velopmental states toward the greater incorporation of neoliberal technologies of the self. Both lines of research, in the end, suggest that we are currently witnessing a set of contrapuntal transformations on the global stage, toward hybrid forms of the neoliberal-developmental or neoliberal-security state.

It is worth asking, in this context: how could such a transformation in fundamental principles of governance around the world, or even in one country, come about? What exactly would have to change, and are such changes actually achievable by design? If a country like Rwanda, in other words, wanted to become more like Singapore, what would it take, and what are the chances that the effort would succeed?

ADVANCING THEORY IN THE ANTHROPOLOGY OF POLICY

Anthropological and other interpretive approaches have been used to examine transformations in governance in the context of how policies function and dysfunction, shape social practice and are shaped by it, define meaning and are reimagined, at a range of levels of social practice (Anderson-Levitt, 2003; Rizvi & Lingard, 2010; Shore et al., 2011). Yet the anthropology of policy is itself constrained by the theories it draws upon, as the dichotomy of structure versus agency maps itself onto these studies in a spatial way. Ideas such as governmentality, *dispositif*, and the social imaginary tend to emphasize the strongly constraining nature of power relationships and structure in ways that make them most appropriate for macro-level analyses. Anthropological studies that emphasize the agency of policy actors, in contrast, tend to focus on the connections and disjunctions between the meso- and micro-levels. Few interpretive studies of policy attempt a unified examination of international, national, institutional, local, and microsocial policy processes all at once in ways that transcend the structure-agency divide. Indeed, existing theoretical approaches do not readily lend themselves to moving continually between and among these contexts.

Here, I sidestep that conceptual and spatial dichotomy by examining the development of political subjectivities through the lens of a new theoretical construct, a model that emphasizes how transformations in governance must necessarily take place through processes of negotiated social learning within and between socially defined communities of practice at all levels of scope and scale.

Governance is at least partially an educative effort, using technologies of power to affect how people see and govern themselves. It requires people to learn certain ways of thinking and behaving in relation to one another—certain forms of social practice to match broader changes in structures of resources and rewards (Bourdieu, 1990). This is particularly the case when significant transformations in governance are under way, such as in the postcommunist states, or in Rwanda as it reinvented itself following the 1994 genocide. The educational aspect of the governing relationship, however, is not necessarily unidirectional from governor to governed. Policies must be performed, and in the process, they produce new and sometimes unexpected realities of relationships and meaning—realities that are often contested along the way (Shore & Wright, 2011).

Governance as an educational process thus involves negotiation rather than straightforward processes of transmission, because new approaches to governance necessarily take shape within multiple interacting communities of practice at all levels of the political hierarchy (Lave & Wenger, 1991). Each community of practice is characterized by its own preexisting set of shared dispositions or group culture, filters that define and redefine how new governing technologies are understood and enacted by policy makers and citizens alike. New ways of thinking and acting—the new subjectivities that underpin a given approach to governance—must therefore be worked out in complex processes of social interaction that are by no means predictable or predetermined.

In the context of this study, conceptualizing transformations in governance in terms of processes of negotiated social learning enables analysis of the connections between, on the one hand, the microsocial sites of negotiation occurring in relation to Rwanda's entrepreneurship education policy, and on the other hand, the larger national and international complexities of the country's shift toward a post-developmental rationality of governance. Following the formulation and transformations of the idea of entrepreneurship education in multiple communities of practice over time, this research shows how policy makers, policy advisers, teachers, and students all belong to multiple social groups, with particular relationships to schooling and livelihoods and the resources at stake in those fields. At the same time, it also illustrates how they bring their diverse preexisting dispositions to bear on the policy process in complex and often unexpected ways. What initially appears as a straightforward rational strategy for resolving a particular national problem of youth unemployment is therefore revealed to be full of social influences and indeterminacies every step of the way.

A perspective on governance as a negotiated process of social learning, in short, enables a unified investigation into how "the small details of social change that are observable in particular locations connect to wider processes of social, economic and political transformations," and it offers new insight into the processes through which we can observe "the emergence of new systems of governing and formations of power" (Wright, 2011, p. 27). A new system of governing—one characterized by an overarching political rationality of regulated self-reliance—is, indeed, currently emerging on the world stage. The Rwandan government's own particular contemporary vision of the ideal citizen's subjectivity, the notion of the orderly entrepreneur, is illustrative of that broader trend in governance.

RESEARCH TIMELINE, METHODS, AND APPROACH

To tell the story of Rwanda's post-developmental transformations, I draw on in-depth observations of, and interactions with, many different groups of people involved in different aspects of Rwanda's entrepreneurship education policy. I began the research in 2008 with written permission from the Minister of State in charge of primary and secondary school education—just a few months after the Rwandan government publicly announced its plans to introduce entrepreneurship education into secondary schools. The project was carried through the end of 2013, three years after the graduation of the first cohort of Rwandan students to receive at least one full year of entrepreneurship education. As a result, the research encompasses aspects of what are conventionally understood as the three phases of the policy process: formulation, implementation, and impact.[7]

In accordance with the particular characteristics of each phase, the research has involved interviews with forty policy makers, curriculum developers, and other influential participants in the policy process; participant observation during the two-year curriculum development process; interviews and observations in eleven classrooms from five different urban and semirural schools in the Kigali area for one academic year; focus-group discussions and beginning- and end-of-year questionnaires with about 400 students;[8] and a longitudinal tracer study at two months, six months, and three years after graduation with a sample of 101 graduates of lower and upper secondary schools.[9] For the latter half of this research process, I was joined by Flora Mutimukeye, a graduate in sociology from the National University of Rwanda, who contributed substantially to this work by helping me understand the perspectives of the students and graduates who participated in the study. More broadly, this research has involved participating in Rwandan life, following the developing public discourse surrounding topics such as employment, entrepreneurship, regulations, and economic growth.

When I began this research in mid-2008, a significant part of my own life as a young adult was already intertwined with the Rwandan youth experience. First arriving in the country in 2002 when I was nineteen years old, I had made friends with young Rwandans of widely varying socioeconomic circumstances, learned to speak French and Kinyarwanda through our interactions, collaborated with them on various informal youth initiatives, and eventually made a permanent home for myself in Kigali. I was deeply touched, throughout all of this, by the struggles of my young Rwandan peers to make a living and create adult lives for themselves. The desire to understand that experience in a more systematic way is what first led me to focus my research on Rwanda's policies for promoting youth entrepreneurship.

Now at the conclusion of more than five years of research, I also see this book as a complement to a recently published study sponsored by the US Institute of Peace, titled *Stuck: Rwandan Youth and the Struggle for Adulthood* (Sommers, 2012), and to other recent work on youth in Rwanda and the region (Abbink & Kessel, 2005; Honwana, 2012; Honwana & de Boeck, 2005; Pells, Pontalti, & Williams, 2014; Smith, 2011). Sommers's research, conducted in 2006–2007 and published in 2012, highlights the plight of rural and urban out-of-school youth in Rwanda, in an atmosphere of both sincere government efforts to counsel youth and what Sommers documented as rising feelings of youth despair. Much of what Sommers's study found is still very relevant in Rwanda today. However, there have also been some significant changes since then, specifically surrounding access to schooling. In November 2008, the Rwandan government announced a policy of Nine Years Basic Education, with the goal of allowing all Primary 6 graduates to automatically continue on to the first three years of secondary school (Senior 1–3, or O-level). In 2012, it was announced that this policy would be extended to Twelve Years Basic Education, by expanding the number of places available for upper secondary school (Senior 4–6, or A-level) in both traditional academic and technical as well as vocational institutions. Although there are clearly still costs involved in attending school and enrollment is not universal (MINEDUC, 2015; Williams, 2013), these policies have paved the way for vastly increased access to secondary schooling.

This study, therefore, adds to Sommers's analysis of the situation of out-of-school Rwandan youth by focusing particularly on the perspectives and experiences of students who are close to graduation from Rwanda's two levels of secondary schooling. I explore how these young students and their futures are being represented in policy language, how the course that was intended to teach them to become entrepreneurs was conceived, how teachers and students received and reinterpreted that course within school walls, and what these young Rwandans have done with these ideas after graduation. Many of the findings from this research are policy relevant; a summary has already been distributed to the government ministries most concerned with these issues,[10] and some concrete policy recommendations are included in the conclusion. More profoundly, however, this is a search for a deeper understanding of the post-developmental landscape of governance that is shaping, and being shaped by, Rwandan youth today.

This book is not about whether Rwanda's effort to teach entrepreneurship has so far been successful. Nor is it about judging the actions of government officials, curriculum developers, teachers, students, or graduates as good or bad, effective or ineffective. The research presented in the following pages instead attempts to understand Rwanda's entrepreneurship education policy from a perspective that looks beyond evaluation of the policy's own immediate stated goals, in order to understand something else: the complex processes of social negotiation and learning involved in introducing such a policy as part of larger transformations in political economy and governance.

The Orderly Entrepreneur: A Policy Landscape in Four Scenes

This book is divided into four parts, each corresponding to a setting in Rwanda in which post-developmental state policies for cultivating the ideal citizen are simultaneously being made and unmade.

Including this introductory chapter, Part I addresses questions of methodology and the national policy-making context. In this Chapter 1, I have argued that an investigation of the internal tensions inherent to the post-developmental rationality of governance requires stepping out of the view of policy making as a linear series of steps, bringing together concepts of governmentality and social learning to offer a unique perspective on the complex, multidirectional, temporally contingent and indeterminate processes involved in shifts in governmental rationalities. Chapter 2 presents this conceptual framework in greater detail, to tell how Rwanda's entrepreneurship education policy took shape through the influence of global models of governance interacting with policy makers' learned subjectivities. In the process, I develop further my argument that exploring the paradoxes found in Rwanda's policy can help us to understand the significance of the recent international rise to prominence of the post-developmental state.

Part II explores the paradoxes inherent to the post-developmental vision of the ideal citizen by examining the details of policy making and curriculum development in Rwanda's Ministry of Education. I focus particularly on a number of episodes in the curriculum-development process that illustrate government employees' struggle to promote creative entrepreneurialism in a way that is both regulated and examinable. Reviewing the historical development of the institution of schooling in Rwanda, Chapter 3 shows how that institutional context influenced curriculum developers to bring to the table certain presuppositions of what a "good" curriculum is and how to write it. In turn, Chapter 4 illustrates some of the dynamics of influence and institutional learning that took place when a new set of participants who did not share the same presuppositions were brought into a second phase of curriculum development. Through these midprocess shifts, I demonstrate how governmental rationalities must work through, and thus may be transformed by, the preexisting subjectivities of actors within specific communities of practice involved in the policy-making process.

Part III then turns to the observations and interviews in five schools where the new course in entrepreneurship was being taught. In these chapters I argue that both teachers and students subverted the policy's purpose of promoting creative yet controlled entrepreneurialism—albeit often unintentionally. Taking up the perspective of teachers, Chapter 5 examines the antipractical and imagination-quashing effects of their attempt to fit entrepreneurship into their expectations of what should happen in a classroom, despite their own sincere belief in the importance of entrepreneurship in students' lives. Moving to the perspective of Rwandan students, Chapter 6 explores how their interactions with the new entrepreneurship course—through neglect and even ridicule—contested the value of such an ostensibly practical and apparently nonacademic course in the school setting. I use the evidence presented in these chapters to demonstrate the ways in which the existing institution of schooling in Rwanda, and the dispositions it cultivates, is at odds with many of the goals of the post-developmental state. Part III thus suggests the kinds of institutional transformations that may—or may not—occur as governments push new developmental policy agendas, and as citizens continue to hold on to more predictable schemas of social and economic mobility.

Finally, Part IV follows Rwandan secondary school graduates beyond school walls. In Chapter 7, my descriptions of the ways these young Rwandans already practice entrepreneurialism in pursuit of diplomas, jobs, and—occasionally—starting actual enterprises, cast new light on policy makers' descriptions of a "lack of an entrepreneurial culture" in Rwanda. In particular, I illustrate how Rwanda's post-developmental regulations may be creating an untenable situation for disadvantaged youth entrepreneurs. Even as young people are being told to exercise initiative and self-reliance, the barriers standing in the way of earning a living are being raised ever higher. Chapter 8 shows how young Rwandans have responded to post-developmental government efforts to both promote and regulate entrepreneurship, as they argue for a different government approach that—if it cannot directly guarantee them a job or start-up capital—should at least guarantee them the conditions they need to create their own.

The concluding chapter discusses how this investigation of Rwanda's entrepreneurship education policy can provide insight into some of the contradictions that may be at the heart of the post-developmental state as an emerging idealized model of governance. Even as the Rwandan government steps up its developmental regulatory regime, Rwandan young people are being trained to exercise the neoliberal dispositions of independent judgment, initiative, and creativity. The jostling and maneuvers that take place over these competing values recall the question introduced at the beginning of this chapter: how expectations regarding work and schooling are transforming in a context in which citizens are expected to be both creatively self-reliant, and compliant, within a process of orderly development.

Chapter 2

Why Entrepreneurship Education?

AT AN AWARD CEREMONY for African entrepreneurship in 2007, the guest of honor—His Excellency Paul Kagame, President of the Republic of Rwanda—was introduced as the "Entrepreneur President." Citing the way in which Kagame has forged an independent development strategy for Rwanda, the host of the event contrasted Kagame's approach to that of other presidents who "are overly influenced by multilateral institutions and bilateral donors" (Fairbanks, 2007).

In an interview after the ceremony, with the lavishly draped banquet tables at one of Kigali's largest hotels serving as a backdrop, President Kagame clearly embraced his new title. "I think it is becoming increasingly clear that entrepreneurship is the most sure way of development," he remarked. "In fact, all activities in terms of development should be hinging on entrepreneurship, because entrepreneurship unlocks people's minds and allows innovation to take place [. . .] Entrepreneurship is about harnessing that and making sure that it takes them to another level, in terms of their development."

As the interview continued, President Kagame linked individual entrepreneurship to entrepreneurialism of the nation. Suggesting that "no one owes anything" to Rwanda, he argued that Rwandans need to develop a new mentality of self-reliance. "We have sought to challenge some of the thinking that is common with many people," he began, "and which has been responsible for in actual fact underdevelopment on our continent, and that is thinking that aid will come and solve everything, or that other people will come from somewhere else and do what we ought to be doing ourselves—for us. Why shouldn't *they* be doing what they are able to do—and there is a lot they can do—to stand up to most of these challenges we face, and be able to raise themselves to higher standards, and achieve more and better, and get out of this poverty that we find ourselves in? So it has to start from the mind, and that is what we have been working on over time. Once the mind gets correct, the rest becomes simple."

"We have also challenged our partners," Kagame continued, "that we appreciate their support, and indeed we do, but it should be support for what *we* intend to achieve for ourselves." The message of the "Entrepreneur President," on this and many other occasions, was clear: Rwanda's government is fully capable of designing and pursuing its own path to development, and the Rwandan population must develop a similar attitude of entrepreneurial self-reliance.[1]

. . .

At the time of this interview as the "Entrepreneur President," President Kagame had already defined an enterprising path of self-reliance for his country, and his government was about to launch a nationwide educational effort to systematically cultivate those values in Rwanda's younger generations. Rwanda's entrepreneurship education policy, publicly announced in late 2007, is unprecedented in the world in its reach and scope. While many other nations have entrepreneurship education programs, the courses involved are usually optional or restricted to particular student populations, such as those in technical and vocational schools (Salzano, Dahn, & Haftendorn, 2006). Rwanda, in contrast, introduced a policy requiring all secondary school students to study the new entrepreneurship course for a full six years—beginning with two periods per week in O-level (the equivalent of seventh to ninth grades in the US system), and increasing to seven periods per week in A-level (tenth to twelfth grades).[2] The course was also slated to be included on the national examinations, which are crucial gatekeeping experiences determining access to higher education. The Rwandan government, in short, was very serious about its goal of developing a "more entrepreneurial" population.

Rwanda's entrepreneurship education policy was decided upon at the highest levels of Rwanda's government, perhaps even within the Cabinet itself. In interviews, Rwandan policy makers described a consistent range of Rwanda-specific national issues that this new course was expected to address. To them the decision to implement entrepreneurship education in Rwanda's schools was an autonomous one, a national policy designed to respond to national needs.

Yet Rwanda's entrepreneurship education policy raises intriguing questions about the cross-border social learning that characterizes public policy making today. What makes it possible, for example, for government officials in Rwanda—or in any other country where a similar phenomenon occurs—to step back and evaluate their own national culture as "nonentrepreneurial"? Why is it that Rwanda's chosen solution to certain specific national issues so strongly reflects similar entrepreneurship-promotion strategies that are already being pursued in dozens of other countries around the world—a confluence of ideas that so often seems to characterize policy making today? And how can one explain the curious way in which, in Rwanda, entrepreneurship education as a policy solution seems to have preceded any formal investigation of the problems it might resolve—reminding us of how, sometimes, "policies go looking for problems" (Stone, 2002, p. 11) rather than the other way around? Theorizing transformations in governance as negotiated processes of social learning, building on the model introduced briefly in Chapter 1, begins to provide a coherent explanation for each of these apparently paradoxical observations, with implications for understanding policy making not only in Rwanda but in much of the rest of the world as well.

In this chapter I offer two different accounts of how the Rwandan government decided to introduce courses on entrepreneurship into its secondary school curriculum. As I expand what is initially a national policy-making narrative outward to consider international dynamics of social influence, I examine the rise of neoliberalism and the ways this form of governmental rationality has profoundly—though not completely—influenced Rwandan policy makers. This one policy, it becomes clear, holds a broader significance for understanding global shifts in dominant forms of governance.

Enthusiasm for Entrepreneurship

"It's an idea that came out in 2005," a Cabinet-level Rwandan official told me as we sat in his comfortable ministry office discussing the entrepreneurship education policy that had just been announced a few months before, in late 2007.[3] "We were conducting the annual investor's conference in Butare, at the National University of Rwanda, chaired by the President," he continued. "We discussed many issues, and had successful entrepreneurs giving their history, how they did it. [. . .] I gave a suggestion that entrepreneurship should be taken as compulsory for all students going to university."

Gesturing broadly, he went on: "It was clear that we had a problem with an entrepreneurial culture, with the entrepreneurship spirit. Rwandans are not good entrepreneurs. I thought it is because of the kind of education they have received—it doesn't open the eyes of people, it teaches them to expect to get a job from the government; they don't learn to create a job by themselves. So I suggested that everyone who goes to university should take this entrepreneurship subject." But, he continued, "it will only be possible if people start thinking of entrepreneurship at [even] a younger age."

"How did you think of this idea?" I asked him.

"I did my studies in Kenya. I'm an economist," he replied. "In Kenya, there is what is known as *jua kali*—people make simple but valuable things, because of their culture—always looking for money. The Kikuyu, the President's tribe, that's their culture. They say that to know if a Kikuyu is dead, all you need to do is throw a coin up in the air near him to see whether he reacts."[4] He laughed. "I looked at this *jua kali* in Kenya and how young people tried to do everything to get money—even students."

"The way it is now [in Rwanda]," he continued, "people expect to finish [studying] and get a job, they don't think about starting their own business. [With an education in entrepreneurship], I expect them to be enlightened, that we can create a job ourselves. Also changing minds—changing that idea that we always need someone to help us. [. . .] This dependence needs to change— students depend on parents until they finish school and look for a job. But instead, students could work even while studying. It will change this dependency."

Not long after the 2005 investors' meeting where this government official first proposed the idea of entrepreneurship education, the United Nations Industrial Development Organization (UNIDO) informed the Rwandan Ministry of Education that there would be a seminar in Kampala on the experience with entrepreneurship education in Uganda and a few other countries. The Ministry of Education accepted an invitation to send a small delegation from its National Curriculum Development Centre (NCDC) to the meeting.

One of the Rwandan participants was strongly convinced by the experience. "We arrived at night, and early the next morning we went directly to visit a school," he recalled during an interview with me.[5] "The students talked to us, they showed us the activities that they had created, within the school itself! Small associations. There was one association, for example, that had a small farm of a few cows—an association of a few students within the school itself. Another association had a store there inside the school. There were other students that had them outside the school—for example, some students had a hair salon. [. . .] There were some that said, today, they don't ask their parents any more for their school fees—they pay by themselves," he continued with admiration. "They had a course to begin with, but their professor gave as home-work that each student would develop a project."

I could see the animation on his face as he remembered the experience. "Personally, I was astonished," he went on, "because here in Rwanda, it's really outside that spirit. Most parents here, when you talk about these concepts, they resist! They say, for example, that if the child starts to know what is money, if he starts to love money, then he risks losing his sense of humanity. In other words, the more one loves money, the less one becomes morally educable. That's still the mentality here. You need a lot of time to change that mentality. . . . You have to see, maybe, the history of the education system."

Yet despite his personal experience and involvement in that same Rwandan education system, this particular Ministry of Education employee saw things differently. "I don't agree—evidently!" he responded, when I asked what he thought personally. "Because of my experience. Me, my children, for example— I train them already to enter into business. My wife has some small business activities; she doesn't have a job. We have a small store; sometimes we supply food to schools. And my children, in the vacations they do this work! They see how there are profits from sales. And they are conscious that it is this money that helps pay their school fees so that they can be educated! They are aware. They are at secondary school—they see, they work, they sell, they look for clients . . . it's already a consciousness raising for them. They know that money doesn't come from nowhere. They know already my own salary. They know that with my salary [alone], they can't survive. So I think, really, that my children are already conscious, and that with time there will be a moment when the others will have to pass through that too."

This enthusiasm for teaching children the practicalities of work, business, and money management came through in the 2005 report he submitted to his superiors at the Ministry of Education. There, he wrote, "The importance of in-troducing such an entrepreneurship curriculum into the Rwandan education system is undoubted" (NCDC, 2005, p. 4). Others at the Ministry of Education apparently agreed, and by 2006 a memorandum of understanding had been signed with UNIDO to collaborate on the development of an entrepreneurship education curriculum.

In 2007, this initiative was confirmed as official policy with the inclusion of one simple line in Rwanda's first Economic Development and Poverty Reduc-tion Strategy Paper (EDPRS): "The curriculum will be revised to include new subjects, such as entrepreneurial skill development, which should enhance the employability of pupils once they have left school" (Rwanda, 2007, p. 58). This was clearly a Rwandan government priority in its own right—important enough to be pushed forward even in the absence of the expected funding. While UNIDO waited for its budget to be approved under the new OneUN system, a directive to immediately begin developing a new entrepreneurship curriculum was nonetheless passed down from the highest levels of Rwanda's leadership in early 2008.[6]

"There was a [government] retreat organized at Akagera Game Lodge, and the political decision-makers went there to discuss and then they gave us this instruction," a Ministry of Education staff person explained to me. "And then we started the work, as technicians."

The course objectives did not come from any particular background study or needs analysis. "We didn't do a lot of research, really, to see how it is going to work," the acting Director General of the NCDC remarked to me as the curriculum development process began. "We only said, 'I think it would be very good if, for example, a Rwandan who has completed three years of secondary school, should have some notion on how to manage a simple business.' [. . .] We are encouraging today our people, Rwandans generally, to be—*not* to rely so much on employment. So we are saying, maybe if you are giving some basic skills on entrepreneurship to this young person—even if he drops out of school, he will have some notion on how he can manage his own small business." Entrepreneurship, it seemed, could be the answer to many of the problems confronting Rwanda's youth.

The Nation's Need for a Spirit of Enterprise

Rwanda's 2007 decision to teach entrepreneurship in secondary schools was both an old and a new policy idea. It built on the key role for the private sector envisioned in fundamental Rwandan policy documents such as Vision 2020 (Ministry of Finance and Economic Planning, MINECOFIN, 2000). Several national-level projects in Rwanda had also already featured some form of entrepreneurship training.[7] But these preexisting projects all emphasized assistance for those who were already interested in entrepreneurship: training of small-scale entrepreneurs, entrepreneurship education for those already in technical and vocational courses of study that were likely to lead to self-employment, and business competitions for young entrepreneurs seeking to start their first enterprises. The suggestion that an entire generation of young Rwandans could be taught to be interested in entrepreneurship was unprecedented.

In interviews I conducted in mid-2008, just a few months after this policy was published, public officials and other opinion leaders in the country consistently explained the importance of entrepreneurship education in terms of two national problems: a culture of dependence on others for work and a crisis of youth unemployment.[8] A Rwandan representative of the Private Sector Federation (PSF), for example, touched on both of these themes as we sat together in his office overlooking the large fairgrounds that now hold Rwanda's increasingly boisterous annual Trade Expo.[9]

"In the mentality of Rwandans," he began, "they don't have this entrepreneurial spirit. You have to look in other countries, even the neighbors like Uganda, where everyone does only business, thinks only about business. Even the student in secondary school [there] prefers to leave school in order to do business. Which is the contrary to here. Here, a man who finishes university, instead of trying to create his own business, he thinks, 'Where am I going to find a job?' He is seeking a job, he wants a job, but not to think: 'How I can create my own job, how I can start a business?'"

Gesturing with some frustration, he continued: "Rwandans don't have that entrepreneurship spirit. So, in order to create that entrepreneurship spirit, one needs an education. And that education should start at the base, either primary school, secondary school, and in the world. To prepare the children: 'There isn't anything but business that helps us to live, there isn't anything but business that is favorable for you.' Because if we are eight million here, there are how many enterprises, or how many [government] ministries that are going to give you work? It's very few. Not even 2 percent, not even 1 percent. And the others, where are they going to go? It's a problem. You have to start very early; teach from the beginning, teach them how to *entreprendre* something, a business. So that even when they arrive up to university, even when they finish university, instead of looking for a job somewhere, instead of looking to be paid a salary of I don't know how much—even better, create his business, his enterprise, create his employment, and of course create employment for others, those who cannot create their own enterprises."

"If we had an entrepreneurial culture," he continued, "that would change a lot of things. Especially unemployment [. . .] because one wouldn't have a lot of unemployed people if people had this spirit of creating their own business, creating his enterprise. Many people think that in order to make a business you have to have a lot of money, a big amount of investment—which isn't true. You can start with almost nothing; with $50 it's possible. We have the experience of many people in Kigali who are rich. We can take the example of Mr. Rujugiro. He's the great rich man—he has cement enterprises, et cetera, many things. He started by selling peanuts! Many people start like that. [. . .] If you start selling anything, on the road, you can start by selling airtime and after one year you change and go like this"—he gestured upward to demonstrate a rise in income—"and after some time you change again and really become someone."

Like this representative of the PSF, many Rwandan policy actors I spoke to talked about a culture of dependence on others for employment. They lamented that too many educated young people looked to their influential relatives to guarantee them some sort of employment, or simply expected the government to "give" them a job after graduation. Arguably, this issue in Rwanda—as in much of the rest of the region—is rooted both in precolonial social structures and in colonial-era patterns of access to employment, exacerbated by the dynamics of Rwanda's own recent history.

Through much of the twentieth century, formal education was the most important, and often the only, path to formal nonagricultural employment. The very few Rwandans who achieved a secondary school or university education were almost automatically guaranteed employment in the country's growing government or some religious and other organizations.[10] In the latter decades of the twentieth century, many countries in the region experienced a transformation in these labor market dynamics, with existing institutions unable to absorb the continually increasing number of graduates. In Rwanda, however, this transformation was briefly reversed by the enormous loss in human resources due to the 1994 genocide. Afterward, the replacement of the country's decimated ranks of professionals became an important government priority (Hayman, 2007).

In the immediate postgenocide context, a large proportion of graduates were absorbed simply in order to ensure the country's basic administrative functioning, and many other graduates were able to find work in international organizations seeking local staff. But within less than a decade after the genocide, that situation had changed again. Most institutions had effectively recruited all the employees they needed, and the government was even pursuing efforts to reduce the government payroll in order to cut budget costs (Green, 2011). By the mid-2000s, the government could no longer be considered a major source of employment for new graduates, but many policy makers felt that Rwandan youth had not yet recognized that reality.

The policy actors I spoke to argued that this continued dependence on formal salaried work, and a related disdain for "small jobs" and informal self-employment, was causing a dangerous situation of youth unemployment in Rwanda. The absolute unemployment rate at the time, using the ILO's definition of employment (at least one hour of paid work in the previous seven days), was actually quite low—only 1 percent overall, for youth aged 14–35 who would like to be working, with somewhat higher rates in Kigali (National Institute of Statistics Rwanda, NISR, 2012, p. 11). Rates of absolute unemployment in Kigali, where most of the promoters of this entrepreneurship policy actually lived, were measured in the same study as 3.6 percent for young men and 7.5 percent for young women. These rates are still quite low when compared to those of other countries in the region (see, e.g., Mains, 2013). Yet in public perception and lived experience, youth unemployment was seen as perilously high—especially considering the role played by idle young men in the 1994 genocide.

In fact, much of what is perceived as unemployment may be the widespread underemployment of youth who would like to be working full-time but are not. Among economically active young adults aged 25–29, for example—an age at which schooling has usually been completed and full-time work is desirable—65 percent were working less than full-time, and 45 percent were working fewer than twenty-five hours per week (NISR, 2012, p. 12).[11] The underemployment figures are similar for the 20–24 and 30–35 year age groups. Much of the available employment for young people is also unstable casual or short-term labor, meaning that even youth with some work experience face frequent periods of intermittent unemployment.

The macroeconomic roots of youth unemployment and underemployment are acknowledged in Rwandan public discourse and policy statements, but blame is also often placed on the attitudes of youth themselves. If young people were only more entrepreneurial and more willing to "start from peanuts," many policy makers asserted, they would be able to create work for themselves. Teaching the spirit of enterprise to Rwanda's youth, they explained, was a commonsense strategy to respond to national needs.

Reconsidering National Autonomy in Policy Making

This way of telling the policy's history—as a national strategy chosen by Rwanda's leaders to respond to specific national needs—is, in many ways, accurate. The Rwandan government has serious concerns about issues such as youth unemployment and developing the business sector, and in response, Rwandan policy makers promoted a policy of teaching young Rwandans to be more entrepreneurial. But there was also something puzzling, a kind of circular logic, to Rwanda's policy discourse: to most people, the importance of teaching entrepreneurship simply justified itself.

The story, as the policy actors I spoke to understood it, went something like this: "because Rwandan culture is deficient in entrepreneurial spirit, the government proposed to teach Rwandan youth about entrepreneurialism." One might ask, what specifically makes entrepreneurship the key factor here? As the UNIDO representative commented at the end of our interview, "Entrepreneurship has become a buzzword. It is basically talked about everywhere."[12] Perhaps—and this is not a criticism, but rather an observation of how policy making often seems to work—entrepreneurship was already defined as the most effective solution, even before Rwandan policy makers had clearly identified the specific national problems that it would solve.

Could there be an alternate way of understanding how Rwandan leaders came to champion the idea of entrepreneurship education, a way that takes into account the interconnectedness of social life and the international circulation of ideas? Rwanda's national entrepreneurship education strategy was not, after all, chosen in a vacuum. Though never representing a single determinant cause of the policy, influences from outside of Rwanda were also present during every step of this decision-making process. A consideration of these influences opens up a fuller picture of the significance of Rwanda's policy in contemporary international dynamics of governance—and, as a result, a fuller picture of the multifaceted social learning that characterizes policy-making processes around the world today.

Efforts to promote education about entrepreneurship have existed since the beginning of the twentieth century. The earliest of these programs were apparently in the United States, explicitly inspired by the US business community's long-standing commitment to the "free enterprise system" (Francomono, Lavitt, & Lavitt, 1988). Through the mid-1900s, there was some further experimentation with the idea here and there (McClelland, 1961). But if one were to make a graph of the number and geographical spread of entrepreneurship education programs over time, the late 1970s and 1980s would mark the beginning of a drastically upward-sloping line. Those years seem to represent the kind of "tipping point" that Gladwell (2000) popularly described as leading to an "epidemic" of rapid social change.

In the 1970s, a university institution established by the US Congress, called the East-West Center, hosted one of the first high-level international workshops on entrepreneurship education, focusing on the Philippines, Malaysia, Indonesia, and India; and President Ferdinand Marcos of the Philippines instituted the world's first government-mandated entrepreneurship course in a state-sponsored formal education system (Nelson, 1977, p. 882). Also in the 1970s, the Indian government decided to support entrepreneurship training among small-scale business owners, an effort that earned praise from prominent international institutions like the World Bank (Paul, Ickis, & Levitsky, 1988, p. 112). Around the same time, the International Labour Organization collaborated with the Swedish business community to develop a course called "Improve Your Business" and offer it in Botswana, Ethiopia, Kenya, Lesotho, Mauritius, Mozambique, Tanzania, Uganda, Zambia, and Zimbabwe (ILO, 2012). By the 1980s, the Thatcher regime in the United Kingdom had begun implementing various initiatives to teach entrepreneurial "values and virtues" to young Britons (Morris, 1991; Yoemans, 2008). And shortly thereafter Junior Achievement, a US-based program encouraging young people to start their own companies, created an international division "in response to increasing requests from other nations" to introduce similar programs around the world (Junior Achievement, 2013).

Diffusionist perspectives on policy making would suggest that this international proliferation of entrepreneurship education programs was due to personal connections and the movement of key individuals among different social groups (Rogers, 2003). Such dynamics surely account for part of the story.[13] But the widespread international growth of entrepreneurship education initiatives cannot be explained by these professional collaborations alone. There was something about the idea of teaching entrepreneurship that must have appealed to an increasing number of international organizations and government leaders, to prompt so many of them in such widespread locales to devote resources to all of these initiatives over the span of just a few years' time.

The idea of entrepreneurship education arguably spread so rapidly during this era because of its affinity with the broader tenets of neoliberalism rising to power in the international field of governance at the time. More than just an economic theory or ensemble of policies, neoliberalism has involved the penetration of a "pervasive style of conduct" (Gordon, 1991, p. 42) into a wide array of different fields of social policy—health, gender, development, labor, and social welfare regimes, among other examples (Shore & Wright, 1997). This style of conduct is exemplified by the metaphor of the enterprise as a life model: applying economic rationality to one's decisions, becoming self-reliant, and in particular accepting responsibility for finding or creating one's own livelihood.

By the 1970s, neoliberal ideas had strong support within the US business community, where the first entrepreneurship education programs in the world—Junior Achievement, followed by DECA and Future Business Leaders of America—originated (Francomono et al., 1988). The first entrepreneurship education initiative of an international organization, the ILO, was sponsored by the Swedish business community, which had recently helped to propel neoliberal ideas to prominence through the awarding of the Nobel Prize in Economics to the neoliberal thinker Friedrich Hayek (Harvey, 2005, p. 22). The United Kingdom's own experience with entrepreneurship education under the Thatcher regime also occurred under direct influence from a neoliberal think tank, amid concern that an anti-business culture was destroying the British economy (Morris, 1991, p. 22). Existing entrepreneurship education initiatives, in other words, involved beliefs about the individual and the economy that were so fundamentally in harmony with neoliberalism that they simply became part of the whole ensemble, spreading widely just as neoliberalism itself rose to prominence on the global stage.

By the time Rwanda introduced its own policy in 2007, the promotion of entrepreneurship through education and training was already in an important sense a prepackaged solution rooted in the neoliberal rationality of governance. As such, entrepreneurship education policies contain within them a number of assumptions about the problems they are supposed to address, regardless of the specific national context. In particular, they emphasize the responsibility of individuals to overcome problems such as unemployment and underemployment rather than government social safety nets or other interventions intended to rebalance the economic structure. Because the neoliberal perspective already contains within it the presupposition that the root cause of economic problems is the suppression of individual entrepreneurial behavior, policies such as entrepreneurship education can be adopted "on faith," without the need for extensive research as to how to address a particular nation's circumstances.

This is perhaps why the decision-making process behind the adoption of Rwanda's entrepreneurship education policy did not involve extensive research into whether or how such a course could really address the specific national or local characteristics of problems of youth unemployment. Such a laborious process was in a way unnecessary, because Rwandan policy makers—long steeped in exposure to neoliberal ideas—already knew that entrepreneurship was the answer.

Conceptualizing Transformations in Governance as Negotiated Social Learning

Rwanda is not the only place where such influences on policy making have been observed, and a number of theories—policy diffusion, policy transfer, new institutionalism, and world culture theory, to name a few—attempt to account for these dynamics (Berry & Berry, 1999; Dolowitz & Marsh, 2000; Meyer, Boli, Thomas, & Ramirez, 1997; Shore & Wright, 2011). Anthropological or interpretive studies of policy have pushed the boundaries of these theories by focusing on certain neglected issues: the power dynamics involved on the international and national levels, policy diversity in specific local and institutional settings, and the ways in which local actors frequently transform and sometimes resist official policy (Anderson-Levitt, 2003; Rizvi & Lingard, 2010; Shore, Wright, & Peró, 2011).

Existing theoretical approaches, however, do not give fully satisfactory answers to the kinds of questions posed at the beginning of this chapter. How do policy makers get "new" policy ideas that simultaneously respond to particular national circumstances and yet strongly echo international discourse and trends? How should we characterize policy makers' relationship to the rest of their country's population, especially in cases where policy makers envision themselves as the vanguard of transformations in national culture? How do policies transform target populations, often at the same time as target populations transform policies?

To answer questions like these, I link political rationality and technologies of power (Foucault, 1991, 2016, 1982, 1988) to the concepts of field and habitus (Bourdieu, 1972, 1990, 1993), two sets of ideas that emphasize structural constraints. These structural constraints are tempered, however, by the multi-plicity of social structures (Sewell, 2005) and the internal dynamics of communities of practice (Lave & Wenger, 1991), which introduce a greater potential role for agency in the policy process. Together, these concepts create a model of social negotiation and social learning that can be employed to understand governing practices at all levels, from the smallest microsocial incidents to the broadest international trends.

SOCIAL FIELDS AND THE RESOURCES AT STAKE IN THEM

We can begin by conceiving of the social world as made up of numerous over-lapping fields or social arenas "within which struggles or maneuvers take place over specific resources or stakes and access to them" (Jenkens, 2006, p. 80; also see Bourdieu, 1993). In a general sense, the major fields in question in Rwanda's policy of entrepreneurship education include the field of governance, the field of formal instruction or schooling, and the field of employment or livelihoods, in which policy makers, teachers, and soon-to-be graduates are all involved in different ways. Each of these fields exists on a global scale, with international implications for the meaning of social practice within them, but they also take on particular local forms.

The resources at stake within any given social field can be understood as different forms of capital.[14] Symbolic capital has to do with acquiring prestige and honor, social capital involves networks of relationships with other people, cultural capital involves knowing "the right way to act" in a given context, and economic capital refers to material resources (Bourdieu, 1986, 1990). These forms of capital can be accumulated and are convertible among themselves, such that one form of capital can be employed strategically to augment another.

These concepts open up the possibility of viewing Rwanda's entrepreneurship education policy not only in terms of national development strategies but also in terms of policy makers' impressions of what is at stake for them in the field of governance. Rwandan governmental actors are conscious that their regime and their country are participating in an international political and economic field in which symbolic capital—reputation and prestige—carries real consequences. After the 1994 genocide, Rwandan government leaders were acutely aware of the need to earn a reputation as a legitimate government deserving of international confidence and assistance with the rebuilding effort. The adoption of a neoliberal approach to economic development was one key feature of the effort to gain international legitimacy, as the Rwandan government promoted structural transformation, growth of the private sector, a shift away from state ownership of enterprises toward a regulatory role, and improved financial management and government administration (Hayman, 2006, p. 133).

A number of sources indicate that the Rwandan government's level of symbolic capital has indeed risen on the international scene because of its acceptance of the neoliberal approach (see, for example, World Bank, 2015; World Economic Forum, 2015). It is a long, slow process to change Rwanda's negative and inaccurate branding in the *New York Times* as a place of eternal "tribal violence" and "ethnic warfare"[15] (Wharton, 1994) to a country where long-term investors can trust that their assets will grow. The promotion of an enterprise culture within Rwanda may play a key role in the image that the Rwandan government and Rwandan population project externally, helping to shape its position in an international field in which important stakes are at play.

A "FEEL FOR THE GAME": DOXA, DISPOSITIONS, AND HABITUS

Social interaction in these fields—in Rwanda just like elsewhere—is like participation in a game of skill, which demands not only knowledge of a basic structure of rules, but also, and more significantly, a "feel for the game," an "acquired mastery, functioning with the automatic reliability of an instinct, [that makes] it possible to respond instantaneously to all the uncertain and ambiguous situations of practice" (Bourdieu, 1990, pp. 66, 104). The more effective our social interactions, the more we are able to access the rewards of particular social fields. The field's structure of power and rewards thus shapes the rules of the game.

Social interactions are creative, not predetermined, but they are still characterized by marked regularities and structure—analogous to the way that musicians can improvise together around certain foundations of melody, key, or rhythm. There is rarely any explicit discussion of the rules that help us to understand one another, come to agreement, and act in ways that are considered effective and socially appropriate. Yet nonetheless, people are able to behave in ways that are intelligible to others, choose effective social strategies, and coordinate their actions—just as so many Rwandan policy makers and other professionals found themselves in agreement about promoting entrepreneurship education, often without ever having explicitly discussed their reasons or the best approach to take.

The concepts of doxa, dispositions, and habitus help to describe how such incidental coordination of thought and behavior occurs and is reproduced within particular social fields. Participation within a particular social field, just like playing a strategic game, involves "investment in the game and the outcome, interest in the game, commitment to the presuppositions—doxa—of the game" (Bourdieu, 1990, p. 66). A shared doxa secures a feeling of fitting into the context of social interaction, knowing what to do and say without giving it great thought, and coordinating with others without explicitly planning that coordination. It involves all of those implicit presuppositions that, while left unstated, nevertheless allow someone to feel that what others are doing and saying "makes sense" in some fundamental way.

The support for entrepreneurship education in Rwanda and elsewhere is a case in point. To them, and to many other people around the world today, it is self-evident that entrepreneurial initiative and creativity are positive qualities that every individual would do well to develop and from which every nation would benefit. To suggest otherwise would provoke serious perplexity in most social circles and might be even be perceived as dangerously countercultural. This state of affairs is a sign that the neoliberal political rationality, and its emphasis on the "spirit of enterprise" and "entrepreneurial culture" has attained doxic status, a level of "undisputed, pre-reflexive, naïve, native compliance," as a fundamental presupposition on an international scale (Bourdieu, 1990, p. 68). Of course, not everyone accepts neoliberal principles on faith—no doxa is completely hegemonic, a point I return to later[16]—but the neoliberal doxa was certainly influential in Rwanda's decision to adopt a policy of entrepreneurship education.

Through participation in particular social fields, under particular material conditions, we take on the doxa of our place in the social game, and in turn, begin to develop patterned thoughts and behaviors that reflect that doxa. These are an individual's dispositions; a disposition is "a way of being, a habitual state (especially of the body) and, in particular, a predisposition, tendency, propensity, or inclination" (Bourdieu, 1972, p. 214). Over the course of our lives, everyone develops a constellation or system of dispositions that shape our social action. This habitus is the mind-body structure that we live in and live through.

Habitus thus implies a holistic way of being and thinking that is learned over time and through social experience (Bourdieu, 1972, p. 72; also see Lave & Wenger, 1991, p. 51). According to Bourdieu, the habitus is "transposable" because dispositions acquired previously stay with us from context to context; "durable" because those dispositions can never be entirely forgotten or erased. Our habitus helps to produce our later actions and reactions, which ultimately often serve to reproduce the same social structures that first defined the habitus. As a result, though actions are improvised rather than being mechanically rule-bound, although they usually do not involve conscious strategic planning, and occur within unpredictable and varied contexts, they nevertheless show significant regularities when actors share a similar doxa and similar dispositions.

I have discussed Rwanda's entrepreneurship education policy in Foucaultian terms, as a technology of power intended to reshape citizens' political subjectivity towards the idealized conceptualization of the orderly entrepreneur. Bourdieu's concepts, as introduced here, permit a greater specification of the dynamic social processes involved in such an endeavor, via an analogy of subjectivity to habitus. The Rwandan policy makers introduced earlier in this chapter clearly share similar values regarding the importance of promoting entrepreneurship. By introducing a policy of entrepreneurship education, they are essentially hoping that the habitus of a wide swath of Rwanda's population will become more like their own—as young Rwandans develop a prereflexive commitment to neoliberal assumptions about the appropriate role of the citizen and the government in economic action, in turn shaping their dispositions in a more entrepreneurial direction.

THE MULTIPLICITY OF STRUCTURES
AND COMMUNITIES OF PRACTICE

While explaining the apparent homogeneity of Rwandan policy makers' ideas is an important piece of this puzzle, it is perhaps even more important to understand why these influential Rwandans—like so many policy makers around the world—set themselves apart from the rest of their own society, believing that *they* understand the importance of entrepreneurship, whereas other Rwandans do not.

The key to understanding the policy maker's perceived role as a catalyst of social transformation lies in seeing social fields not as encompassing and homogenous, but rather as made up of a multiplicity of structures (Sewell, 2005) or communities of practice (Lave & Wenger, 1991). Rwandan citizens are all participants, for example, in the same international and national fields of governance—with their particular overarching structures of power, rules of the game, and resources at stake. But this does not necessarily mean that they have all developed identical doxa and dispositions, nor that they all share a single cohesive "culture." For, within any given social field, and intersecting among fields, there are many types of intermediate social structures. These structures "exist at different levels, operate in different modalities, and are themselves based on widely-varying types and quantities of resources" (Sewell, 2005, p. 140). Individuals come into association with them in diverse ways and combinations, subtly shaping their habitus in ways different from those of their peers. It is from this diversity of social experience that the possibilities of social learning and social change are born.

The more one looks into the social structures that shape all of our lives, the more the boundaries seem so overlapping and intertwined that they are blurred. The concept of a community of practice (Lave & Wenger, 1991) provides a way of thinking about these social groups and structures without being restricted by artificially exclusive notions of belonging. The term *community*, Lave and Wenger (1991) explain, principally implies joint participation in some kind of social activity "about which participants share understandings concerning what they are doing and what that means in their lives and for their communities" (p. 98). A family is a community of practice, as is a classroom, a school, a workplace, a profession, a multinational religious body, and so on. Any given individual thus belongs simultaneously to multiple communities of practice, with different scopes and sizes of membership (see Figure 5).

Association with a given community of practice is not just an issue of physical proximity or geographically defined space. It does not even necessarily depend on direct personal relationships with other members of the community, but it may be in relation to contact with their ideas (through written, oral, or visual "texts"), a sense of shared goals, or sharing of other group features and experiences. Membership or participation in a community of practice is not a fixed state, but rather a continuous process, and individuals do not participate in equal ways. Some may be more central or participants, and others peripheral; some have more social expertise in the group's modes of practice while others are more like novices; some members may be more closely wedded to a group's shared features and more conforming than others. Individuals have a degree of freedom in their ability to voluntarily associate with different communities of practice; their membership in a certain set of communities is never totally dictated from birth. Furthermore the multiple communities of practice to which a

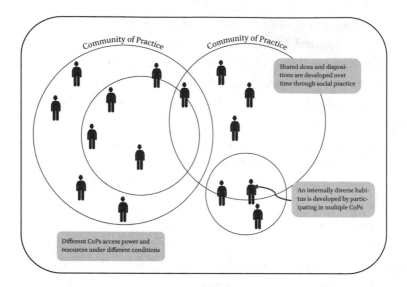

Figure 5   Communities of practice (CoPs) within a field

given individual belongs may be variously encompassing, overlapping, or even in conflict with one another. Each person's habitus is a record of that multifaceted social experience, endowing us with a repertoire of doxa and dispositions that we may selectively play up in different contexts, according to the needs of the moment.

This conceptualization of social structure as simultaneous membership in multiple communities of practice allows us to understand how Rwandan policy makers came to adopt a neoliberal-influenced policy like entrepreneurship education later than in many other countries, but also in a relatively stronger form. It can also help us understand these policy makers' simultaneous and sometimes contradictory emphasis on law-abiding behavior, which was to emerge so strongly over the course of the research described in later sections of this book.

Rwanda's original implementation of neoliberal structural adjustment was interrupted by the 1990–1994 conflict and genocide (Uvin, 1998). Yet the country's history of social and political turmoil had also laid the foundation for a reintroduction of neoliberal ideas by a new generation of Rwandan policy makers. The social dislocation of Rwandans, beginning with the first massacres just after independence in 1959, had pushed many Rwandans into the diaspora, where they developed deep personal and professional experiences in other policy contexts (Schweisfurth, 2006). As a result, when the postgenocide government came into existence, it drew on a disproportionately large pool of Rwandans who had pursued their studies, and often a significant part of their professional careers as well, in other countries. To the extent that these countries and professional communities had been influenced by neoliberalism—which was certainly the case in such places as Uganda, Kenya, South Africa, the United Kingdom, and the United States, and within a number of professional fields connected to economics—members of the Rwandan diaspora had learned and incorporated into their own habituses many of the presuppositions characteristic of the neoliberal doxa.

When these highly educated Rwandans from the diaspora then returned to Rwanda and began to rebuild Rwanda's contemporary academic, economic, and governing institutions, their very participation would have influenced these institutions in a neoliberal direction. And even those policy makers who had never left Rwanda were similarly exposed to the neoliberal doxa and dispositions through their strong associations with international organizations, transnational academic and professional discourse, and media channels. Neoliberalism may, in fact, have been one of the few perspectives they all held in common despite their diverse experiences, strongly influencing their commonly held "feel for the game" of governance. Whether or not they were consciously aware of the tenets of neoliberalism, and whether or not they purposely intended to introduce neoliberal policies, these presuppositions would have served as a foundation for common understanding within the postgenocide regime's new community of practice.

Neoliberalism was not the only broad set of convictions these policy makers may have shared, however. They also shared a social exposure to the patterns of authority and hierarchy characteristic of Rwanda's historical disciplinary state, as described in Chapter 1. Even those who had left Rwanda or were born outside it brought some vestiges of disciplinary ideals with them as part of their family and diaspora communities of practice. Policy makers thus had two major commonalities of social practice to draw upon—neoliberal and disciplinary doxa—as they set about determining new policy directions for Rwanda. And as the successes of post-developmental states like Singapore have become increasingly acclaimed on the world stage, Rwandan leaders had a contemporary model to draw on that fit with their orientation toward strong-state policies.

The participation of Rwandan policy actors in multiple different communities of practice both within and outside of Rwanda can also explain the kind of "dual consciousness" (Fanon, 1967) that many expressed in their interviews. Though they self-identified as Rwandans, they simultaneously looked at Rwandan "culture" from the alternate perspectives they had gained through their social experiences outside the context of mainstream Rwandan values. When Rwanda's security situation had finally stabilized and UNIDO offered to support in the development of an entrepreneurship education program, Rwandan policy makers were in an ideal position to envision an engineered transformation in their own culture, moving it in the direction of increased self-reliance and entrepreneurial initiative, while never fully relinquishing the disciplinary convictions that continued to hover in the background.

Governance as Teaching, Governance as Learning, Governance as Negotiation

Policy makers in Rwanda and around the world believe that well-designed policy can produce important social transformations. And this can be the case—but not always to the same degree, or even in the same direction, that they imagine.

Change is a continuous feature of social reality—albeit sometimes in such a slow form as to be almost imperceptible. Specific social structures or communities of practice are associated with particular doxa and dispositions, and ordinarily, this ensemble seems to remain largely the same over time. But individuals and groups may borrow or appropriate systems of thought and action from one structural complex they belong to and apply them to another—just as Rwandan policy makers have arguably appropriated the idea of entrepreneurship education from elsewhere in order to use it to transform the Rwandan context. Because of the overlap and intersections among social structures with different characteristics, "reproduction is never automatic. Structures are at risk, at least to some extent, in all of the social encounters they shape" (Sewell, 2005, p. 143). As social structures intersect, and as people interact within and among them, one may observe processes of transformation "in which numerous microscopic changes finally give rise to structural change" (D'Hooge, 2008, p. 538). The introduction of a new social policy does indeed have the potential to bring about change, because it introduces new norms of thinking and behaving into various communities of practice.

Whether these changes occur and in what form, however, is difficult to predict. All social interactions involve indeterminate processes of learning and negotiation. New ideas may change social practice, or existing social practices may overcome or transform the new ideas. Newcomers to a given social context may bring alternate social understandings into play—elements from their own distinct social history and repertoire of dispositions—that other members learn from as well.[17] Or newcomers may assimilate to the group, "gradually assembl[ing] a general idea of what constitutes the practice of the community," until they eventually demonstrate a social mastery that is indistinguishable from that of other full practitioners (Lave & Wenger, 1991, p. 95). Most often, it is a mixture of the two.

Meaning is therefore "inherently socially negotiated" among these members and knowledge of the social world is continually "produced, reproduced, and changed in the course of activity" (Lave & Wenger, 1991, p. 51). Napier (2003) refers to this process as the "creolization and re-creolization" of policy ideas as they pass through and are modified in each successive decision-making context. An idea that is as hegemonic as doxa in one community of practice may become mere orthodoxy in another, as interaction among diverse members helps even central participants develop some self-awareness of their assumptions and a "recognition of the possibility of different or antagonistic beliefs" (Bourdieu, 1972, p. 164).[18] Participants in a community of practice, at all points in the spectrum of mastery, are continually involved in re creating—and therefore sometimes altering—the social meanings that shape their practice.

Rwandan policy makers, in other words, may wish to introduce a new post-developmental doxa and new dispositions into Rwandan schools and young Rwandans' lives—but this outcome is by no means guaranteed. Those who must execute the policy decision—curriculum developers and teachers around the country—will interpret national intentions through their own social experiences, perhaps with unexpected results. And while policy makers plan to educate youth in new directions, Rwandan youth may have a thing or two to teach policy makers in turn. It is through the complex negotiations within and between these communities of practice that Rwanda's contemporary post-developmental state is beginning to take shape.

Part II
Creativity and Controls in the Curriculum

Figure 6 A curriculum development seminar under way

Source: Photo by author.

Chapter 3

Codifying Entrepreneurship for O-Level

THE CURRICULUM DEVELOPERS arranged around the conference table—most of them teachers on their school break—followed along as the director of one of the units at the National Curriculum Development Centre sat next to the projector screen and began flicking through his slides.

"After an introduction, we will talk about classic pedagogy and active pedagogy," he began, gesturing to opposite sides of the room to illustrate the metaphorical distance between the two approaches. "We are just trying to push our mind to work on the possibility of using active pedagogy in our contexts—I don't mean only in entrepreneurship, but in our pedagogical context in general."

His audience nodded and he continued: "We know that the main objective of classic pedagogy is clear, without any ambiguity. The clear objective is just to transmit the content. [. . .] There are some difficulties in this kind of teaching. [. . .] For example, we said we would like to create someone able to develop our country, to participate in development, building our nation [. . .] but when he is [only] able to define a concept, can we say he will be able to solve some of our problems?"

"I think we are in the classic system, until now," he concluded a few minutes later. "Even though we are discussing the active system, but we are still so rigid. Everyone here is aware that the classic pedagogy is continuing to influence us, we continue to be so limited by our principles."

Pausing to check that his audience had agreed with his condemnation of the classical approach, he asked: "Are there questions about the classic method before we advance?"

At this invitation, the curriculum developers stirred and began to raise their hands. "It seems to be a good system!" the first called out, in a tone of voice that managed to sound simultaneously ironic and sincere.

Another seconded the implied challenge: "Before we talk about the active method, can you give us, what are really the inconveniences of the classic method?"

A third curriculum developer laughed, joking: "I remember, even my ex-teacher at university was saying the active method is good, but he was using classic methods to tell us!" Several people in the room chuckled knowingly.

Turning to a serious tone again, a fourth colleague remarked: "Surely [being able to use active pedagogy] is about having the right materials and means, but it is also about changing the mentality and attitude. That is difficult. That classic system is embedded in our minds."[1]

· · ·

As Rwanda's National Curriculum Development Centre (NCDC) set out to create the new entrepreneurship curriculum in 2008, it was clear that the course needed to be practically relevant. After all, as the NCDC official quoted in the previous chapter so clearly stated, this course was intended to give "some basic skills on entrepreneurship" to every young Rwandan so that "even if he drops out of school, he will have some notion on how he can manage his own small business."[2] And the General Objectives for the three-year course to be offered in O-level (grades 7–9) were, indeed, described in terms of specific things that graduates were expected to be able to do:

At the end of the lower secondary school level, the student must be able to: (1) Exercise commerce; (2) Pay taxes, charges and import duties in accordance to Rwandan norms; (3) Perform small enterprise's accounting; and (4) Develop and implement an income generating project.

These course objectives were a clear reflection of the government's vision of encouraging self-employment and orderly entrepreneurial activity among O-level graduates.

By the time the final syllabus had been prepared, however, that feeling of on-the-ground practicality had largely faded into the background. In the subsequent pages of the O-level curriculum, unit after unit indicated that the greater part of students' time should be spent merely learning the "definition" and "importance" of a given list of terms. Something got lost, in other words, along the way from the policy proclamation to the codified curriculum. Tracing the deviations and detours that led to this unexpected policy destination provides yet another level of insight into the kinds of paradoxes involved in the contemporary rise of post-developmental governance, in Rwanda and elsewhere.

In this chapter, I examine Rwanda's entrepreneurship curriculum development process in light of one of the curriculum developer's comments: that "the classic system is embedded in our minds." Drawing on the concepts of field and habitus discussed earlier, the following pages explore the social context within which the Rwandan curriculum developers working on the O-level entrepreneurship course had learned to view their task through an examinations- and credential-oriented lens that rewarded only a particular type of knowledge. As this initial team of curriculum developers brought their own ingrained dispositions to the process, they created a curriculum that reinforced the importance of credentials and controls at the expense of creativity—arguably jeopardizing one of the central policy objectives of the post-developmental state.

Imagining the Graduate Entrepreneur

The Rwandan government's decision that entrepreneurship should be taught in the first three years of secondary school (O-level) was publicly announced in late 2007. Bringing the course to schools around the country, however, still required several steps: developing a detailed syllabus, creating guides for teachers and students, training teachers, and distributing the materials to schools. In July 2008, the NCDC hosted the first curriculum development workshop for the O-level entrepreneurship course, beginning a process that was ultimately to last about eight months.

Just a day or two after the start of the workshop, the director in charge received me in his office to explain how the process would work.[3] "We intend to spend about fifteen days," he began. "We have invited some teachers from secondary schools, we have invited people from the Bank of Rwanda we have invited someone from Rwanda Revenue Authority, we have invited someone from [the business development center] CAPMER—and all of them are now seated trying to conceive this particular curriculum."[4]

"Now this first week," he continued, "they are trying to analyze what we call a leaver's profile: a person who has completed three years of secondary school in Rwanda and has done [studied] entrepreneurship—what profile should this person have?" He gestured beyond the brick walls of the building: "'He will be able to do this, he will be able to do that, he should be . . . ,' you know? Then from this profile, we shall be looking at the skills that this person should be able to be having. Then after the skills, we start going deep into the program or curriculum environment now, where we put the objectives, the global or general objectives, the specific objectives, the content, the methodology, and how we shall evaluate. You see? So it is still in its infancy, really."[5] The NCDC's curriculum development process seemed to be highly focused on practical outcomes, with the topics and teaching methods deriving logically from a vision of what graduates should be able to do once having completed the course.

Following this short briefing, the director accompanied me to another building on the NCDC campus, where a dozen people were squeezed around a U-shaped table strewn with papers and bottles of water. The blue light from a projector reflected off of their faces as they worked in small groups around a few laptops.

After introductions all around, I sat down with one of the groups to see what they were working on. The group was made up of three teachers and an NCDC curriculum developer, and the document open on their computer showed that they were working on a theme titled "Introduction to Accounting." They had identified two "competencies" related to accounting—elaborating a budget and managing stock—and the partially blank page on the screen showed that they were trying to list the "tasks" related to each one. All of the discussion was taking place in French, with some Kinyarwanda thrown in here and there to clarify a point.

On the other side of the room, another group—this one including not only teachers but also a representative from the National Bank of Rwanda (BNR), from the Rwanda Revenue Authority (RRA), and from the customs agency MAGERWA—were discussing the theme "Commerce." To the side, a third group was working on "Initiation to Commercial Law."

I soon learned that the group had already finished discussing the "school-leaver's profile," the vision of what "a person who has completed three years of secondary school in Rwanda and has studied entrepreneurship" should be able to do. Interestingly, however, it turned out that not much discussion had actually been necessary: in fact, high-level government decision makers had already designated the basic elements of the expected graduate's profile prior to the start of the curriculum development process.

"Before we began," one of the NCDC curriculum developers explained to me, "MINEDUC had asked us to introduce certain themes into the curriculum: commerce, commercial law, accounting, taxation, clearing and forwarding (that means customs, duties and importing), and project or enterprise planning and management." I noted the prominent emphasis on laws and regulations, which was the focus of three out of the six expected themes.

I asked him to tell me more about the origin of this instruction, and he continued: "This directive was handed down directly from the Akagera retreat with government leaders. We were called in for a meeting with the Director [of the NCDC], who told us the decisions that had been made at the Akagera retreat and that the curriculum was to include these subjects."[6] The promotion of entrepreneurship had apparently become such a key policy priority that even the Cabinet had gotten involved in deciding what the course should include—and a major part of what they considered relevant to the practice of entrepreneurship in Rwanda was an understanding of the extensive regime of business regulations that the government was then still in the process of consolidating.

During the first day or two of the workshop, the curriculum developers followed these instructions, settling on a vision of the course as "enabling the country's future citizens not only to become creators of their own employment but also people who give employment to others, and all of this in respect of the laws and regulations related to the creation and management of income-generating projects" (NCDC, 2008, p. 3, my translation). "At the end of O-level," the school leaver's profile continued,

the student should be capable of: (1) exercising his rights and obligations; (2) paying taxes, charges, and customs duties in respect of norms; (3) elaborating and executing a revenue-generating project; (4) negotiating a bank credit; (5) managing a bank account; (6) correctly declaring merchandise at customs; and (7) exercising commerce. (NCDC, 2008, p. 4)

Dutifully following the government's instructions, the curriculum development workshop participants had written the profile in such a way as to include an emphasis on legal issues, taxation, and customs, as well as other aspects of the practice of entrepreneurship. In that sense, the new course seemed well on its way to fulfilling the post-developmental objective of educating a generation of orderly entrepreneurs.

Dwelling on Semantics

If the first step of the curriculum development process had resulted in decidedly post-developmental objectives for the entrepreneurship course, this was not to last long. From that point on, the curriculum quickly turned in a different direction—toward an unambiguously "disciplinary" (Foucault, 1975) form of knowledge that could be easily linked to examinations and credentials. This shift began, paradoxically, while curriculum developers were trying to follow NCDC procedures specifically designed to encourage thinking about knowledge in terms of attitudes and skills rather than just information. As the curriculum development consultants tried to follow that designated procedure, however, they often seemed to get stuck at the level of semantics, slipping back into what seemed to be an ingrained habit: the primary importance of establishing correct terminology above all other considerations.

On the day I joined the curriculum development workshop, one member of my group explained that each group had first chosen one of the themes from the school leaver's profile and then, from that, had identified corresponding competencies and a set of tasks for each competency. Pointing to his laptop, he continued: "We have to think about each task in terms of three elements: *savoir*, *savoir-faire*, and *savoir-être*"—knowledge, know-how or skills, and "know-how-to-be" or attitudes.

Our group, working on the theme "Commerce" had decided to focus on two competencies ("Exercising Commerce" and "Exploit Different Markets—National, Regional, and International") and had already finished describing four tasks related to the former: (1) choose the commerce to undertake, (2) register yourself at the commercial registrar, (3) complete the documents related to buying and selling, and (4) calculate the different taxes and charges to pay on their commerce. Thinking back to the strong emphasis on regulations in the school leaver's profile, I noted that the exercise of commerce also seemed to involve a surprising number of bureaucratic tasks.

Their first competency complete, the group moved on to the second. One of the participants typed: "Competency: Exploit different markets (national, regional, and international)" and hit the Return key a few times. The group then began to discuss how to fill in the required categories for this new element of the curriculum:

BNR Consultant: The first task is "categorize the markets (domestic, regional, international)."

Teacher 2: For *savoir*, we can put: "define the different types of market."

Teacher 1: We have to look for words that are about tasks and not just knowledge.

Teacher 2: So, "identify the different types of market"?

He typed the phrase in the blank space waiting next to a bullet point. They continued:

BNR Consultant: The next one can be "explain the advantages and disadvantages for each type of market."

Teacher 1: Anything else?

Teacher 2: Maybe two is enough. So for *savoir-faire*, it could be "choose the appropriate market for their commerce."

The others nodded and he added the sentence to their list. There was a pause while they thought of other items to add to the *savoir-faire* list:

Teacher 1: We need at least one more.

Teacher 2: Once they choose the market, they have to sell.

BNR Consultant: Write: "Present products on the domestic market."

Teacher 1: And "good quality."

Teacher 2: [*Writing*] "Present superior quality products in the domestic market."

Teacher 1: What about *savoir-être*?

Teacher 2: Ummm . . .

BNR Consultant: Is there anything?

Teacher 1: We can't just leave one of the categories blank![7]

The discussion had begun to seem a little like a school workbook exercise, with blanks that each had to be filled in with the correct word.

I strained a little to overhear the discussion taking place on the far side of the table. There, the group working on the theme "Commercial Law" had identified one competency, which they titled "Create an enterprise (legal aspects)." As the group members argued about how exactly to formulate a second competency, they seemed to be even more focused on issues of terminology than my own group. At first they proposed writing "defend his rights and obligations," but then another group member argued that it should be "*respect* his rights and obligations" instead. After some minutes spent discussing the relative merits of the words *defend, respect,* and a few alternative options, they finally settled on the phrasing: "*identify* his rights and obligations."

After the amount of energy these two groups had spent on seemingly simple questions of word choice, what I saw as the deeper issue—the actual skills an entrepreneur might need to develop in order to put this knowledge into practice in the Rwandan context—seemed almost beside the point.

Somewhat later, each group made presentations on its lists of tasks. A few of the curriculum developers asked the NCDC staff for clarification on the difference between a notion, a concept, and information, arguing that another group was using the terms incorrectly. At another point, there was a loud discussion about which particular verbs to use when framing their instructions for the categories of "knowledge" and "know-how." The final settlement was a compromise, as someone suggested: "For the first year, we can tell them to 'identify' and 'list.' In the second year, it becomes 'describe' and 'give examples,' and then in the third year we can tell them to 'explain' and then 'do a mini-project.' So we will use them all."[8]

The purpose of this whole process, according to the NCDC staff, was to ensure that they arrived at a practical curriculum that would develop new skills (*savoir-faire*) and attitudes (*savoir-être*), beyond just transmitting information (*savoir*) to students. But the curriculum developers seemed to have reinterpreted their task as one focused centrally on determining the appropriate terminology to use while filling in each blank space on their lists. This cannot just be explained away as halfhearted effort—on the contrary, those in the conference room seemed highly engaged in the process, with an atmosphere of concentration and friendly discussion and debate. What they chose to debate *about*, however, was something far removed from the questions of practical application that had initially seemed so central to the process.

"Defining" an Appropriate Pedagogy

As the workshop continued, the curriculum developers converted these sets of tasks, knowledge, skills, and attitudes into bullet-pointed lists of the "specific objectives" and the "contents" of the course, enumerating the different topics to be discussed in class. There seemed to be an inexorable tendency to emphasize the terms and categories originally listed as knowledge (*savoir*), while questions of know-how and attitudes were quickly sidelined without much notice given to the fact. Soon, the contents of the course began to seem like little more than a list of terminology and information to be learned.

Toward the end of the second week, the conversation then turned to the issue of what sort of pedagogical guidance should be given to teachers. But interestingly, in contrast to the extensive discussion of what should be included in the contents of the course—and how exactly to phrase each bullet point in the syllabus—the issue of pedagogy seemed of minor importance to the curriculum developers.

The NCDC curriculum developers instructed the workshop participants to use "the active methodology" in which "the student is the center of the learning process." But when they asked the participants to give examples of active methods before beginning their work, the group quickly got into somewhat of an argument about whether it was more correct to use *brainstorming, remue-méninges,* or *jeu de questions-réponses.* Finally, the group arrived at some agreement that the "active method" implied using one of a few designated approaches: "group work," "brainstorming," "documentary research," or a "discussion guided by the teacher" that would lead students to "discover the definition by themselves."[9]

Once this list of pedagogical techniques had been fixed and defined, it seemed that no one felt much of a need for further in-depth discussion of the particular learning experiences that would be necessary to develop the specific skills and attitudes they had identified earlier on. Instead, workshop participants seemed to just dutifully rotate their pedagogical instructions among the established set of "active" methods. One such decision making process took place as participants were reviewing the following part of the syllabus for the module on commerce (see Table 2):

Teacher 1: Is there any activity that corresponds with 3.4? [Quality of the products on the market]

Teacher 2: *Ntayo* [there isn't any].

Teacher 3: So we have to search one to propose, we can't just say—"it's not there."

He used his finger to trace each of the surrounding activities in the syllabus— "through debates and discussions, learners will define," "basing on information research, learners will give the definition," and "by concrete examples the

Table 2   Excerpt from the O-level syllabus

Specific objectives	Contents	Teaching/learning activities

Differentiate various types of commercial discounts	3.3. Commercial discounts
	· Definition
	· Types of commercial discounts
	  · Cash discount
	  · Grace period
	  · Trade discount
		Basing on information research, the learners will give definition and the types of commercial discount

Identify an appropriate quality of the product to be offered on the market	3.4. Quality of the products on the market	
Explain the requirements for a successful sale	3.5. Conditions to success in selling · Knowing the behaviors of customers and their needs · Listening to customers' opinions · Satisfying customers' needs · Treat the customers well	By concrete examples the learners will give out conditions to success in selling

Source: NCDC (2008), p. 7.

learners will give out conditions to success"—apparently looking for an approach they had not yet used. They continued:

Teacher 3:   What about "by brainstorming"?
             [*There was a general murmur of agreement among the group, and the group secretary started writing: "By brainstorming, learners will identify—"*]
Teacher 2:   [*Interrupting*] In the specific objectives it says "identify" so the activity can't be identify, it has to be explain. [*Pausing to reconsider*] But then what are they going to explain? It's not *explain.*
Teacher 1:   It's *identify.*
Teacher 4:   It has to be *identify* or *discover.*
Teacher 1:   With *brainstorming*, it has to be *identify.*[10]

Yet again, their discussion seemed to evolve around questions of terminology—this time, the correct verb to associate with a particular pedagogical technique.

There was no discussion of the educational experiences students would need in order to "be able to run a small size business" (the module objective), to "be able to explain the operations in the buying and selling of goods" (the unit objective), or even to be able to "identify the appropriate quality" of the products a given business should offer (the specific objective in question). No one wondered out loud, for example, what kind of activity would help students understand the concept of distinguishing between different levels of quality, much less help them to practice that capacity. There was no discussion about the abilities that might be involved in becoming capable of analyzing specific markets in order to be able to determine "the appropriate quality" of a particular product to be sold. This particular specific objective might not have been of transcendental importance in the overall context of the course, but the absence of discussion on these considerations seemed significant—here and throughout.

As the curriculum development process progressed, the syllabus expanded to include a long list of terms, including *commerce, product, marketing, 4 Ps, banking system, trade license, statute, customs declaration, material requisition note, LIFO, FIFO, corporate income tax, fiscal taxes, value-added tax, creativity, originality, initiative,* and *SMART objectives,* among many others. Many of these terms had been the subject of significant debate during the workshop, as the curriculum developers discussed the appropriate phrasing for each one. But the question of which pedagogical approach to use in order to teach each concept often amounted to the same issue in the end—basically any approach would do, so long as it implied that students would "discover the definition" or "discover the answer" in the end.

The behavior of these curriculum developers began to seem puzzling, to say the least, as I observed their work over the following weeks and months. After all, this course was supposed to prepare young Rwandans to start and manage their own businesses—but, from my perspective as an outsider, nothing about the curriculum development process so far seemed to be focused on cultivating actual entrepreneurial behavior. Yet these participants were clearly working hard to create a good product. Virtually everyone was offering their ideas, often debating points extensively before eventually agreeing on how to give teachers and students the best possible guidance—even as the curriculum seemed to be moving farther and farther away from considerations of how to develop the practical abilities of an entrepreneur. To comprehend what happened during this curriculum development process, I now turn back to the concepts of field and habitus, discussed in the previous chapter.

Dispositions, Habitus, and Shared Experience in the Rwandan Field of Schooling

A curriculum is not, obviously, simply the output of some programmed computer; it is inevitably created by people with their own personalities and personal histories. Participants in a given curriculum development process, however, bring to the table more than their individual idiosyncrasies. In many cases, they also share professional and educational experiences that shape—often at an unconscious level—the curriculum they produce (Apple, 2004; Bourdieu & Passeron, 1990). It becomes crucial, then, to ask, who are the writers of this curriculum, and what learned social experiences have brought them to this role?

The workshop participants involved in designing Rwanda's first O-level entrepreneurship curriculum came from a small range of professional and educational backgrounds. Some were direct employees of the National Curriculum Development Centre. Most, however, were full-time teachers of economics and accounting in Rwandan secondary schools who had been brought in for a short-term consultancy. Only a few participants had professional careers outside of the Rwandan formal school system, and these were mostly from government regulatory agencies interacting with the business sector. None of the curriculum developers had introduced him- or herself as a practicing entrepreneur.[11]

Further, all of the O-level curriculum developers had in common a significant period of experience within Rwandan schools. The majority were Francophone Rwandans or Congolese, either fully Rwandan educated or immersed in Rwandan schools for years as part of the large contingent of Congolese secondary school teachers who had come to Rwanda since the outbreak of violence in the eastern Congo in the 1990s. A few others had been born outside of the country or had left as children during an earlier period of violence, but most, if not all, of them had returned to Rwanda for secondary school or university. No one involved in the O-level curriculum development process had been educated outside of East Africa, though several hoped that one day they would have the opportunity to earn a master's degree elsewhere.

As former students and as education professionals, those involved in the O-level entrepreneurship curriculum development process were deeply immersed in Rwanda's field of formal instruction, a social field with a shared history of lasting significance. To advance to this level in their chosen professions, they had undoubtedly developed a "feel for the game" of schooling, an "acquired mastery, functioning with the automatic reliability of an instinct" (Bourdieu, 1990, pp. 66, 104). They had become, in other words, "masters" of the appropriate ways of thinking and behaving in Rwanda's field of schooling—strongly shaping, perhaps in largely unconscious ways, the doxa and dispositions that structured every one of their social interactions.

To understand Rwanda's 2008 O-level entrepreneurship curriculum development process, then, one needs to understand something about the shared experiences that may have influenced these curriculum developers' presuppositions about what a "good" curriculum is and how to create it. In the following sections, I offer a reconsideration of what happened during the O-level development process by showing how the field of schooling in Rwanda has historically come to be defined by two principal characteristics: first, a perspective on knowledge as that which can be defined and memorized, and second, a valorization of examinations and credentials to a far higher degree than the knowledge itself gained along the way. The conditions under which formal schooling developed in Rwanda, I argue, established an institutional culture that exerts a persisting influence on its participants—and on their actions in the social world—to this day.

DISCIPLINE AND SOCIAL MOBILITY IN PRECOLONIAL AND COLONIAL RWANDAN SCHOOLS

Rwanda has a long history of formalized education systems promoting the standardized transmission of particular forms of knowledge. This codified approach to knowledge and learning arguably took shape more than two hundred years ago within indigenous Rwandan institutions and was further developed and embedded in Rwandan society through the advent of colonial-era mission schools. In both types of institutions, the motivations for learning were not just for the sake of gaining knowledge. Instead, formalized learning was closely tied to opportunities for status advancement that have indelibly shaped popular understanding of the purpose of schooling in Rwanda.

Prior to colonial intervention in the late nineteenth century, a diverse set of social groups within the territory roughly corresponding to contemporary Rwanda were being progressively consolidated under a central kingdom (Newbury, 2009; Vansina, 2004).[12] Among many other formal institutional features, this precolonial Rwandan kingdom had established a system of increasingly formalized education called *itorero*,[13] with centers for training in warfare, dance, poetry, and other arts. Many local chiefs hosted *itorero*, as did the King's court (Bale, 2002; Barber, 2007; Codere, 1973; Erny, 2005; Peck, 1970). Disciplinary codes were embedded in every aspect of the *itorero*. Military exercises were highly disciplined affairs, as was the learning of poetry and dynastic recitation. Accurate usage of difficult vocabulary and proverbs, and the correct recall of extended official accounts of history, were highly valued. Barber (2007) writes, "Every aspect of verbal art was named and consciously mastered" and "the creation, transmission, and differentiation of genres was regulated by the state" (p. 59).

While most young people involved in the *itorero* were probably already of high social status, there was the possibility of selection from other social groups as well—the very word *itorero* means "the place where one is chosen" (Bale, 2002, p. 36). The *itorero* thus opened up possibilities for social status advancement among some selected Rwandan youth—with capacity and merit measured according to the dominant values of the aristocracy (Maquet, 1954, as cited in Erny, 2005, p. 110). In that sense, the *itorero* was a bureaucratic institutional innovation comparable to other bureaucratization processes that were occurring elsewhere in the world around the same time (Foucault, 1975; Weber, 1978), beginning to rationalize social hierarchies via a more externalized system of evaluating conduct. And one of the key characteristics valued by the Rwandan central state was respect for authority.

European visitors of the time were struck by the strong consolidation of Rwandan hierarchy and rule—to the extent perhaps of overstating the case in their accounts (Newbury, 2009). But even if obedience to authority was not universal in Rwanda (Waldorf, 2007), it was a value being consistently communicated and reinforced by the ruling state. The dynastic poetry that youth learned in the *itorero* conveyed the exalted position of royal authority:

> *The King is neither a common nobleman*
> *Nor can he be a simple prince of the blood;*
> *He is the exalted and he dominates human beings. (Iliffe, 2005, p. 162)*

Although youth in Rwanda made their fair share of mischief, deference to authority was drilled into young Rwandans of all classes as they grew up, through instruction and example. "When the ruler gives an order," one observer remarked, "he must be obeyed, not because his order falls into the sphere over which he has authority, but simply because he is the ruler" (Maquet, 1954, as cited in Prunier, 1995, p. 57). The *itorero* was just one of the Rwandan institutions that instilled this sense of honor and respect for authority.

Around the same time that the *itorero* system was being consolidated in Rwanda, fundamental changes in European social systems and approaches to education were also already well under way. Foucault has called this transformation the rise of the "disciplinary" state, which implied not only new bureaucratic forms of discipline through mechanisms such as examinations but also a new degree of state supervision of "the welfare of the population, the improvement of its condition, the increase of its wealth, longevity, health, etc." (Foucault, 1991, p. 100). By the mid-nineteenth century, a number of European governments had established new public programs in areas such as health care, old-age pensions, and some provision for the unemployed (Esping-Anderson, 1990; Hennock, 2007). Furthermore, nearly every European government already considered itself responsible for providing at least a primary education to its population (Deacon, 2006).

In most cases, these new European government-sponsored education systems built on the example of existing provisions for basic schooling sponsored by both Protestant and Catholic churches (Power, 1991). As a result, when Christian missionary activity increased in central and eastern Africa in the nineteenth century, followed shortly thereafter by the division of the region into German, British, and Belgian colonies, there was already some measure of agreement between the missions and colonial governments that basic education should form a part of the colonial enterprise. The form of that education, in turn, was conceived of largely in terms of priorities and practices current in Europe at the time. Yet it was also heavily influenced by colonial-era racism and the need to maintain a position of domination over colonized populations. The result was the propagation of education systems throughout Africa that contained a number of contradictions at their core.

The first European-style schools in Rwanda were established before the turn of the twentieth century by missionary societies, with the greatest and most widespread influence exerted by the Catholic White Fathers order. By 1923, the White Fathers mission reported 267 elementary schools, with almost twenty-four thousand pupils. The Phelps-Stokes educational survey of the region at the time noted that "it is probable that many of the 'schools' are merely catechetical centers," focused more on oral religious instruction than on academic preparation (Jesse Jones, 1923, p. 291). The Protestant mission elementary schools, in contrast were numerically much less significant, with a total of about 1,300 pupils (Jesse Jones, 1923, p. 292). As these numbers suggest, the Catholics were particularly successful at achieving an early large-scale expansion of basic schools that focused on religious conversion through education in Catholic doctrines, as well as on a certain level of literacy and numeracy.

In an extensive historical study conducted by French ethnologist Pierre Erny (2001),[14] the diaries and letters written by the leaders of these missionary societies, as well as by some of the first literate Rwandans, reveal a social context in which the initial expansion of Catholic basic schooling was directly influenced by the aspirations of the less powerful for an opportunity to change the social order. The missionaries were perceived early on as a group with a distinct position of wealth and status. Similar to the existing Rwandan aristocracy, they were exempt from hard manual labor and able to exert authority over others. Participation in missionary schools, and especially the advancement to higher academic levels through good performance on school examinations and acquiring the attendant credentials, was thus quickly associated in the Rwandan public eye with "protection against the exigencies, justified or unjustified, of their chiefs" and with an automatic improvement in social and economic status—to a degree never before possible in Rwandan society (Erny, 2001, p. 24).

As the first groups of Rwandans became literate within the mission schools, they were also incorporated into specific nonagricultural functions within the small mission and colonial settlements. A priest, Father de Lacger later recalled:

The humble serfs were thus elevated to the situation of educated literates, secretaries, interpreters, just as much before the eyes of their indigenous chiefs as before their European masters. They were even invited to present their candidacy for the priesthood, which elevated them with one bound to the level of their own teachers. What a sudden advancement in their condition! What an incredible gain in prestige and even in well-being! (Erny, 2001, p. 38, my translation)

The opportunity that the mission schools posed for social advancement thus seems to have figured strongly in their widespread expansion.

The Rwandan aristocracy had originally rejected the missions and their schools, and had encouraged punishment and shunning of those who attended (Erny, 2001). However, the success of the Catholic schools in attracting the Rwandan masses, and the surprising social transformations that almost immediately accompanied their expansion, quickly prompted the King to partially reverse his position. Within a few years, the King had demanded schooling for his own sons and pages, coexistent with the court's ongoing *itorero*, under the condition that the missionaries teach nothing of their own religion (Erny, 2001).

HIERARCHY AND THE LIMITATION OF SOCIAL
AND EDUCATIONAL MOBILITY

Colonial-era schooling in Rwanda was largely an affair of the missions, but with a few key interventions from the colonial powers that further consolidated the importance of educational credentials for social advancement.[15] The Belgian administration that came to power after World War II reached a new agreement with the mission representatives, offering government subsidies in exchange for slightly greater influence in the schools' operations. In particular, the colonial government emphasized its preference for a strongly hierarchical system with limited access to the upper levels of schooling, controlled at each stage by a strict process of selection.

On the basis of his analysis of Belgian colonial documents, Erny describes the fears behind this hierarchical educational structure:

A constant preoccupation, though undoubtedly not spoken aloud, ran through the Belgian education policy: that of avoiding at any price that Africans should arrive at a level of instruction in which they could compete with their colonizers; according to the principle: "no elites, no trouble," education was never more than a necessary evil. As a result, [. . .] a principle of progressivity [governed the system]· the emphasis was on an elementary education for the masses, and only opening upper tracks under conditions of extreme prudence and parsimony when specific needs appeared: "*education should only distribute the knowledge that the indigenous will be able to use in the social role that each is called on to play.*" (Erny, 2001, p. 88, my translation, emphasis in the original)

The principle of progressivity that Erny mentions here, that of limiting the form of education to the kind of work available to (or supposedly "appropriate" for) the Rwandan masses, led to a triage system with extremely limited places at the secondary school level. This fit well with the objectives of the existing Rwandan elite, which also preferred to impose certain limitations on educational access and thereby preserve its social position. As a result, at the time of independence from Belgian rule, in 1962, a total of around 280,000 students were studying in Rwandan primary schools, while only 726 students were enrolled in all grades of Rwanda's secondary schools combined, with the expectation that there would eventually be around 100 secondary school graduates each year (Erny, 2001, pp. 226–227).

In such a situation, in which only a tiny percentage of primary school graduates were permitted to continue their studies, every graduate from secondary school was essentially guaranteed a salaried position with the government or mission structures. For the rest, the primary school cycle was supposed to be complete in and of itself, oriented toward the agricultural domain that would necessarily be most graduates' field of work. But this state of affairs was not easily accepted by those who had entered the schooling system hoping for an advancement in their position, only to be shut out of its higher levels.

In the 1950s, the White Fathers order carried out a study of young Rwandans who had not progressed beyond primary school, arriving at the following conclusions:

The boys who have done no more than two or three years of primary school [. . .] adapt quite easily to traditional life and work [. . .] [But] the boys who have completed their primary studies (5 or 6 years): these cause a big problem. These adolescents of 13 to 16 years old, who know how to read and write and speak some words of French, no longer adapt easily to traditional life [. . .] manual work puts them off. [. . .] If he is Tutsi and from a well-off family, his parents and friends of the family engineer a way to find him a little desk job with the chief or the subchief, or he becomes a house worker, roadman, agricultural monitor, etc. [. . .] Among the adolescents who are Hutu or from poor families, some, especially if they live far from the centers, go back to work in the fields. But often they do not last long before becoming bored and leaving their hillside, taking the road to Uganda or going towards the urban centers. In Uganda, they will work in the plantations. In the centers, they will search for a job that is not too hard, or live as dependents of a member of the family, or become vagabonds, or steal [. . .] In summary, one can say that the entire youthful generation of Rwanda-Urundi that has finished primary school aspires to secondary school and even to university-level studies. If that possibility is closed off to them, they want an occupation that is less tiresome and more profitable than the work of a farmer or laborer. This is the anguishing problem of post-school youth. (Erny, 2001, p. 224, my translation)

By independence, Rwandan schools had thus become a gateway both to unprecedented opportunities for social advancement and to potentially bitter disappointment.

THE PEDAGOGICAL INFLUENCE OF THE CATECHISM

The developing significance of formal Western-style schooling in Rwanda was tied not only to its role as an unprecedented route to improved socioeconomic status but also to the particular means by which students could obtain that advancement. While the criteria for advancement in the mission schools were not completely impartial, the means that was most directly under students' control was exemplary academic performance.[16] This performance was measured in two ways. On the one hand, students' careful adherence to school norms influenced teachers' personal opinions of students, which were a crucial factor in selection. On the other hand, performance on examinations, while not completely determinant, played a part in the system of triage at every stage of schooling. The promise of socioeconomic advancement that schooling apparently offered was thus heavily dependent on mastery of particular types of behavior and forms of knowledge.

Significantly, as defined by the Catholic missionaries who ran the majority of schools in Rwanda, good academic performance was not measured in terms of intellectual creativity or insightful analysis. Instead, the Catholic schools placed an emphasis on the correct restating of preformulated information, as "the catechist instructors taught as they themselves had been taught, the essential being the word-by-word memorization of the texts to be learnt" (Erny, 2001, p. 33, my translation). This interpretation of knowledge—as that which can be codified, memorized, and repeated—undoubtedly drew upon and reinforced the existing arts of recitation developed by the Rwandan aristocracy through the *itorero* system (Barber, 2007). While training in most of Rwanda's ritual texts and poetry would have been limited to the few who participated in the *itorero*, however, under colonialism an increasingly wide segment of the Rwandan population gained access to another ritual text: the Catholic catechism. Together, these poetic and catechism pedagogical styles have created a limited, but firmly ingrained, repertoire of dispositions for teachers and students that continues to shape the entire field of education in Rwanda up to the present day.

It is difficult to identify exactly which version of the catechism was used in colonial Rwanda, not least because of the partial and inadequate translations into Kinyarwanda that were only improved over time (Shorter, 2006). However, given the most common catechisms in circulation in the early twentieth century, and the general features of traditional Catholic pedagogy (Kössler, 2009; Willey, de Cointet, & Morgan, 2008), we can suppose that the catechism would have included a set text divided into chapters focusing on a progressive succession of topics. Each of these, in turn, would have opened with one or more definition-oriented questions such as "What is faith?" or "What is God?"—questions intended to clarify key terms and definitions that would then be employed in slightly longer and more complex passages. Only the teacher would have had access to a printed catechism, if at all. The content was fixed and intended for memorization, offered in the traditional call-and-response format in which the teacher posed a question and the class responded in chorus with a preformulated answer (Erny, 2001; Shorter, 2006).

The catechism's style of transferring codified knowledge extended even to the upper levels of colonial Rwandan schooling. For those students who successfully passed beyond the primary level of the catechism and basic literacy, and were selected for the seminary, their curriculum began with courses in "religious instruction, French, Latin, history, geography, elementary science, arithmetic and music" and then narrowed in the upper level to a focus "restricted almost entirely to theology and philosophy" (Jesse Jones, 1923, pp. 291–292). Despite the apparent intellectual rigor of this program of study, the pervasive racist judgments of the time strongly influenced the goals and methods of the teachers. Because it was "generally accepted that after puberty the intelligence of young Blacks could not progress further," the entire education system considered it "useless to give too much emphasis on discursive and critical reflection; instead, the emphasis was put on passive memorization and recitation by heart" (Erny, 2001, pp. 36–38, my translation). Thus, even the upper levels of Rwandan Catholic schools continued to emphasize memorization and recitation—not because of limitations in literacy as was the case in the primary schools and catechetical centers, but because of the supposed intellectual limitations of the students.

In the lead-up to independence and for decades thereafter, this pedagogical orientation continued to influence the entire Rwandan education system. In a context where traditional academic schooling was seen as essentially the only path for individual socioeconomic mobility, the whole pressure of the system continued to be focused on obtaining the highest examination scores possible. And those examination results continued to be dependent on the mastery of a form of knowledge that had changed little since the initial catechetical centers were introduced. Erny writes of his own experience encountering some secondary school students in the mid-1970s, during the time that he was teaching at the National University of Rwanda:

Teaching remained, setting aside some meritorious exceptions, terribly formal, abstract, passive, bookish, founded on copying, memorization, group recitation, crude verbalism, and parroting. I remember that, in walking one day around Butare [the town where the original National University of Rwanda was situated, now called Huye] I met a group of young students who were coming back from their classes. I asked them what they had learned that day. They showed me their notebooks, and the lesson of the day was titled "the Orography of Rwanda." On the previous page was the topic of "Hydrography." In another notebook, I found exercises on "phraseology." [. . .] The lessons, whether of geography, or history, or grammar, were methodological carbon-copies of those of the catechism: one asked a question and the response was, by preference, given in chorus. (Erny, 2003, p. 57, my translation)

It is not difficult to see the similarities to the O-level entrepreneurship curriculum described earlier—where yesterday's orography, hydrography, and phraseology have become today's management terminology of the 4 Ps, LIFO, FIFO, and SMART objectives.

"PLUS ÇA CHANGE . . .": SCHOOLING IN POST-GENOCIDE RWANDA

The period surrounding 1994 was a time of drastic social upheaval and widespread personalized violence in Rwanda. Yet despite the complete social disruption provoked by the 1994 genocide, the overall structure of rewards in Rwanda's field of schooling—and thus the underlying doxa and dispositions encouraged by the system—changed little for almost two decades after the genocide.

Indeed, one of the most significant reforms instituted by Rwanda's postgenocide government has arguably served to reinforce the role of examinations in Rwandan schools—though this is widely regarded as a positive transformation. Specifically, the new regime launched an immediate campaign to increase the transparency and fairness of the examinations at each level of schooling, which had previously involved a great deal of ethnic, regional, and personal favoritism (Rwanda National Examinations Council, 2012). Uniform national examinations were established, and for the first time the criteria for grading and assigning places in schools were publicly explained. Students also now take their examinations under a numeric code, rather than writing in their names, and of course their "ethnic" designation is no longer mentioned.

These efforts had the effect of making the examinations even more important than ever before in Rwanda, as the recognized objective arbiter of opportunities for educational—and thus socioeconomic—advancement. Since the mid-1990s, results on the national examinations have been reported publicly each year and have determined who would be awarded places in the higher-quality, and usually less expensive, state secondary schools. Examination scores also provided nongovernmental and governmental organizations with a merit-based measure on which to condition need-based grants to secondary schools. Finally—and perhaps most crucially in the eyes of most students—the Senior 6 national examinations determined who would receive a government scholarship to attend Rwanda's prestigious public universities or even to be sent to other universities around the world.[17] Despite these changes in the examination system, however, until recently there was little discussion of changing the measurement approach itself, which continued to focus largely on definitions and recall.

At the same time as traditional examinations maintained their central importance in the Rwandan system, pedagogical practices had also remained essentially unchanged. Numerous recent initiatives in Rwanda have focused on promoting a shift in schools toward a more "active" pedagogy. These include a number of Innovation for Education projects funded by the United Kingdom's Department for International Development (MINEDUC, 2013); the Rwanda Education Commons, an online forum to promote teacher collaborations and improvements in teaching practice; and recent efforts to transform Rwanda's national examinations toward a more constructivist approach (Gahigana, 2008; Gahigana & Kagame, 2008; Kwizera, 2009, 2011). But these initiatives were introduced precisely because both the Ministry of Education and certain international organizations recognized that pedagogy in Rwanda had remained just as definitions driven and memorization focused as it was decades ago.

When the O-level entrepreneurship curriculum developers first began developing the syllabus in 2008, therefore, Rwanda's field of schooling was thus still heavily influenced by the missionary and colonial conditions under which it first developed, and by some of the longer-standing disciplinary features of Rwandan society and the *itorero* system before that. Teachers and students alike continued to interpret educational credentials as a form of symbolic capital that could be traded on for a chance of advancement in socioeconomic status—becoming more upwardly mobile through access to paid employment. And those credentials were still dependent on examinations that rewarded certain dispositions, including regarding the teacher as the central authority on knowledge, and treating knowledge as that which can be defined and memorized.

These were the social conditions of the *itorero* and of the first Catholic mission schools, and these were the social conditions within which the curriculum developers themselves were later educated. As one of the curriculum developers in this chapter's opening vignette mentioned, they are not so much conscious pedagogical choices as prereflective issues of attitude and belief that have become "embedded in their minds."

Controlling Creativity: Curriculum and Textbooks

After three weeks of discussions focused on terminology and definitions, the O-level entrepreneurship workshop participants succeeded in completing a syllabus detailing the specific objectives, contents, and pedagogical activities for each of the units of the course. The NCDC staff and workshop participants had not consulted any other existing entrepreneurship materials from around the world as they worked on the O-level curriculum.[18] But if the workshop participants had done a more extensive comparison with other entrepreneurship curricula, they might have remarked that Rwanda's syllabus was shaping up to be quite different from existing materials being used in other countries, in two respects: the extensive amount of time and detailed attention given to government laws and regulations, and the almost complete neglect of any issues related to entrepreneurial creativity.

A content analysis of Rwanda's 2008 O-level course makes clear its distinctive characteristics as compared to two other entrepreneurship curricula used in the region: Uganda's entrepreneurship education course recently developed under guidance from UNIDO (National Curriculum Development Centre Uganda, NCDC, 2000a, 2000b), and the International Labour Organization's program Know About Business (KAB; Mann, Nelson, Thiongo, & Haftendorn, 2008), which is now being used in dozens of countries around the world, including in Kenyan TVET schools. Based on an analysis of the curricular objectives, titles of sections, lists of content to be covered, and suggested activities, Figure 7 compares the approximate percentage of course time devoted to two different aspects of entrepreneurship instruction: governmental laws and regulations regarding business activities (controls) on the one hand, and entrepreneurial resourcefulness and innovation (creativity) on the other.[19]

The differences among the three curricula are stark, particularly with respect to issues of regulations and controls. In comparison to KAB and the Ugandan entrepreneurship curricula, Rwanda's O-level curriculum spends more

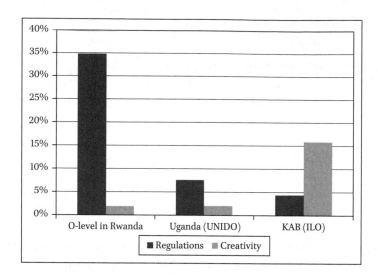

Figure 7   Percentage of course time intended to be spent on regulations versus creativity

than four times the percentage of class hours on issues of governmental laws and regulations: a recommended 55 out of 158 class periods, or more than one-third of the total course time.[20] These topics include detailed discussions of business taxes, customs procedures, and legal issues related to contracts and business disputes. In contrast, the other two curricula devote very little time to such regulatory questions, discussing them briefly at the level of principle, or simply mentioning them in passing as issues to keep in mind.

Figure 7 also shows the relatively limited degree to which the Rwandan O-level curriculum addresses creativity in opportunity-recognition and problem solving, arguably one of the fundamental abilities of effective entrepreneurs (Robinson, Stimpson, Huefner, & Hunt, 1991), and a key issue in the economic theory underlying neoliberalism, as introduced in Chapter 1. Time devoted to teaching "creativity" is much more ambiguous in a curriculum, and therefore much harder to count. The figure reflects a count of any curricular topic that explicitly concerned terms such as *creativity, innovation, resourcefulness*, and *problem solving*, as well as any recommended activities that might develop these abilities.

Differences in the amount of time devoted to questions of creativity are particularly noticeable between the Rwandan O-level curriculum and the International Labour Organization's KAB program. The Rwandan syllabus devotes less than 2 percent of total course time to this topic—principally to offer definitions of the terms *creativity* and *innovation* as part of a long list of entrepreneurial qualities. In contrast, Know About Business calls for at least 16 percent of its total course time to be spent discussing or practicing issues of entrepreneurial creativity, including one entire module with numerous exercises devoted to the topic.[21]

The final 2008 Rwandan O-level entrepreneurship syllabus thus clearly echoed the historical features of education in Rwanda—instructing teachers to focus heavily on respect for government authority, this time in the context of business regulations and procedures, while treating creativity as not much more than another term to be defined.

This trend was carried through to the development of student textbooks and teacher's guides later in 2008, the final phase of the curriculum development process. Despite some efforts to include student-centered activities, these materials largely ignored many of the practical capacities that seem most centrally important to entrepreneurial behavior: insightful analysis of opportunities, strategic planning, independent initiative, bootstrapping improvisation, and creative problem solving, to name a few. These aspects of entrepreneurship, so hard to define and even harder to control, simply did not seem to fit well within the curriculum developers' conception of how to develop appropriate content for a textbook. Instead, they focused on the terminology and basic information that would eventually be examinable at the district and national levels.

On the other hand, closely following the syllabus, the textbook writers devoted a significant amount of attention to a range of bureaucratic, regulatory, and legal issues relating to entrepreneurship. These became, in fact, some of the most "practical" lessons in the textbooks—as they taught in detail about different specific Rwandan laws to follow and even gave full-page examples of different forms to be filled out. However, while they are certainly applicable to life beyond school walls, these lessons also required little deviation from existing Rwandan educational practices. No independent investigation or problem solving would be necessary, no role plays or field visits. A chalkboard and chalk, notebook and pen, would suffice for teaching students how to fill out forms and follow rules. "Practical" teaching about business regulations, it turned out, was quite compatible with a school system still focused primarily on definitions and memorization.

With this sort of material as a supplement to the syllabus, students could be expected to demonstrate a practical expertise in current Rwandan business norms, such as naming specific Rwandan regulatory agencies, explaining the details of particular Rwandan laws and regulations, and even describing or reproducing examples of certain bureaucratic procedures. Students could also be expected to be able to list and define the qualities of a typical successful entrepreneur—being sure to mention creativity. Indeed, students would have been well prepared for the examination given in the first trimester of the 2010 school year, which began by asking students to "define the entrepreneur."[22] The O-level curriculum developers, it turns out, seem to have had a good understanding of the kind of knowledge these potential future entrepreneurs would need—at least in order to pass their final examinations.

The Synergy of Credentials and Controls

The O-level curriculum development process described in this chapter might have raised a number of questions for any outside observer. How did a course with such down-to-earth initial goals of promoting entrepreneurial practice end up focusing so strongly on theoretical and calcified forms of knowledge? Why is it, that although these participants tried to follow the NCDC guidelines on producing a practical and learner-centered curriculum, their discussions still tended to focus primarily on issues of terminology and taxonomy? Why did the curriculum developers focus most of their efforts on developing a list of "content" for the course and accord relatively little attention to the question of the pedagogical methods that could help students develop such understanding, skills, and attitudes—even though pedagogical recommendations are an integral part of what the NCDC conceives of as a syllabus? And finally, why did a course that was intended to produce entrepreneurs give so much attention to orderliness and regulations while virtually ignoring the qualities of resourcefulness and creativity that are so integral to entrepreneurial practice?

By considering the history of schooling in Rwanda and carrying forward the model of governance as negotiated social learning, presented in Part I of the book, it is possible to propose an answer to these questions. The argument is this: while none of the curriculum developers were intending to subvert the design of a curriculum capable of inspiring creative entrepreneurial behavior, their ingrained conceptualization of what constituted "a good education" was in many ways essentially anti-entrepreneurial, inevitably shaping the kind of curriculum they produced.

Who curriculum developers are, as actors with particular social histories, influences in many ways the kinds of curriculum they collectively produce. The participants in the O-level curriculum development process were all strongly influenced by the presuppositions that have historically come to characterize Rwanda's field of schooling. A focus on codified knowledge, examinations, and credentials, had—in other words—become part of their own ingrained doxa and dispositions, limiting and structuring the very range of educational goals that were even available for their consideration. When the NCDC brought these individuals together to develop the new entrepreneurship curriculum, it was these ingrained dispositions that came to the fore and shaped their collaborations.

Within the new community of practice constituted to create the curriculum, a negotiation had to take place. On the one hand was the procedural guidance from the NCDC that was intended to encourage the production of a more student-centered and practically relevant form of curriculum. On the other hand, and in significant contrast, was the participants' embodied knowledge of the familiar "rules of the game" in Rwanda's field of schooling. The ideas of active pedagogy were expressed in words, but there was no one in the group who had experienced them to such a degree that they unconsciously embodied them in their habitual dispositions and actions. Active pedagogy was a "text" that had "circulate[d] without its context" (Bourdieu, 1999, p. 221), open to misinterpretations and reinterpretations under the conditions of a new social field.

Without the tension between these two sets of social instructions ever becoming the subject of explicit debate, an unspoken settlement was quickly reached in which "relevance" was reinterpreted in terms of the "practical" requirements of codifying examinable knowledge about entrepreneurship and government regulations. In the process, the more elusive aspects of the practice of entrepreneurship—such as creativity, initiative, and independent problem solving—were either calcified or set aside.

But the eventual O-level entrepreneurship curriculum did more than just prepare students for examinations and credentials—it also strongly reinforced the regulations and controls that represent the "developmental" aspect of Rwanda's post-developmental state. This was the product of a second set of

instructions—the guidance received from high-level leadership that the curriculum should address business laws and the regulatory framework—instructions
that seemed to fit in much better with participants' existing disciplinary- and
credentialist-influenced habitus. Government goals of encouraging obedience
to laws and regulations turned out to be quite compatible with the credentialist focus on examinable knowledge expressed in lists of terms and definitions.
Rwanda's 2008-level curriculum development process thus arguably registered
the presence of three distinct visions for the purpose of Rwanda's entrepreneurship education policy: (1) transmitting a fixed body of knowledge that can be examined and on the basis of which credentials can be awarded, (2) encouraging
obedience to government laws and regulations, and (3) cultivating the qualities
of entrepreneurial and creative self-reliance. Representative of different logics
of governance, each of these education policy priorities could be expected to
coexist in a certain degree of contradiction with the others. The observations
discussed in this chapter suggest, however, that this triangulation of tensions
is not evenly balanced. The imbalance lies in the synergy created between the
priorities of credentials and controls—the stronger this connection grew, the
more completely the creative aspects of entrepreneurialism seemed to be marginalized.

As a result of this synergy between credentials and controls, Rwanda's
O-level entrepreneurship curriculum represented more a technology of the
developmental state approach to governance than it did the neoliberal or post-
developmental goals that the Rwandan government has more recently been trying to promote. As curriculum developers' existing dispositions exerted their
strong influence on the process, the O-level entrepreneurship curriculum became something that would reinforce, rather than revolutionize, the existing
significance of schooling in the Rwandan context. This observation illuminates
the necessarily piecemeal and incomplete nature of any process of shifting
from one fundamental rationale of governance to another. For no matter how
straightforward the new set of goals and rationales may appear in policy documents, such efforts at change necessarily involve multidirectional and indeterminate processes of social learning in specific institutional settings and social
groups.

In the O-level curriculum development process, the social histories of the
curriculum developers, and the instructions introduced by high-level policy
makers, resulted in a strongly disciplinary-oriented curriculum. Those same

elements played a very important role in the A-level curriculum development process as well—but this time with very different results. In Chapter 4, I continue with an examination of how a confluence of changes in Rwanda's field of schooling resulted in the development of a radically different A-level entrepreneurship course, suggesting that one day, creativity might just take precedence over controls.

Chapter 4
Reimagining Entrepreneurship for A-Level

THE O-LEVEL CURRICULUM development process, aimed at the first three years of secondary school in Rwanda, was complete around February 2009. By August 2009, Rwanda's National Curriculum Development Centre had begun work on an A-level entrepreneurship syllabus intended for the final three years of secondary school. But the A-level curriculum took shape in a noticeably different direction, even as it covered some of the same topics.

To illustrate one major difference between the two curricula, we have only to turn back again to the topic of product quality. During the O-level curriculum development process, we listened in on a group discussing how to teach this topic. "By brainstorming," they had suggested, "learners will identify an appropriate quality of the product to be offered on the market."[1] Period. Having filled in the empty space on their draft syllabus, the O-level curriculum developers simply moved on to another topic.

The eventual A-level syllabus also included the learning objective "analyze the quality of the product/service/processes of a business." But this is where the resemblance ends. In the right-hand column describing the suggested teaching and learning activities, the A-level curriculum developers wrote:

The teacher brings several examples of locally-produced products to the classroom (e.g., chapattis, tomatoes, eggs, mandazi, etc.). The learners should analyze these examples to see whether they are good quality products or not, and in what respect. If they notice quality defects, they should analyze the steps that have been gone through to produce the product and try to suggest how to guarantee better quality at each step. (*4 Allocated periods*)

And:

Let half of the learners assume the role of the owners of the school, and the other half its "customers." The owners are interested in knowing what their customers (clearly describe who these customers are) think about their school (what they are happy about and what they are not happy about). Ask the "owners" to enumerate the various ways in which they can get this information (examples: observation, survey, records, focus group/meetings, suggestion box), and use those methods to ask the opinion of the 'customers' about the things they would like the school administration to improve on to provide a better service. Together, they should make a plan for how to improve the school based on the information collected. (*4 Allocated periods*). (NCDC, 2009, pp. 52–53)

Gone was the sense of dutiful filling in the blanks from the O-level curriculum. Gone was the automatic rotation among the few pedagogical techniques that had been designated as "active" and "learner centered." These new activities certainly involved brainstorming, group work, and a discussion guided by the teacher. But rather than just citing these terms, the A-level curriculum developers actually demonstrated what they would mean in action.

The difference between the eventual O-level and A-level syllabi does not end there. Where more than one third of the O-level teaching materials were devoted to offering detailed information on topics like registration and taxation, the A-level syllabus hardly mentioned government regulations at all. Instead, it focused on concepts such as social responsibility and business ethics through activities such as the following: "ask learners to propose how they would finance provision of roads, water, schools, health service, security etc. in their locality," and "discuss three or more case studies showing different ways businesses have proactively contributed to the social and environmental context" (NCDC, 2009, pp. 56–57, 59). Gone were the detailed legal terms and the lists of regulatory institutions. Gone were the pages upon pages of example forms to be filled out.

In the final A-level curriculum, creativity seemed to have won out over controls. We would be justified in wondering, "What happened here?"

. . .

The O-level and A-level curriculum development processes may have led in different directions, but their implications for the study of shifts in governmental rationalities are similar. By contrasting the outcomes of the same entrepreneurship education policy processes at two different points in time, the following pages illustrate that a change in the rationality of governance cannot come about automatically or in a single abrupt transformation. Instead, it must work through established institutions and communities of practice characterized by

their own group cultures, and through the preexisting assumptions and dispositions of the individual policy makers—whether those at the highest levels of
leadership, or the regular day-to-day public servants working within them. The
result may often be a very piecemeal and partial shift, as policy makers in different public institutions come to embody the new dispositions to very different
degrees and in different combinations, and as conditions in larger social fields
change in uneven ways around them.

Changes in the Social Field of Schooling in Rwanda

When the National Curriculum Development Centre (NCDC) set about creating the A-level entrepreneurship curriculum in 2009, there had been no change
in the explicit policy instructions they originally received with regard to the
O-level curriculum. But the context had changed, in three significant ways: first,
in the approach of the national examinations system, altering the structure of
rewards in the field of education; second, in the exposure to external texts, influencing the NCDC's own institutional doxa; and finally, in the community of
practice that the NCDC was able to draw upon in order to create the new curriculum. These changes opened up possibilities for imagining new forms of "good
practice" in curriculum development, with a drastically different outcome.

NEW RULES OF THE GAME? SHIFTING APPROACHES
TO EXAMINATIONS

In 2008, just as the O-level entrepreneurship curriculum development process
was being launched, a significant change in the public discourse surrounding
examinations had begun to take shape in Rwanda—with the potential to alter
the entire structure of rewards in Rwanda's field of schooling. Early that year,
the Rwandan National Examinations Council (RNEC) had decided to make fundamental changes to the country's high-stakes national exams, which largely
determine access to high-quality public secondary schools and universities, by
focusing more on "analytical questions" rather than on those that are strictly
memorization based (Gahigana, 2008; Gahigana & Kagame, 2008). The RNEC
Executive Secretary explained in press interviews:

The aim is to change the old style that has been characterized by closed questions where
students have been giving narrow answers. [. . .] [T]he new set-up will enable students
to write detailed essays on a given question, [. . . which] requires deeper thinking [. . .

and] understanding of the critical issues of the country. [. . .] We know that in the short term students might have difficulties in adjusting to the new standards, but in the long run it is good for the nation in terms of competitiveness, as far as the East African labour market is concerned. (Gahigana & Kagame, 2008)

The RNEC Executive Secretary was aware of the potentially broad significance of these changes, stating that "one of the reasons for changing the national exam structure is because of the pressure it places on education reforms" (Gahigana, 2008). After nearly a century of examinations based on recall, it appeared the Rwandan education system was going to attempt a shift toward a more open-ended approach to measuring knowledge.

Although the first announcement of these changes formally predated the O-level entrepreneurship curriculum development process, it took some time for them to become widely understood. It was not until the O-level entrepreneurship curriculum was complete that the new approach to examinations began to play a role in conversations at the NCDC. At a training in the new O-level curriculum for a small group of teacher trainers, one of the first items on the agenda was a discussion about attempts to shift toward a more active and learner-centered teaching style.[2] The teachers present in the meeting at first argued not only that using "active pedagogy" requires too much time and expensive materials but also that it would condemn their students to failing the national exams:[3]

Teacher 1:   This [active] method for sure is good, because it helps students to be analytic and critical. But when you look at the way the exams are set, they are prepared in a way that means students are supposed to be taught using the classic method and not active. So if you use only the active method you might end up by not getting any students passing the exam!

Teacher 2:   I think that the examiners are not aware of what's being done as active pedagogy. At the national level, the examiner says: "The answer is like this, I've read it in this book; if the student doesn't say it like this exactly, then I give 0 out of 5!"

These teachers clearly felt that one of their primary obligations to students was to help them gain their credentials by doing well on the national examinations, and that using an active or learner-centered approach to teaching would jeopardize their ability to accomplish that objective.

It was only when other participants argued that Rwanda's examination system itself was changing that many of the participants began to acknowledge that teaching with an active pedagogy might actually be feasible:

NCDC Staff 1:   Let me comment about that. First of all, in this group we have people who have been sitting exams from Senior 6, and we also have some markers on exams here. [...] For a couple of years, some examiners used to set it so they want students just to memorize their courses. But nowadays, the National Examinations Council has been going to teachers to train them about how to set exams that require students to think. For example, when I say "define commerce," it is different from "what do you mean by the term commerce?" Or when I say "discuss," you don't want to just bring what the teachers taught you.

Another teacher concurred:

Teacher 3:   We are [exam] markers too, we don't just teach. In the past it was difficult, they told us what [the answer] had to be, et cetera. Now there is improvement, even in the level of taking into account the idea of the student. The marker is not a slave to what is already determined—the child has the right to think of a new idea, and you can take that into consideration. That doesn't pose a problem, it's possible.

Suddenly, there was a newfound agreement that the national examinations had begun to change in a way that was more compatible with learner-centered instruction.

With this realization, the tone of the conversation also began to turn. While some of those present continued to insist that "active methods" require time and resources that they do not have, others started to become more vocal champions of the idea:

Teacher 4:   I just wanted to say, about the issue of the time used [for active methods], actually the group active work takes less time because everyone is involved, they are all thinking. In classical, either they are all quiet and thinking about something else,

> or they are shouting and making noise and classroom control
> becomes hard.

By the end of this conversation, as one teacher put it, "We know that the active method is the best; we know that all of us here are the ambassadors." The group seemed to have accepted, at least at the level of principle, that they should be making more of an effort to engage students in learning beyond simply drilling them in lists of terminology and definitions.

As these comments show, the transition between the O-level and A-level curriculum development processes occurred at the same time as a significant— though perhaps not yet widely experienced or understood—shift in Rwanda's field of schooling. The ultimate rewards at stake in the system had changed little; students were still vying for the higher-level educational credentials that, they hoped, would guarantee them socioeconomic status advancement through access to good jobs. But the means for attaining those credentials was beginning to change, requiring demonstration of more independent thought and creative analysis in order to perform well on the national examinations. However partial and unevenly implemented at that stage, this shift in the approach to examinations was enough to lay the groundwork for a change in the doxa itself of the community of practice working on the entrepreneurship curriculum.

TRAVELING TEXTS

A second new influence on the educational context was an expanded degree of exposure to the ideas and dispositions of other communities of practice, with regard to pedagogy, the production of educational materials, and the teaching of entrepreneurship itself. In the preparations for the O-level curriculum development process, there was very little reference to entrepreneurship education materials that had been developed in other contexts. However, by the time the NCDC began its preparations for the A-level curriculum, that dynamic had changed, catalyzed by a textbook evaluation training sponsored by the United Kingdom's Department for International Development (DFID).

"Texts"—whether written, oral, or visual—can travel from one community of practice to another. As within the O-level curriculum development process, there is a likelihood of misunderstandings and limited influence when such texts have been introduced into different social realms, without bringing along "the field of production of which they are a product" (Bourdieu, 1999, p. 221).

However, that is only one side of the story; such texts also have the potential to catalyze changes in social practice, especially when they are accompanied by convinced practitioners of the ideas and dispositions they convey. This is in fact what occurred in the lead-up to Rwanda's second phase of entrepreneurship curriculum development.

Just two months before the A-level entrepreneurship curriculum development process began, as part of the ongoing DFID project Reform of the Procurement and Provision of Learning and Teaching Materials for Primary and Secondary Schools in Rwanda (NCDC, 2010), a team of DFID consultants led participants from the NCDC through a textbook evaluation process. Aiming for direct professional relevance, the DFID team gave the group of NCDC staff who were working on the entrepreneurship materials the assignment of evaluating a British General Certificate of Secondary Education (GCSE) textbook titled *Setting Up a Business* (Denby & Hamman, 2009).

This exercise constituted a double social influence on the NCDC community of practice. First, the very presence of experienced DFID educators allowed the NCDC staff a chance to collaborate with education professionals who had gained a great deal of practical experience with the principles of active pedagogy. Second, the textbook they analyzed together also brought the NCDC staff into contact with the ideas and methods of yet another distant community of practice, writers at the second-largest publisher for secondary education in the United Kingdom.[4] The British business textbook included in the workshop expressed markedly different presuppositions from the Rwandan O-level curriculum, particularly regarding the importance of attracting students' interest through relevant examples and eliciting their participation—two key features of learner-centered pedagogy.

During the textbook evaluation training, the NCDC staff read through only the introduction and a single chapter of the 170-page British textbook. Yet this in itself represented more in-depth contact with external educational materials than they had had during the entire O-level curriculum development process. After reading, they then filled out two columns on an evaluation checklist—one representing the rating for the British book and another with comparison ratings for Rwanda's own O-level entrepreneurship curriculum. The NCDC staff's responses on that evaluation checklist reveal their recognition of a number of ways in which the O-level curriculum fell short in terms of their goal of offering a learner-centered course capable of inspiring entrepreneurial activity.

The British textbook, one NCDC staffperson noted, had "plenty of activities that are of a wide variety *and* are relevant, interesting and practical"; in contrast, the Rwandan entrepreneurship materials featured "very few exercises, assignments and activities."[5] The British textbook had "regular and sufficient exercises, which are well-designed and helpful to the pupils," whereas the Rwandan materials, this NCDC employee felt, had "some exercises of this type, but they do not cover a majority of the topics or there are problems with their design and usefulness." The British text and illustrations, he thought, "consistently emphasize the development of skills," but in the Rwandan materials "the attempt to develop skills is not very successful." The British textbook "encourages a genuine understanding and appreciation of the subject [and] problem-solving exercises and activities are plentiful," whereas the Rwandan materials "attempt to encourage problem-solving, the attempt is not always successful."

These and similar comments filled out on the NCDC staff members' evaluation checklists suggest a growing realization that the O-level entrepreneurship curriculum did not meet the objectives of learner-centered practical relevance they had set for it. When one of the NCDC curriculum specialists later told me about his participation in the textbook evaluation training, he implied that the process had opened his eyes to seeing their own curriculum in an entirely new light. Whereas before the team had been largely satisfied with the O-level curriculum, he said, he had "noted many shortcomings in the entrepreneurship materials."[6] The doxa of the NCDC staff, in effect, had been transformed by the exposure to this textbook evaluation process—and he seemed determined that the A-level curriculum be written differently.

NEW MEMBERS OF THE NATIONAL CURRICULUM DEVELOPMENT CENTRE'S COMMUNITY OF PRACTICE

Finally, a number of changes also occurred during the same time period in the community of practice responsible for developing the entrepreneurship curriculum. Not only was there a greater inclusion of individuals and texts coming from other national contexts; there were also changes in the composition of the curriculum development team due to the Rwandan government's decision to switch from French to English as the primary language of instruction, as well as increased involvement of the UN Industrial Development Organization (UNIDO). Together, these changes served to increase the presence of ideas and practices influenced by neoliberalism, with a distinct effect on the resulting A-level curriculum.

Not long after the DFID textbook evaluation training, the NCDC staff set to work with an added vigor to organize a workshop for developing the A-level entrepreneurship curriculum. This time, however, their preparations were different. They visited other institutions and obtained examples of entrepreneurship curricula that were being used in other countries, including the ILO's *Know About Business*. They pursued contacts with a team of MBA students from Harvard Business School, who were interested in developing some case studies of Rwandan entrepreneurs for a secondary school started in Rwanda by another MBA graduate. And whereas previously they had allowed me, as a researcher, to be largely a silent observer of the process, they now suggested that since I had a background in education and some business training, I should offer presentations on practical methods for teaching entrepreneurship.

The NCDC also set about gathering the team of consultants who would develop the new A-level entrepreneurship curriculum. Because of a change in language policy, however, they could not simply include the same people who had written the O-level materials. After more than eighty years of using French as the language of instruction, Rwandan secondary schools were told they would shift to English, beginning with the classes entering Senior 1 and Senior 4 in January 2009.[7] As a result, while the O-level curriculum was developed by a group of Francophone professionals, who had been educated primarily in Rwanda and the Democratic Republic of the Congo, for A-level the NCDC had to bring together a new group of teachers and curriculum developers who were comfortable working in English—in most cases, because they had been educated in Uganda, Kenya, and Tanzania.[8] Though a few of the participants in this new phase were carry-overs from the O-level curriculum development process, even most of these people had been educated outside of Rwanda for long enough to become comfortably bilingual in French and English. Unlike the O-level curriculum developers, the resulting new group also had some members with higher educational degrees (MAs and, in one case, a PhD), a few of which even were earned outside of East Africa.

The community of practice involved in the A-level curriculum development process was also influenced by the increased involvement of the United Nations Industrial Development Organization (UNIDO). Though a supporter of entrepreneurship education in Rwanda from the beginning, UNIDO had not played a very central role during the preparation of the O-level curriculum.[9] However, as the preparations for the A-level curriculum development process began, the increased presence of a UNIDO consultant began to catalyze new discussions on the focus of the entrepreneurship curriculum, particularly regarding the curriculum's emphasis on regulations and taxation.

Regulations and Taxation

In a transition phase between the development of the O-level and the A-level curricula, the NCDC convened a meeting in April 2009 to evaluate the O-level materials and train a small group of teacher trainers. The possibility that the A-level entrepreneurship curriculum development process would take a new direction first became apparent on the second day of this meeting, when the UNIDO representative, a consultant from Uganda, arrived.

In one of his first presentations, the UNIDO consultant touched on the issue of taxation and regulations, but in a manner far different from the extensive and detailed instructions on the topic found in the O-level curriculum. Rather than arguing that students should learn about these topics as part of becoming entrepreneurs, he commented about the need to develop a more limited regulatory regime in order to cultivate a propitious environment for entrepreneurship:

There should be a simple and inexpensive regulatory regime. Let's say the learners want to start a vegetable growing business—the school administration should let them do that. It would be naive of you to teach entrepreneurship, otherwise.[10]

The UNIDO consultant's perspective was not only manifestly in line with neoliberal thought; it also seemed to echo his personal experience of an uncomplicated Ugandan regulatory environment. At numerous points during his presentations, he gave examples of small businesses sprouting up here and there, in Ugandan schools and on Ugandan streets, with little capital and no hassles other than the struggle to work and earn a profit. Not once in his examples did he mention regulatory constraints such as registration and taxation in the Ugandan context.

When issues of Rwandan government regulations continued to come up on the third day of the April 2009 meeting, however, the UNIDO consultant began to express more directly his surprise at the amount of time that the curriculum was giving to the subject. During a discussion on the different legal types of companies in Rwanda, for example, he at first stepped into the conversation to assist with the terminology in English: "There is sole proprietorship, partnership, [. . .] and private limited liability company. Partnership is informal, not registered."

Hearing a few objections, he clarified: "Some are registered, others not."[11]

The murmuring in the room increased in volume. "Seeing the Rwandan law," one teacher interjected, "all businesses must be registered, so I don't think it's good to tell students that there are some businesses not registered. That is not in the law."[12]

At first the UNIDO consultant simply accepted this correction and went on. As he continued perusing the syllabus during the group's presentation, however, he began to seem more and more perplexed at the seemingly interminable list of institutions and regulations that a business would have to deal with simply to begin operations:

UNIDO Consultant:	Then look, on page 25: "Identify institutions that are to be sought in order to carry out registration at the trade registry." I thought—that is very full! [*The syllabus lists "Institutions concerned (Notary, RRA, Banks, Rwandan Commercial Registration Services Agency RCRSA, MINICOM)"*[13]]. I don't know what was meant there. Are these the institutions that are involved in registering a business?! When I'm going to register a business [. . .] what do I need to do?
NCDC Staff 1:	Yes, you see, when you want to register with the trade registrar, there are some institutions that you need to have their documents. [. . .]
UNIDO Consultant:	Even if I am starting a kiosk? A small trading boutique?
NCDC 1:	No, no. This is for big companies.
UNIDO Consultant:	Exactly. This is where we want to be clear. Are we teaching our learners about big companies? Or about small businesses, in their communities? Otherwise we are teaching them about things they cannot see.

At this point, another teacher interjected:

Teacher 1:	These days, *everyone*, even those who just have kiosks, is obliged to register. Last time, they were chasing after

people to make them register. *Every single person* has to be registered here at the business registrar. Everyone.

Teacher 2: And everyone has to have a TIN, a Tax Identification Number. [...]

Teacher 3: And everyone who goes to Congo, who brings something back. He has to declare that, and he has to have a TIN number. [...]

UNIDO Consultant: But wait, let me ask again: is our Senior 1 student going to get a TIN number?

Teachers: [*Speaking together*] Yes ...

NCDC Staff 1: I mean, according to these guys, *everyone* who practices commerce needs to have a TIN number. Needs to register.

UNIDO Consultant: This is a requirement??

Teachers: [*Speaking together*] Yes.

UNIDO Consultant: Even these small shops?

Teachers: [*Speaking together*] Yes! Mmm!

UNIDO Consultant: Okay.[14]

After this conversation, the UNIDO representative appeared to have finally accepted the Rwandan reality, but a number of participants continued mulling over this exchange, and in the coming days they began to join the UNIDO representative in questioning the emphasis on taxation in the O-level curriculum. The first of these were two teachers (Teachers 4 and 5) who were educated almost entirely in Uganda but had lived long enough in Rwanda to draw some comparisons.[15] They argued that Rwanda's comparatively high level of government regulations could in itself be discouraging to entrepreneurship students, even if the course itself were able to motivate them.

UNIDO Consultant: We as teachers should do everything to motivate our learners, to build their confidence, to give them opportunity to *act*! To practice. So that when they come out, they are able to act, they are able to put into practice what they learned. [*He pauses, seeing that others have comments to make.*] Yes, sir?

Teacher 4: You may find that students have the knowledge and they are motivated, have self-confidence and the model for acting, but there are some kind of restrictions. Like, maybe you will find government policies which will hinder those practical activities. Now I don't know what we can do to tell them about those policies [...] Let me give you an example. I may be having small capital like 500,000 Rwf [$830] to start my own business. But you find that I have to pay, like, four or five types of taxes and my capital is already finished, so what am I going to do? You find there are some policies that restrict people from engaging in small businesses. So we may go and teach all these things, but—

UNIDO Consultant: But the environment is not convincing for the learners to put in practice what they have learned.[16]

The UNIDO representative turned to the NCDC staff present at the meeting:

UNIDO Consultant: I think the other point he is raising is, you know, there are some government policies which may prohibit learners from undertaking some activities. Either there are administrative procedures—like if he wants to start a small business, even wants to start a small kiosk or even become a hawker. These hawking boys make a lot of money! These ones who sell their wares in cartons, hey?

Teacher 5:   [*Interrupting quietly*] They can't allow that.

UNIDO Consultant: Huh?

Teacher 5:   [*Louder*] They can't allow that here!!

NCDC Staff 2:   It's so difficult to use that kind of activity in our context nowadays, but in school it is possible. There are no taxes when it is done in the framework of teaching and learning. I know that, for example, if there is a workshop in mechanics or electronics; I know when you bring your radio or your TV to be fixed, they do it and you pay and there is no tax. Like at [X technical and vocational school].

Teacher 5:   But is it one single man who owns [that workshop]? No. It is a government school. But here we are focusing on one single student who wants to start a small business. What then?[17]

Rwanda's high level of taxes and regulations, these participants were asserting, was simply incompatible with the goal of promoting entrepreneurship through schools. No matter how effective a curriculum they would create, and no matter how good their teaching, the regulatory environment itself was discouraging.

The April 2009 meeting ended without any particular conclusion being drawn on these issues, since the participants were not asked to create any document together that might codify their ideas. But the UNIDO representative did make written recommendations after the workshop, suggesting, among other things, that the issues of taxation and regulation should not be given such importance. "The units on taxation," he concluded after a series of detailed remarks, "could be reduced to focus on general awareness about taxation and why they should pay as well as the basic taxes payable by a micro and small business."[18] By this point, many of the changes he was proposing would be impossible to accomplish for several years, as the O-level syllabus and textbooks had already been printed and distributed to schools. His suggestion that the emphasis on taxation in the curriculum be reduced did, however, come back in the next phase of curriculum development, this time for A-level.

In August 2009, the NCDC convened its new group of consultants and curriculum developers to begin developing the A level syllabus. Outwardly, the NCDC staff structured this new process in almost an identical way to that of O-level. An NCDC curriculum development specialist opened the workshop with a description of the "steps to go through in order to develop a program," explaining: "First is to research to identify the needs of the training. [...] After we see what kind of person we want, we need to look at the profile of their functions, the synthesis of capacities that the students should have."[19] As he moved to the next slide in his presentation, the projector showed a familiar-looking table with columns for "duties," "tasks," "knowledge," "skills," and "attitudes." "After the profile of functions or duties," he explained, "then we go to the profile of qualifications. Each function can be subdivided into tasks, activities, knowledge, skills or abilities, attitudes, etc."[20]

As the curriculum developers pursued these by now familiar activities, they began to raise questions about issues that had simply been taken for granted before. This time, unlike at the beginning of the O-level process, there was no Cabinet-level directive concerning the central purpose of the course and the "school leaver's profile." As a result, to a degree far beyond what had occurred in the O-level syllabus, the envisioning of the A-level graduate profile involved in-depth discussion about what kind of entrepreneur the course should develop and how that could be done. By the third day of the workshop, participants had finally settled on a phrase framing the purpose of the course:

To produce a self-reliant citizen who is capable of identifying and exploiting viable business opportunities and contribute to the development of the society for the mutual and just benefit of her/himself and others.[21]

It soon became apparent, however, that there was little agreement regarding what students should learn in order to become capable of "contributing to the development of society" as entrepreneurs.

To begin with, one small group suggested that entrepreneurs' contributions to development included "providing quality services, declaring and paying taxes, respecting business rights and obligations, and taking care of the environment." This rather comprehensive list might have gone unremarked in the original O-level workshop. But for the participants in this new community of practice—particularly one from Kenya (Consultant 1) and two others who had studied in Uganda (Consultants 2 and 3)—something did not seem quite right:

Consultant 1: Before we [finalize this list of tasks], why are we emphasizing on taxation?

NCDC Staff 3: Because Group 2 said that the main activity is to contribute on this development—and you can't do that as an individual unless you pay taxes. And we see that the central goal includes a contribution to the development of society.

Consultant 1: Yes, but in the elaboration of this curriculum I think we are giving undue emphasis on paying taxes. In fact, maybe some of these people will be paid or given subsidies, and not pay taxes. That can come later. The problem we have is to teach entrepreneurship so that people can *get into* viable businesses—to give people the skills to create and run successful businesses.

Consultant 2: I agree, because what we really need is not the person who understands taxes very well, but—

Consultant 3: How does he contribute to development without paying taxes? [*Pausing, then thinking aloud*] It's true, he *can* do it. When you create a job for this man, when you make it possible for someone to buy something at a fair price. Even churches, they don't pay taxes but they develop the society.

Consultant 1: The problem isn't that people don't know *how* to pay taxes. People pay their taxes in Rwanda. The problem is to *have* enterprises that *can* pay taxes: expand the tax base.[22]

And that was that. Over the next few minutes, different participants suggested ways to reduce the focus on taxation or relocate it as a minor topic under what they considered more centrally important issues.

In the end, the A-level syllabus would designate just a few class periods, out of a total of 545 class periods over the course of three years, for discussing issues of business registration and taxation (NCDC, 2009, pp. 43, 56).[23] And even in these sections of the syllabus, in contrast to the O-level curriculum's focus on top-down government regulation, the eventual A-level curriculum devoted much more attention to business social responsibility. The focus overall was not on how state laws exert control over such issues, but rather on training the individual entrepreneur's inner sense of ethical decision making and self-control. As a result, while the O-level curriculum essentially took on the characteristics of a disciplinary technology, emphasizing surveillance and control of the state through bureaucratic administration, the A-level curriculum instead came to echo neoliberalism's focus on self-responsibility and other "technologies of the self" (Foucault, 1988, 1991).

Creativity, Problem Solving, and Resourcefulness

Once the issue of taxation had been resolved in the A-level curriculum development workshop, the conversation turned to completely different issues. In particular, as they moved further into a consideration of the capabilities an effective entrepreneur would need, the A-level curriculum developers began realizing that they did not know *how* these abilities could actually be taught. As they began, for the first time, to raise the question of how to cultivate entrepreneurial capacities such as opportunity recognition, problem solving, and innovation, they finally began to work in earnest on the kinds of active and learner-centered methods that might lead to their development.

This process of rethinking the pedagogy of the A-level entrepreneurship course began with a few participants wondering aloud about certain issues that, they noticed, the O-level syllabus had simply seemed to take for granted:

Consultant 1: [*Comparing the O-level syllabus and part of the draft A-level syllabus under development*] Here it says, "Identify business opportunities." It is difficult to identify opportunities, and this does not have an established method. [...]

NCDC Staff 4: I've [also] been pushing myself on how one can teach a student how to be creative. How can we teach creativity? And how to be innovative? Can we really get the content for how to teach creativity?

At first, these signs of the emergence of a different perspective seemed to be quickly subsumed under the same definitions- and content-oriented focus that had so characterized the O-level materials:

Consultant 2: Like here [*looking at a book*], there are some steps of creativity that we can put. [...] Here they are giving about the definition of creativity, the five steps of creativity: open perception, processing, insight, implementation, and application. And so on. So there is content for it.[24]

For the time being, the group still seemed comfortable with the idea that a definition and list of steps was sufficient for teaching about creativity. Reassured that the appropriate "content" existed, the group moved on to another issue. The question of how to develop creativity in practice, however, would return later on.

By twelve days into the A-level curriculum development process,[25] the group had settled on a draft for the entire syllabus of the course. But some of the NCDC curriculum specialists guiding the workshop were not satisfied. Referencing what they had learned during the DFID textbook evaluation training a few months earlier, they remarked that the overall approach of the A-level draft syllabus seemed nearly identical to that from O-level, as Table 3 illustrates.[26]

I learned about the NCDC staff's dissatisfaction with this result when one of the curriculum developers came to meet me a few days before the next phase of meetings. Showing me the draft A-level syllabus, he asked me if I would reformulate the specific objectives of each unit "to be more practical and effective," and also help them "relook at the teaching and learning activities."[27] The contents column in the middle of the syllabus, he explained, was adequate and could remain unchanged. I agreed to make an attempt at the first few pages and give it to him to see if it was useful—in one step making a symbolic move from

Table 3   Excerpt from a draft of the A-level syllabus on Day 12 of the workshop

Specific objectives	Content	Teaching/learning activities
By the end of this theme, learners should be able to: · Define entrepreneurship · Enumerate qualities of an entrepreneur · State the benefits and challenges of entrepreneurship	1. The concept of entrepreneurship 1.1 Meaning of entrepreneurship 1.2 Meaning and qualities of an entrepreneur 1.3 Benefits of entrepreneurship 1.4 Challenges of entrepreneurship and their possible remedies	Through brainstorming sessions, learners will give the meaning, qualities, benefits, and challenges of entrepreneurship. The teacher will moderate suggestions given by the learners and help them to come up with clear answers for each term.

Source: Unpublished draft document from NCDC curriculum development workshop, September 2009.

being a largely silent observer to becoming an "expert" participant, bringing my own—perhaps up to that point largely unacknowledged—doxa and dispositions into a position of greater influence within the process.

As I worked on the assignment the NCDC coordinator had given me, I first proposed extensive changes to the specific objectives in the first few pages of the syllabus, trying to connect them more directly to aspects of entrepreneurial practice. Instead of just saying that "learners should be able to define entrepreneurship," for example, I introduced additional objectives calling for students to be able to demonstrate what it would mean to carry out work with initiative or creativity; to identify and describe examples of new businesses, products, or services; and to distinguish between employment and self-employment—three aspects of typical definitions of entrepreneurship.

Still working with those first few objectives, I then gave particular attention to developing a few examples of what I thought would be more engaging classroom activities, such as the following:[28]

Organize students in small groups where they will each show someone doing a particular kind of work, choosing from among the list they developed during the previous lessons. The first half of the role play should show what that work looks like when it is done in a routine way. The second half should show the work being done with the entrepreneurial qualities of initiative and creativity.

And:

Explain that [one] aspect of entrepreneurship is developing new products, services, and processes or technologies. Brainstorm with students examples from their own locality or elsewhere of someone inventing and marketing a new product, service, or technology.

I also proposed a number of activities that would require students to go out of the classroom to discuss particular topics with practicing entrepreneurs and suggested that the curriculum include case studies illustrating specific challenges faced by entrepreneurs and asking students to propose their own strategies and solutions.[29] In many of these activities, I included elements that reflected my personal interests in ethical decision making and social responsibility.

In short, my contributions promoted both learner-centered constructivist pedagogy and a sense of individual responsibility. Though this did not occur to me at the time, it seems likely in retrospect that these ideas essentially served to reinforce the neoliberal-influenced perspectives already being brought to bear on the A-level curriculum development process.

At the prompting of the NCDC staff, I presented a few example pages containing these ideas to the curriculum development consultants at the beginning of the next workshop. Though I knew that my suggestions might be somewhat naive, I was still caught by surprise at the degree to which some of the workshop participants objected to them, finding the ideas to be radically and unrealistically different from the accepted norm:[30]

Consultant 4: These objectives are very long and numerous! [. . .] We should diminish them to be closer to how the objectives are formulated briefly in other curriculum books. [. . .] You need to see the reality; it might take them two years to do all these activities! They might ask them to do too much. We can select the most important ones. [. . .]

NCDC 3: I agree that if we're not careful will propose too many activities. Because our children, even at university, they aren't habituated to work. And really this [approach] is new.

As other faces around the room showed their disapproval of my suggestions, the environment in the workshop room was almost combative. I wondered if I should just concede the point in order to let the curriculum development process proceed on its own path.

"But," the coordinator from NCDC continued, "we should confront these challenges. We need materials and training and we should put this in our recommendations. This course can't stay theoretical. We want to make a change in students' lives, even in the society."

The NCDC coordinator then asked the curriculum developers to use the example I had prepared in order to propose their own changes to the syllabus. "Now what can we do?" he went on. "Take our syllabus and try to make it more practical. You have an example; it's not fixed, but try to use it as an idea. Make it much more practical, don't worry if—don't be afraid of writing something too long, we can always shorten the text later."

With some doubt still apparent in their expressions, the participants returned to their small groups. Under the insistence of the NCDC staff circulating among the groups, they soon got down to work, attempting to reformulate the objectives and activities for different sections of the syllabus.

The ensuing discussions exemplified the partial, stop-and-go nature of social learning, as participants both experimented with the new approach to the pedagogical activities and simultaneously continued to pursue some of their more habitual concerns. Parts of the conversations involved enthusiastic proposals of different ways of teaching the content:

You could discuss family structure with them, how the family functions, how it is guided: people can't just do what they want. Then you move from the family to talking about the management of different types of organizations. [. . .] I can write an opening story for the unit on this.

While in other cases, the discussion again returned to issues of terminology and definitions:

We shouldn't include team building. It's not one of the four commonly recognized management functions. [. . .] Will this syllabus be accepted if we use different labels and terms from what is acceptable? There are only four managerial functions: planning, organizing, leading, and controlling.

By and large, however, the groups did as the NCDC coordinator asked, spending several days coming up with ideas for reorienting the objectives and pedagogical activities in a more "practical" direction.

As I sat in on different groups' discussions over the following days, I noticed the change in focus from the earlier O-level curriculum development process. Before, the sole necessary justification for including a topic or term in the content was verification with other members of the group that it was the correct academically recognized formulation. Now, however, such discussions focused almost exclusively on the question of how to help students understand new ideas and be able to put them into practice.

"How can we simplify these accounting things to be really useful to them?" one participant asked, for example—for the first time opening up space for discussion in what had previously been a rigid approach to teaching accounting. "Not teach the complicated theory of different types of journals, et cetera, but to help them see how to keep a general journal with all the essential information, keeping it chronological and accurate?"[31] "Other fields have things like internships," another curriculum developer mused, "so why don't we make a practical exam for this? Like, a student has to create their own business, and then the teacher goes to examine that business to give them marks."[32] The doxa of the group was clearly changing, regarding the importance of the conventional definitions- and examinations-focused structure in relation to a course that, after all, aimed not at providing students with a certificate in order to get a job but at their developing certain capacities so that they could create one on their own.

By mid-November 2009, the workshop participants had come up with a complete syllabus that showed just how much had changed, in terms of their conceptualization of the relative importance of the three competing goals for schooling. The objectives and content had moved far away from the traditional understanding that schools would award credentials largely on the basis of memorized lists of terms, definitions, and typologies. In their place, the teaching-and-learning activities had taken on much greater importance in the syllabus, with detailed suggestions unique to each specific learning objective. A great number of these suggested activities gave importance to the goals of cultivating creativity, problem solving, and resourcefulness:

The teacher will guide the learners to use the approaches of observing, interviewing, reading books or periodicals, and investigating on the Internet in order to develop their own new business ideas, technologies, processes, products, and/or services. (7 allocated periods)[33]

In order to help them understand the managerial functions, ask the class to decide a goal they would like to achieve together [. . .] Then, make an in-class game where learners have to form teams and prepare a certain quantity of some simple item (such as identical drawings of something, etc.). They have to make a plan to reach their production goal, organize their team members into different functions/activities for achieving their responsibilities, and have a manager who helps supervise and control their activities. See which teams are more efficient and effective in reaching their goals, and analyze with the class after they complete the game what techniques worked well, etc. (7 allocated periods)[34]

Each group should review the business ideas they developed in Senior Four and choose the idea that they think will be most effective. With the help of the teacher, each group will write down a business plan according to their business idea. (63 allocated periods)[35]

Visually, the A-level syllabus also reflected this new focus on original learner-centered pedagogical activities. Both syllabi featured three columns: the specific objectives, the content to be taught, and teaching-learning activities. Whereas the bulk of the text in the O-level syllabus appeared in the "contents" column, in the A-level syllabus the third column on teaching-learning activities had been widened to cover half of the page, to accommodate its varied and detailed suggestions of what teachers could do to help students develop their understanding and abilities.

This emphasis on activities related to creativity, resourcefulness, and independent problem solving was also carried through to the development of the A-level entrepreneurship textbooks. There, although curriculum developers were still concerned with writing the paragraphs of text that counted as the "content" of the course, they also included numerous exercises and activities based on the proposals made in the syllabus. At one point, the curriculum development team even left their workshop room to interview practicing entrepreneurs in the surrounding neighborhood, collecting stories that they could use as part of the lesson plans they were developing. They also eventually incorporated into the texts a number of case studies developed separately by the group of Harvard Business School MBA students mentioned earlier, who were in Rwanda developing their own entrepreneurship course materials for a school started by a Harvard MBA graduate and who had liaised with NCDC for background information and advice. Together, these initiatives gave a new feeling both to the process of writing the textbooks and to the products themselves.

Fittingly, the A-level entrepreneurship curriculum development process concluded one day with a practical activity in a Kigali-area school. There, the Harvard Business School students videotaped one of the curriculum developers as he put into practice the case study method, demonstrating for his peers how their materials could be used in schools around the country to promote a new school culture of student-centered discussion and independent problem solving.

Hanging in the Balance

The distinction between Rwanda's O-level and A-level entrepreneurship curricula could hardly be much clearer. From the more than 30 percent of course time devoted to issues of government regulations in the O-level curriculum, the new A-level curriculum addressed related topics in just 4 percent of the 545 class periods expected to be spent on the course—and many of these in fact focused more on personal ethics than on government rules. And while the O-level curriculum addressed creativity only once, as one element in a list of terminology to be learned, the A-level syllabus suggested that teachers provide multiple opportunities throughout the three years for students to understand and experience creative problem solving in practice. With these changes, the new community of practice involved in the A-level curriculum development process seemed to have definitively asserted the primacy of creativity over controls.

Rwanda's A-level entrepreneurship curriculum development process differed significantly from the O-level process precisely because this phase of curriculum development took place in a context in which both the community of practice and the surrounding field of schooling had changed, significantly increasing the social prominence of neoliberal influences. A different form of knowledge was beginning to be valued on Rwanda's national examinations, altering understandings of the relative value of different approaches to teaching. The NCDC staff had learned from more in-depth contact with entrepreneurship materials developed by communities of practice in the United Kingdom and elsewhere in the world.[36] And new participants, with dispositions gained from other neoliberal-influenced countries, were placed in prominent guiding roles from the beginning of developing the A-level curriculum. In this context, even those who had participated in the earlier O-level entrepreneurship curriculum development process found themselves "playing up" the more neoliberal aspects of their habitus—dispositions that they had developed in other social settings but perhaps had seemed irrelevant or inappropriate until conditions in their community of practice had changed.

In the end, the O-level curriculum exemplified strong disciplinary tendencies, suggesting that young people should learn the terminology and techniques related to the same kinds of commerce that are already so widely practiced in Rwanda, and that the state would be watching to make sure that their own entrepreneurial efforts abide by the rules. The A-level curriculum, in contrast, became almost entirely neoliberal, suggesting that young people should practice creating their own forms of employment, with personal choice and self-interest tempered only by some encouragement toward social responsibility and ethical decision making. Neither curriculum, by itself, truly represented Rwanda's post-developmental goals of cultivating a generation of entrepreneurs who would simultaneously be creatively self-reliant and willing to follow state guidance and regulations.

This indeterminate outcome echoes some of the tensions that Baildon (2009) signals as key educational policy challenges for East Asian post-developmental states. In particular, he writes, the post-developmental state must manage "the tension of advocating critical and creative thought and innovation while setting firm limits on what is acceptable (Lim, 2006, as cited in Baildon, 2009, p. 69) and balance "flexible education that creates the adaptive, flexible citizen" with "the social discipline desired by the post-developmental state" (Baildon, 2009, pp. 71–72). Striking such a balance is not easy, and Rwanda's O-level and A-level entrepreneurship curricula seem to have ended up each on opposite extremes of the scale, as a result of the microdynamics of policy making at two different moments in time.

Under the Rwandan school structures that prevailed at the beginning of this research, such a curriculum outcome could have resulted in two different tracks of entrepreneurship education. If the curriculum were to be fully implemented and absorbed into students' own dispositions—and this is a big "if," as I show in Part III of this book—one might have expected to see the Rwandan youth who completed only O-levels obediently paying taxes but practicing fairly unoriginal and perhaps not very growth-oriented forms of entrepreneurship. In contrast, the smaller percentage of students who entered A-levels each year would largely turn their focus to developing more practical and imaginative capacities in innovative entrepreneurship.[37]

However, recent changes in Rwanda's schooling system have made this educational class-based divergence unlikely. Soon after implementing the full entrepreneurship curriculum, the Rwandan government took ambitious steps to provide universal access to twelve years of basic education, vastly expanding the number of teachers and classrooms, and pumping significantly increased funding into the secondary school system in order to make it possible for students to attend lower secondary schools without paying school fees. Though other costs, such as uniforms and school materials, still apply and may continue to prevent some students from attending secondary school (Williams, 2013), the

Rwandan government clearly seems interested in helping all students gain access to a full secondary education, including everything that the A-level entrepreneurship curriculum might have to offer them.[38]

Far from being intentional, Rwanda's indeterminate entrepreneurship curriculum outcome is evidence of the unpredictable social complexities of policy making as a state's numerous administrative organs, and the individuals within them, improvise multiple ongoing social negotiations in which different rationalities of governance prevail, or are transformed in the process. To forge public policies imbued with the tension-filled synthesis that post-developmentalism implies, policy makers must to some extent embody both neoliberal and disciplinary dispositions simultaneously. But the O-level and A-level curriculum developers both missed that post-developmental mark: one group giving too much emphasis on orderliness and controls, the other virtually ignoring government regulations in favor of entrepreneurial initiative and creativity.

Despite their contradictions, both of these curricular materials were distributed to schools by the end of the 2009 academic year. The balance of the entire course's educational and governmental priorities was thus still undetermined as students began to study entrepreneurship in earnest within Rwanda's secondary schools, the subject of Part III of this book.

Part III

Educating Entrepreneurs?

Figure 8   Copying down notes, School A

Source: Photo by author.

Chapter 5
Chalk and Talk Lessons in Entrepreneurship

ABOUT FORTY SENIOR 3 students sat calmly in the tight rows of rough wooden desks that filled the classroom. Although the hems of their clothes were fraying, each one was dressed in the full school uniform, tie and all—perhaps anticipating the discipline prefect's next visit.

After a few moments, a slim teacher with graying hair walked through the door. Without a word to the rest of the class, he gestured at one of the students to clean the blackboard, and then began delivering one of the first entrepreneurship lessons of the year. Almost immediately, the students took out their notebooks and began copying down the lines of text that appeared, one by one, in chalk on the board:

> *a) Types of Industry*
>
> *Food processing industry: It includes all industries which transform agricultural products into food products. The raw materials that are used are products from animals or plants that undergo more or less complex transformations before being brought to the market.*

The teacher wrote fluently, his arm moving from one word to the next, one line to the next, one section of the board to the next. Only the squeak of the chalk and a few whispered comments here and there broke the silence:

> *In this category we can put meat industry, fish industry, fruits and vegetable industry, fatty crops industry (oil, yoghurt, butter), grain and amylaceous processing industry (malt, flour, bakery . . .) animal food, making breweries (alcoholic and non-alcoholic) and other food industries (chocolate factories, confection, spices, etc.)*

Ten, twenty, thirty minutes into the class, there had still been no word out loud from the entrepreneurship teacher. All of the students, except two who were whispering in the corner, continued to copy with great concentration:

Manufacturing Industries: Chemical industries, metal wood, rubber and plastic products, transportation equipments, first transformation of metals, non-metallic mineral products, food and drinks, furniture, paper, leather, machines, tobacco, textile, printing and publishing, oil and coal, electrical products, various manufacturing industries.

Outside somewhere, the whistle blew, ending the class hour. The teacher ignored it and kept writing. All of the students stayed seated, continuing to copy quietly, while their peers from other classrooms began to stream past the window.[1]

. . .

If educational policy making in Rwanda were on a linear track, the next stop after curriculum development would be "implementation in schools." Of course, the reality was much messier. Introduced as a policy idea in late 2007, by February 2009 the O-level entrepreneurship curriculum had just been completed, and printed materials would still not arrive in schools for several more months.[2] Yet O-level teachers had already been instructed to begin teaching the course starting in January of that year. Not yet sure what exactly they were expected to teach, they scrambled to find photocopies of business and entrepreneurship textbooks from Uganda or notes from their own university studies in accounting and management to structure their first lessons. Meanwhile, by the beginning of the 2009 school year,[3] the Ministry of Education had just decided that entrepreneurship should also be offered at A-level. The A-level syllabus, as a result, was not published until the end of 2009 and the A-level textbooks would not be distributed to schools for more than a year. It was not until the 2010 academic year that the majority of schools across the country offered a full year of the course in both O- and A-levels.

This is the year, therefore, that I set out to visit schools in the broader region surrounding the city of Kigali, to find out what was happening as teachers began to put the new course into practice. Over the course of the following ten months of the academic year, together with my research assistant Flora Mutimukeye—a sociology graduate from the National University of Rwanda—I spent every school day observing in eleven different classrooms where entrepreneurship was being taught.

These classrooms were diverse in a number of different respects (see Table 4). Five of them were Senior 3 O-level classrooms, five were Senior 6

Table 4 Characteristics of the schools and classrooms in this study

School	Type	Catchment area	Level offered	Exam Performance	Family socioeconomic status	Classrooms	Language
A	Public day	Semirural	O-level	Low	Low (55% have no electricity)	A01: Senior 3	English
						A02: Senior 3	English
B	Public day	Rural and urban	O-level	Average	Mixed (47% have no electricity; 27% have electricity and a TV)	B03: Senior 3	French
						B04: Senior 3	French
C	Private day	Urban	O- and A-levels	Low	Middle (54% have electricity, 38% also have a TV)	C05: Senior 3	French
						C06: S6 Auto	French
						C07: S6 HEG	French
D	Public boarding	Rural and urban	O- and A-levels	Average	Mixed (61% have no electricity; 30% have electricity and a TV)	D08: S6 PCM	English
						D09: S6 HEG	English
E	Public day and boarding	Primarily urban	O- and A-levels	High	Middle-high (75% have electricity and a TV, 30% have cars)	E10: S6 MCB	French
						E11: S6 HEG	English

Notes: There were 473 students in eleven classrooms. 469 of whom agreed to participate in the research. The participants were 58 percent male, and 42 percent female, with an average age of 17 years in Senior 3 and 20 years in Senior 6. Because this was a period of transition for Rwanda's new language-of-instruction policy, roughly half of classrooms were still studying in French while the other half used primarily English. Senior 6 classrooms specialized in different academic tracks: Auto = auto mechanics; HEG = history, economics, and geography; MCB = math, chemistry, and biology; PCM = physics, chemistry, and math.

A-level classrooms in the humanities and sciences, and one was a Senior 6 auto mechanics classroom.[4] One private and four public schools were included in the study, with varying levels of performance on the national examinations.[5] And although all of the schools were within the greater municipality of Kigali, some were located in rural settings, while others were in the middle of the city—and all of Rwanda's provinces were represented to some degree in the student populations of these schools.[6] The socioeconomic status of these students was also diverse, with 47 percent living in homes without even electricity, and on the other extreme, 11 percent living in homes with electricity, a television set, and a family car.[7] In total, 469 students participated in this part of the research.[8]

The teachers included in this study had, in many respects, even more diverse backgrounds than their students (see Table 5).[9] Three of the teachers had studied primarily in Rwanda, two had significant educational experiences in the Democratic Republic of the Congo, and two were fully educated in Uganda. They had university degrees in economics, business, or management—but also in French linguistics, dentistry, and geography. Most of the teachers spoke only

Table 5   Entrepreneurship teacher characteristics

School	Entrepreneurship teacher	Classroom(s)	Nationality	Primary academic language	University degree
A	Jacques (male)	Senior 3 B Senior 3 C	Rwandan	French	Congo, Burundi: seminary; dentistry; BA, management
B	Nadine (female)	Senior 3 A Senior 3 B	Rwandan	French	Rwanda: BA, management
C	Eliphas (male)	Senior 3	Congolese	French	Congo: BA, French linguistics
	None	S6 Auto			
	Paul (male)	S6 HEG	Rwandan	English	Rwanda: BA, economics and geography education
D	Samson (male)	S6 HEG S6 PCM	Ugandan	English	Uganda: BA, business education
E	Eugene (male)	S6 MCB 3	Rwandan	French	Rwanda: BA, management
	Geoffrey (male)	S6 HEG 1	Ugandan	English	Uganda: BA, economics education

Notes: All names are pseudonyms. Congo refers to Democratic Republic of the Congo. HEG = history, economics, and geography; MCB = math, chemistry, and biology; PCM = physics, chemistry, and math.

one European language well, and this was not always the language they were asked to teach in. Six of the teachers were male, and only one was female.

The findings that I discuss in this and the following chapter are particular to these schools and these particular classrooms. Through the window of these diverse settings, however, we can also gain a glimpse of the landscape of entrepreneurship education around the country—a landscape that took shape far differently than policy makers originally imagined.

By the 2010 academic year, the entrepreneurship teachers in all of these schools had received the National Curriculum Development Centre's syllabus, together with its lists of objectives, content, and pedagogical activities. And yet in many ways, what happened in the entrepreneurship classes that year represented a fundamental transformation of the goals of the official curriculum. This Part III of the book is about how and why that transformation took place, as both teachers and students reinterpreted the entrepreneurship education policy on their own terms, and about the implications of that transformation for Rwanda's post-developmental state.

Variations on the Theme of "Chalk and Talk"

With the introduction of the new entrepreneurship course, the government of Rwanda clearly expected its teachers to become ambassadors of the entrepreneurial culture so often discussed in policy documents. By "talking up" the benefits of entrepreneurship, one might say, and by building students' entrepreneurial knowledge and skills, the government hoped that teachers could help to convince increasing numbers of young Rwandans to take an entrepreneurial path, becoming "job creators" rather than "job seekers."

Yet inside classrooms all over the country, teachers had to interpret for themselves what the government expected them to do with the new course and how to accomplish it. As they settled into their own teaching styles, a pattern in their interpretations and choices became clear, regardless of the apparent differences between the O-level and A-level curricula. The policy's goal of talking up entrepreneurship was all well and good, the teachers seem to have decided, but there must be sufficient "chalking up" as well: ensuring that chalkboards were regularly filled with the definitions and descriptions that students could copy down into their notebooks, and then study for later examinations.

There is a long research tradition of ethnography in formal schools, including a significant number of studies conducted in central and eastern Africa.

Many of these studies have documented a widespread pedagogical style in which "teachers teach; students listen" (Fuller & Snyder, 1991; Stambach, 1994). As I have illustrated in the previous two chapters, in the discourse of Ministries of Education and donor organizations, this approach to teaching is often criticized (Tabulawa, 2003). However, a number of researchers (Barrett, 2007; O'Sullivan, 2004; Vavrus, 2009) have also sought to investigate these practices from teachers' perspectives, as I do here, examining the system of constraints and rewards within which such a pedagogical approach makes sense.

In this chapter, I introduce the schools and many of the teachers observed for this research. In the process, I explore how these teachers carried out yet another transformation of the entrepreneurship course's purpose and significance in Rwanda's post-developmental state. For, by just a few weeks into the year, these teachers had already defined "creativity" and moved on to other topics, even as they seemed to spend every day underlining in chalk the word *credential* in the course's triad of purposes. When put together, these teachers' methods create the impression not of a cacophonous variety of individual pedagogical styles, but of a harmonious blend of variations on a single theme: chalk and talk—classify, define, transmit, explain. Understanding the development and significance of that harmonizing motif is the central purpose of this chapter.

VARIATION 1: NECESSARY NOTES

Set in the midst of fields and modest mud-brick houses on rutted dirt lanes, when one walks through the opening in a line of bushes that serves as School A's entryway, the orderliness presents a striking contrast.[10] The buildings are relatively new, with evenly placed red bricks, clean metal roof sheets, and well-constructed windows. The paths are bordered with stones, and the bushes always seem to have been freshly pruned.

A few years ago, a foreign governmental organization contributed funds to build these classrooms and expand what used to be only a local primary school into a full secondary institution. Even after this expansion, the school at first was attended only by local students who had received relatively low scores on their primary school exams. But soon, other students from the city and nearby towns, whose parents did not want to send them far away to a boarding school, began to take advantage of this inexpensive secondary school closer to home. With its majority rural student population, however, the school continued to perform below the national average.

"They have a very, very low level," Jacques, the entrepreneurship teacher from School A remarked to me one day after class.[11] "So low that we have difficulties advancing with the courses, to make them assimilate the courses [...] In English, but even in French, and even in Kinyarwanda! They have a problem of comprehension. For that reason, you have to give a lot of examples, a lot of examples."

"You see what I did yesterday, to give them a start and then help them understand," he continued enthusiastically. "I even tried to bring them an example! You're going to laugh at me a bit. Me, I started a little project—I started crocheting. You see!" He rummaged around in the sack by his feet and took out a piece of crochet work and needles. Peering at my face with a look of mischievous delight, obviously enjoying my surprise, he went on: "I even make trousers for babies, everything. So I showed the class: 'This is my project.'"

But even this wonderful bit of teacher idiosyncrasy served a limited pedagogical purpose. Jacques's first responsibility, as he described it to me, was to help students "assimilate the course." This orientation held true in nearly all of the classrooms I observed. Practical examples, exercises, and the occasional group activities, if offered at all, were usually done in service of better retention of the teacher's notes or were regarded as an "extra" that was something to fill the time if that week's notes were completed ahead of schedule.

The primary pedagogical importance of notes—formulating them, writing them on the board, talking about them, copying them into notebooks—was apparent in every classroom observed in this research. The vignette from the beginning of the year at School A that opened this chapter illustrated that importance. And little changed as the year went on.

One Monday morning, my research assistant Flora and I squeezed our knees under one of the rough wooden desks that crowded the classroom in crooked rows and watched as students took a history test and then began copying notes on "the Aims (Objectives) of the United Nations." Their hands moved silently across the page, mimicking their history teacher's own arm movements as she wrote in chalk on the board.

In this school, as in nearly every other secondary school in Rwanda, it was the teacher who moved from class to class rather than the reverse. As a result, no teacher's efforts at personalization, not a single map or poster, had altered the classroom's bare walls. When the history teacher completed her lesson, she simply gathered together her notebooks and left the room. The students chatted quietly while waiting for the next teacher to arrive.

A few minutes later, Jacques walked in to begin his entrepreneurship class. Greeting the students with a nod, he began:

T:[12] Last time we saw sectors of production: agriculture . . . [*he paused, waiting for the students to complete his list*]

SS: Fishing.

T: And secondary. But the tertiary sector is among important of all: Trade, Transportation, Banks and Insurance. About transportation, what does it help us do?

SS: Get around.[13]

His review of the previous lesson continued for a few more minutes, after which Jacques turned around and began writing on the board:

Unit 4: Resources needed to run an enterprise

1. Manpower and capital

1.1 Manpower　　　　　*1.1.1 Meaning*

He continued:

T: Manpower refers to workers who are engaged. *Main d'oeuvre*, a hand that works, a workforce. In an enterprise, you will need manpower—

SS: [*Several students raise their hands and snap their fingers, trying to get the teacher's attention*] Teacher! Prof! Wait![14]

Jacques turned, eyebrows raised at their impertinence.

Hastily, the students explained that they missed the previous class. They wanted to know how many pages of their notebook they should skip in order to fill in those missing notes later on.

Nodding as if to acknowledge this as a legitimate reason for their interruption, the teacher bent his tall frame over another student's desk. Flipping through her notebook, he located the previous day's notes and then straightened up again: "Reserve three pages. Quiet now, please." Turning, Jacques continued copying notes on the board:

1.1.2. Manpower refers to a group of workers who are engaged or who are waiting for recruitment into the framework.

1.1.3. The analysis of the skills for the needed manpower: Not only the entrepreneur has to determine the number of workers, but he also has to define the profile of each worker in order to respect the principle of "the right man at the right place."

As Jacques continued writing, the students settled into their task and stared up at the board, their hands moving along the notebook page. For many, the process seemed automatic: glance at the lines of chalk and then copy down a few words, all the while chatting quietly to their friends.[15]

. . .

As I allowed myself to be lulled into the same sense of mechanical note taking as the students around me, I reflected on the way the students had so urgently called out to the teacher just a few minutes before. The students obviously saw the question of reserving blank pages of their notebook, for copying down the missed notes later on, as a crucial issue. And as the weeks wore on, I began to understand them: with not a single other reference material in the classroom, no textbooks, and certainly no educational displays, their notebooks were the only source of information that most of them would ever be able to access to prepare for the national examinations at the end of the year.[16]

VARIATION 2: CALL-AND-RESPONSE

Some parts of Kigali, a capital city with more than one million inhabitants, offer hidden surprises. Tucked in between densely populated neighborhoods, you sometimes come across a valley filled with banana trees and long grasses, partially concealing mud-brick houses behind them, as if you have found a pocket of rural life in the midst of the bustling urban city. School B's environs always seemed like one of those discoveries. Situated on a steep hillside and surrounded by mostly empty fields, it was just beyond one of Kigali's most densely populated neighborhoods, on the rural outskirts of the city but seemingly poised just on the cusp of urbanization. Its students also came from two worlds—some walking long distances from their rural homes over the hills beyond, others coming from the midst of the markets and businesses below.

At seven forty-five in the morning one Thursday, the entrepreneurship teacher—Nadine—entered one of the Senior 3 classrooms wearing a brightly colored dress and matching head wrap. The class was in the midst of a series of lessons on business finance. In a previous class, she had introduced the topic by discussing how a business gets capital, using her own particular call-and-response style:

T: Now you might have a project, but no money. You have to find *kuh*—
SS: Capital!

T: Capital. And that comes from the *buh*—

SS: Bank!

T: But the bank has conditions too. Can you get the capital just by going in, wearing a good suit, chic, and saying—? No. They have to first ask for the *gah*—

SS: Guarantee!

T: That you have the best *id*—

SS: Ideas!

T: But you don't have the *muh*—

SS: Means!

T: To put them in *ak*—

SS: Action!

Nadine often employed this pattern of speech, apparently eliciting participation from almost all the students in the classroom. And yet, on a closer look, students did not seem to have to work very hard to supply the words the teacher wanted. The responses had a sort of automatic quality, as if their minds were half-occupied with other thoughts.

This class period, Nadine continued with another issue related to business finances: accounting and the balance sheet.

T: Today we will look at . . . [*looking in her own notebook*] the balance sheet.

She begins to write on the board:

Balance Sheet

1.1. Definition

The balance sheet is a table representing the situation of an enterprise's assets on a given date.

Active	*Passive*

T: The balance sheet has two arms, the left one, which is—

SS: Active!

T: And the right one, which is—

SS: Passive!

T: Did you eat enough for breakfast? You are weak! You should eat well in the mornings. You! You don't have your own pen? You come to school without a pen?

SS: [*All laugh, including the one who had been trying to borrow a pen.*]

The teacher continued her notes while the students quieted down and began copying from the board:

Analysis of the Passive of the Balance Sheet

The passive of the balance sheet brings together the resources, the resources that are included in a balance sheet come in particular from:

* *either the owner of the enterprise (capital)*
* *or from a lender of funds (provider of money)*
* *or from an ordinary vendor*

These are the external resources coming from the exterior to the enterprise. They allow for growing the realized profits and conserving them in the enterprise (internal resources). The profit benefits in reality the owner, if he uses them he increases the resources that he puts at the disposition of his business. The ensemble of these resources that have been given to the business by the owner is the capital. The assets on the passive side can be classified in two ways:

* *by the nature of the service providers*

Passive	Owner's capital	Capital
		Profits
	Required capital	Lenders of funds
		Vendors

* *by the character of the resources*

Passive	External resources	Capital (creditor)
		Lenders of funds
		Vendors
	Internal resources	Profits

Nadine continued to write at a furious pace on the board, moving on to an analysis of the "active" side of the balance sheet, while the students focused on copying as quickly as they could. After another ten minutes, Nadine suddenly turned around and began talking:

T: The passive is the capital, profits, lenders of funds, and venders. The active is buildings, furniture, inventory, bank accounts, petty cash, and postal checks. Do you follow?

Flustered, the students seemed unsure of where to direct their attention, as they struggled to finish copying the notes:

SS: [*Distractedly*] Yes . . .
T: [*Briskly*] Okay, then we go to the exercises.
SS: Eh! [*They exclaim in dismay, perhaps because in reality, they have not understood at all.*]

Ignoring their objections, Nadine pressed on, writing:

> **Exercise No. 1**
>
> *In an enterprise there is 60,000 francs in cash, merchandise for 300,000Rwf, and furniture for 40,000Rwf. Make the balance sheet.*

T: Where will the cash go?
S(m):   [*Raising his hand*] Passive![17]
T: [*Frowning in disapproval*] Is that right?
SS: [*In chorus*] No! Active!

Nadine drew a table on the board and began filling in the three items, calling to students each time to tell her where to put them. Soon, she announced:

T: Okay, on to the second exercise!

She turned back to the board and writing rapidly:

> **Exercise No. 2**
>
> *Establish a balance sheet based on the following information:*
>
> *· building = 100,000Rwf*
>
> *· furniture = 50,000Rwf*
>
> *· merchandise = 70,000Rwf*
>
> *· supplier = 40,000Rwf*
>
> *· client = 35,000Rwf*

· *bank account = 60,000Rwf*

· *profit = 15,000Rwf*

T: Now tell me which is which, we'll put A or P. Building!
SS: Active! Passive!

The students shouted out their answers for each item on the list, quickly adapting to any slight frown or raised eyebrows on the teacher's face by changing their response to the other option. As the exercise continued, they got into the rhythm of things and began to get the correct answer more often. But no one, I noticed, paused to ask or explain why the balance sheet had to be organized in this way.

Without further explanation, Nadine soon turned around and began to erase the values next to each element in her original list, changing the amount of money assigned to each one. Their homework, she said, would be to make a balance sheet using these new values.

As students settled into the task of copying the new exercise into their notebooks, I noted that the they would not need to think for themselves about the meaning of active and passive to complete their homework; all they would need to do was copy the balance sheet the teacher had just written on the board and simply replace the values on each line.[18]

.   .   .

As the class wrapped up, I overheard a few muttered comments from the students around me, confused about why something called "supplier" would belong in the "passive" category. The lesson, I reflected, had left me perplexed, and I was not exactly a novice at balance sheets. Teaching in French, the teacher had naturally used the French terminology of *active* and *passive*, which seemed somewhat less self-explanatory than the English terms *assets* versus *liabilities plus owner's equity*. But if the students left the lesson with less than a useful understanding of a balance sheet, it was due to more than just difficulties with the terminology.

On the one hand, I realized, though the students had been participating and giving answers throughout the class, they were almost never required to produce an answer that was truly based on their own reasoning. At first, their participation consisted of completing the teacher's words in chorus, using the clues of the first syllables she gave them in her habitual speech pattern. Later, their participation amounted to a choice between two alternatives, in each case allowing the students to automatically self-correct on the basis of nothing more than the expression on the teacher's face. The students' homework, as I have already pointed out, would also require little more than a bit of arithmetic on their part. In other words, this teacher was often extremely active and engaging—but she, like most of the other teachers I observed, "engaged" the students primarily in repeating her own train of thought.

I also realized that, as the lesson rolled along at the teacher's vigorous pace, no one had yet discussed one key question—why an enterprise would want to record this information in the first place. The unit just before the one she was discussing was titled, in the syllabus, "Why Study Accounting?" but the teacher had never asked students to reflect on that question themselves, nor had she answered the question in much practical depth. By the end of their lesson on the balance sheet, the students might have known roughly which categories of things to put on which side of their paper, and how to add them up—and they had been drilled enough on these issues to confront any one of the typical examination questions that could have been asked on the topic. But without the crucial understanding of the purpose of all those activities, it seemed unlikely that they would apply the information to help them more carefully manage the finances of their *own* businesses.

This outcome seemed especially surprising because I happened to know that this entrepreneurship teacher really cared about whether these students could manage their own finances and run a business well. "With the genocide of Rwanda," Nadine commented to me another day, "there are children living by themselves, and this helps them know how to manage their resources." She explained with evident approval that a few students had even started small activities in their homes, raising chickens and rabbits, and she spent some time describing to me her ideas for a school garden that could generate some revenue for each class.

Nadine clearly believed that, by teaching entrepreneurship, she could help her students improve their household economic situation. But could her call-and-response style of teaching, I wondered, really accomplish such a goal?

VARIATION 3: LABORING OVER LANGUAGE

Situated in the middle of a mixed-income urban neighborhood, School C was a private school, but not one of the expensive private schools catering to children of the elite. Started in 2002, the school somehow managed to have the air of being simultaneously unfinished and already dilapidated—with partial foundations for as-yet-unbuilt classrooms facing classrooms with dirty walls and missing window panes.

School C followed the national curriculum but took in mainly students who had not scored high enough on their Primary 6 or Senior 3 examinations to be admitted into the more prestigious public schools. Its student body included a few from families with middle incomes who wanted their children to study close to home, but many students had quite modest means or were very poor. A full 30 percent of the students had sponsors paying their school fees—religious groups, nongovernmental organizations (NGOs), and government agencies supporting those orphaned by AIDS or the genocide.

Despite the fact that students were aware of their school's low academic reputation—and thus their own low chances for academic success—students wore their uniforms conscientiously and for the most part were self-motivated and self-disciplined. This was especially apparent in the older classes, where students were often left alone for multiple hours each day as one teacher or another was waylaid by another overlapping job. But when teachers did show up, many seemed quite knowledgeable and committed to teaching as a vocation.

On one day early in the school year, I sat together with about forty-five other students in the school's only Senior 3 classroom. The walls were dirty white; the black border painted along the bottom edge had been turned a brownish gray by chalk dust and dirt. As is the norm in most Rwandan schools, there were no educational posters decorating the classroom—just a few scattered samples of student graffiti. To my left, six large windows let in plenty of light, though each one was missing at least two panes of glass. No one seemed much bothered by this less-than-inspiring physical environment, however. The students simply waited patiently at their desks for the next class to begin.

When Eliphas, the entrepreneurship teacher, arrived a few minutes late, he immediately issued vigorous instructions:

T: Erase the board, if you have finished. [*Pointing to the student in charge of cleaning the board*] Get up! [*Addressing the other students*] Put away your computer science notebooks and get out entrepreneurship.

When one student did not move quickly enough, Eliphas immediately sent her out of the classroom. His manner was brisk and strict, but not unkind, as he began the lesson, speaking in French:

> T: What did we study last time?
>
> S(m):   Classification of enterprises.
>
> T: Put that in a sentence. Go ahead, repeat it. But before that—what is the chapter that we're studying right now?
>
> S(m):   The enterprise.
>
> T: Very good. We have tried to define an enterprise, even if the definition wasn't exhaustive. [*He pauses, waiting for students to supply the definition*].
>
> S(m):   [*Reading from his notebook*] It is an organization that produces goods and services.
>
> T: [*Writing the full definition on the board as he repeats it*] A commercial organization that produces goods and services. What does *commercial* mean?
>
> S(m):   To create [*mispronouncing the word in French; the teacher asks him to repeat it three times*].
>
> T: Create what? Create business. Who can explain to us why, in Kinyarwanda?
>
> S(f):   *Kwihangira imirimo* [to create their own jobs].
>
> T: Not so disorderly. Raise your hands.
>
> S(f):   *Kwikura ubukene* [to take yourself out of poverty].
>
> T: [*Writing as he says the phrase aloud in French*] To improve our daily life. Who does commerce?
>
> S(m):   The seller and the vendor.
>
> T: They are not opposites, what is the opposite of seller? What are the criteria for classifying enterprises?
>
> S(m):   The dimensing.
>
> T: Say it correctly.
>
> S(m):   The dimension.[19]

The class was quickly beginning to seem not just like a review of the previous notes students had copied in entrepreneurship but also a lesson in French grammar and pronunciation.

As he delivered this French-focused entrepreneurship lesson, Eliphas spoke confidently and orchestrated rapid exchanges with students, whom he often called by name:

T: I told you that each one should try to create your own enterprise.

SS: Yes [*some laughter*].

T: I have a plan, let's say, to create a salon. I want an employee for women, one for men, one for pedicures, and one for receiving clients and dealing with the money. What kind of enterprise is this, by property?

S(f):   Private.

T: By dimension?

S(m):   Small.

T: I want five students to create an idea for a small enterprise. Because we have said that every enterprise begins with a dream. For my salon, I don't yet have the money ready, but I have the dream. Five people! Raise your hands.

SS: [*In Kinyarwanda*] We don't understand the question.

T: We said at term beginning that one objective of the course is to create enterprises. I want five students to create an idea for a small enterprise. [*He pauses, seeing students' hesitation*] Two can speak in French and three in Kinyarwanda [. . .].

S(m):   [*In Kinyarwanda*] A tailor's workshop.

S(m):   [*In Kinyarwanda*] A studio in charge of everything—sound setup, and why not even do the videotaping too?

S(m):   [*In French*] A canteen.

Eliphas pressed for some improvement in this first attempt in French:

T: Prepare yourselves already for the national examinations. Don't just say one word, say a sentence.

S(m):   [*Laboriously, in French*] A canteen, where students from the school—

T: Which school?

SS: [*Silent*]

T: Others, continue to think about this.

As the entrepreneurship teacher pronounced this conclusion to the discussion—"continue to think about this"—his instruction seemed double sided. Continue to think about your business idea, yes. But also, crucially, continue to think about how to improve your French in order to perform well on the upcoming examinations.

. . .

The entrepreneurship classes we observed often seemed to be just as much a question of laboring over language as discussing the substantive content of the course. This was not surprising—most students came from families in which only Kinyarwanda was spoken in the home, and school was the only place where they had both the need and the opportunity to practice another language. Unlike in eastern Congo, where this entrepreneurship teacher was from, most Rwandans share Kinyarwanda as a common language, making foreign languages like French, English, and Swahili unnecessary for day-to-day life.

In school, however, as some students were set to complete their education in French and others were transitioning to English, language was a crucial issue and often a determining factor in performance on the national examinations. In that context, the entrepreneurship class—as well as history, biology, geography, and every other class—was fair game for extended discussions of grammar, vocabulary, and pronunciation. Whether or not students were able to clearly understand the topics that were discussed in their entrepreneurship classes, of course, is another question entirely.

VARIATION 4: DELIVERING DICTATIONS

School D lies just beyond one of the city's newer neighborhoods, where large houses are continually sprouting up in what used to be fields and lots with modest homes. Originally founded just after the 1994 genocide, as a private school to accommodate the large number of Anglophone students coming back to Rwanda from Uganda, Kenya, and Tanzania, there was quite a wide range in socioeconomic status among School D's students. On the one hand, the school was known to attract the children of a number of powerful families in government and business. On the other hand, many other students coming from rural areas had very modest backgrounds and struggled to pay their school fees each trimester.

The students at School D were unusually independent and had a reputation for indiscipline. They often seemed to set their own schedule, and more than any other school in this research, their attendance reflected their estimation of the worth of each class. As I discuss further in the following chapter, both of the classrooms we observed in this school were rarely full during the entrepreneurship periods.

Despite—or perhaps because of—these habits, the students seemed to relish discussing the topic of disciplinary systems and employee management in the business setting, as I sat in their entrepreneurship class one day:

T: Now we have looked at motivation, now how do you manage discipline?

S(f):   Rules.

T: Rules, regulations. What causes indiscipline?

S(m):   Big heads!

T: What is "big head"? What causes indiscipline?

S(m):   Poor background.

S(f):   Home background.

S(m):   Low payment.

S(f):   Peer pressure

S(m):   Love.

T: Let us listen to him—he can explain love!

SS: [*Laughter*]

The students were clearly relaxed and enjoying the question. Having gotten their attention with this initial discussion, however, Samson soon settled in to begin dictating lines from his own notebook:

T: [*Dictating*] "Management of Discipline: It is vital that discipline of the employees and their leaders is observed and enforced." [*Repeating, pausing between each phrase*] "Management of Discipline . . . It is vital . . . that discipline of the employees . . . and their leaders . . . is observed and enforced."

[*Pausing to comment*] So you observe the behavior of your employees and you put rules.

Next! "Causes of indiscipline among the employees . . . Causes of indiscipline . . . among the employees. First: Weak management . . . Weak management."

After each phrase of dictation, the teacher repeated his words, watching students' pens to see if they were following along. While he waited for them to finish each line, he liked to add a few additional comments on the side:

T: You just sit in the office and relax, you don't know what is going on, you manage funds poorly, embezzle them—you yourself are indisciplined, so your workers will be too.

Next! "Inconsistency in enforcing discipline . . . Inconsistency . . . in enforcing discipline."

Today you come and you say break time should begin at twelve thirty p.m., and then the next week, students will not go for break at all, then the next week they start at one [o'clock]—there is no consistency, you're always changing.

As Samson offered these comments, some students made eye contact; others daydreamed, their gaze drifting out the window.

Indeed, as these short repeated phrases washed over us in waves, it often seemed useless to keep track of the logical connection of ideas. It seemed easier, as I took notes alongside the students, to just disconnect the brain to allow for the free flow of words from the ear down to the ink in our pens; in the meantime both our eyes and our thoughts could wander. As soon as we heard the teacher say "Next!" however, we all jumped back to our notebooks:

T: Next! "Defective work culture . . . Defective work culture . . . For example: late-coming, rudeness, absenteeism, among others . . . Late-coming, rudeness, absenteeism."

Someone explain about late coming. You are the manager, you come late, you leave early. That is indiscipline, when they need you, you are not around.

Next! "Excessive authority on the part of management . . . Excessive authority . . . on the part of management. . . . Favoritism." When one sees he is paid less than another, he wonders why. Next! "Lack of procedures for handling employees' grievances."

A few minutes later, the teacher stopped his dictation, noticing that the students' attention had wandered. Two students were having a private conversation, turned sideways in their seats. Another was doodling on her paper while her deskmate looked at some photographs under the table. A few others looked out the window or just stared into space, their pens poised somewhere near the notebook as they waited for the next sentence:

T: You have had enough?

SS: Yes . . .

T: So we will continue next time.

As Samson packed up to leave the classroom, the students got up from their desks and milled around, discussing with their friends whether or not to attend their next class in the computer lab.

.   .   .

Despite his somewhat monotonous dictations, Samson did have a distinctly practical interest in this topic. "When you're still studying, you have big hopes," this recent graduate from a university in Uganda had told me on another occasion. "You think, 'When I finish studying, I'll get a job in such-and-such a company,' they have those hopes. But with low-developed countries, employment is a problem. [There is] widespread unemployment. When you get out, you can take one to two years without being employed where you [apply] to go!"

"I have been telling them," Samson went on, "even when they are employed somewhere—paid employment is not   okay, paid employment should just be done for [a little] while, because paid employment does not make you develop." He had in fact followed this strategy himself, he told me, setting aside some money from his first teaching job to start a "beverage depot" that sells crates of sodas and beers to restaurants and shops. When he moved farther away from his home, in Uganda, he left the depot in the charge of his brother. Proudly, he explained that through its earnings he was able to supplement his own income as a teacher and even pay his brother's university fees.

This teacher clearly had his students' futures in mind as he taught his course, and what was more, he had experienced the process of starting and growing a business himself. Perhaps he imagined his students as one day running their own large companies, drawing on what they had learned about employee management starting in his classroom in secondary school. And yet I couldn't help chuckling a bit to myself as I thought about how his students had spent an entire hour copying down a dictation about how to discipline employees—even as they hardly seemed capable of disciplining themselves. No matter how practical the topic, these classroom dictations often seemed oddly divorced from reality.

VARIATION 5: TRAINING IN TERMINOLOGY

Founded in the 1970s, School E was the longest-established school included in this research and among the strongest public schools in the country. This school also had the highest percentage of wealthy students in the study, with the vast majority of students living in homes with electricity, and almost one-third even having a family car. Today, more than half of the students from School E live in Kigali and go home each afternoon, while the others come from districts around the country and stay in the school's dormitories.

Situated on a hillside with well-paved roads near one of the city's commercial centers, School E had expanded little by little over the years, with new paths and blocks of classrooms eventually making quite a large campus. The school was organized and fairly disciplined, but students were not passive—they talked and asked questions, and they often were not afraid to contradict their teachers. Though plenty of students, like their peers in all of the other schools where I observed, seemed to never touch a book, this was also the only school where I saw the library—which was large and well stocked with tables and benches—chock full of students studying independently.

The Senior 6 math, chemistry, and biology (MCB) classroom where I carried out some of my observations was crowded with desks, three-quarters of them filled with boys. These were serious students, many hoping to become doctors and open private clinics of their own one day. During the midmorning break, many of the students had out their notebooks, busily copying or reviewing their notes while chatting with friends.

Some minutes after the bell rang to signal the end of the break, the entrepreneurship teacher, Eugene, arrived and quietly asked the students to erase the board. His low voice seemed to get the attention of only the closest few desks of students, as he began his lesson about "business planning":

T: Before noting this, let's see "the project" first. What does project mean?

At first, no one answered, as they continued working and chatting about other things:

T: What does project mean?
S(f): [*Raising her hand, then reading from her notebook*] An ensemble of
       activities that gives preponderance to—

T: To objectives. Is that what you saw last time? Today I brought you an
example of a project, but first we'll look at what it includes in general.
[...] Who can write on the board?

At this prompt, most of the students took out their entrepreneurship notebooks
while one boy went to the front of the room. Eugene handed him his notebook
without a word, and the student turned his back to the class, beginning to
write lines of chalk on the board. A low undercurrent of chatting permeated
the room, a backdrop to the sound of rustling papers and pens, as the students
began to copy.

Eugene sat down to watch the proceedings from the side of the room:

The Difference Between Plan, Program, and Project

*It is not unusual to hear one document being interpreted at different times and
places in terms of a plan, program, or project. In order to avoid this kind of confu-
sion, we must come back and bring a greater degree of precision regarding the
nomenclature of each term.*

Eugene had apparently decided that one of the most crucial bits of information
his class needed to know in order to understand the topic of business planning
was the terminological distinction between the words *plan*, *program*, and *project*. The minutes ticked by as the student continued writing up lines of chalk on
the board:

Plan: *A plan is an indicative document that establishes precisions about the
probable evolution of a [business] for a given period. It defines the objectives that
one hopes to attain, and the best way to get there.*

Program: *This can be defined as an ensemble of organized activities with a
precise objective in time and space.*

Project: *This is an ensemble of activities that, in relation to available resources,
envisions achieving certain advantages. It is therefore an ensemble of activities
that give preponderance to immediate and precise objectives. Projects can be
considered as partial solutions to fundamental problems.*

Wearily dotting the last period of the definition of *project*, the student writing
on the board looked around for the first time in several minutes. Noticing that
the teacher had stepped out of the room, he put down the chalk and sat down.

The other students continued to chat around him, many of them having long abandoned their notes.[20]

.   .   .

Eugene, like the other Senior 6 teachers we observed in Schools C, D, and E, seemed to relish introducing difficult vocabulary into his notes. Whether or not his sentences always made sense, they were filled with terms like *preponderance, anti-cyclical, disequilibrium, hierarchization,* and *structural conditions.* Seemingly a shy man, without the loud voice and commanding presence of some of the other teachers, I reflected that Eugene might have relied partly on his specialized vocabulary to bolster his status as an authority in the room.

The students, in turn—though assertive and even rebellious in certain other ways, as I discuss in the next chapter—accepted with little question their teacher's role as the source of the terminology and definitions that they would have to learn. These, in fact, were the times when they seemed most cooperative and satisfied with the entrepreneurship course, as they copied down words and concepts that—just like in their biology and chemistry classes—would obviously require some study to master.

But wading through all this terminology on a day-to-day basis made it easy to forget the main topic of this lesson—and in fact, of the whole entrepreneurship course. Business planning, after all, is about planning a business, not just about defining the word *plan.*

Understanding the Theme of "Chalk and Talk"

The musical technique of "variations on a theme" often came to mind as I reflected on the teaching of entrepreneurship in these Kigali-area schools. The teachers I observed undeniably had unique personalities—Jacques was droll with a dry sense of humor, while a second teacher from School E, Geoffrey, indulged in frequent antics in search of the comic laugh; Eugene was shy and retiring, while Nadine was lively and vigorous with a loud voice. And their favorite pedagogical techniques differed in some ways as well, as the vignettes in this chapter illustrate. Yet the underlying theme of these entrepreneurship classes was often the same—a melody of some sort, to be sure, but a fairly repetitive one.

Entrepreneurship teachers gave lists and definitions, offered up their notes for copying, and talked through them. Simple topics seemed to drag on from one week to the next, and students were rarely asked to think for themselves. Teachers frequently lamented the lack of "documentation" to help them prepare their notes in entrepreneurship, but even after sets of textbooks had been distributed to O-level public schools, only once did I see an entrepreneurship book actually opened within classroom walls.[21] The teachers, in turn, almost never asked students to do the activities proposed in the syllabus or teachers' guides. The focus was on blackboard and notebook, chalk and pen, teacher's words and students' copied notes.

Most of these teachers had some personal entrepreneurial experience outside of the classroom, and they were all enthusiastic about the topic. They genuinely believed that entrepreneurship was important for their students' lives. And yet, somehow, that enthusiasm for the practice of entrepreneurship was nearly always buried under the exigencies of conveying definitions and covering the content of the course. In the midst of all this, the disciplinary tendencies of Rwanda's school system took over nearly completely, making the course much more about a controlled and orderly process of transmitting information than an opportunity to cultivate entrepreneurial creativity.

The educational theme of chalk and talk is certainly not unique to Rwanda, as the literature on schooling in Rwanda and the surrounding region, not to mention elsewhere in the world, amply demonstrates (see, e.g., Rubagiza, Were, & Sutherland, 2011; Stambach, 2000; Uworwabayeho, 2009; Vavrus, 2003, 2009). But the entrepreneurship education policy was designed to encourage different pedagogical dispositions—to develop students' skills, not just academic knowledge, and to orient their learning toward self-employment, not just performance on examinations. It is worth questioning how, in the context of a course with such eminently practical aims, so many of these teachers interpreted their responsibilities largely in terms of notes to be copied and memorized.

Educational policies and curriculum are socially produced texts that require reinterpretation in each new social context. The potentially powerful influence of such texts—whether written, oral, or visual—as means for changing both individual and group dispositions is widely assumed. As governments and organizations develop educational materials, they hope that their syllabi and textbooks will help to shape teacher practices and, from there, be transmitted in such a way as to mold students' attitudes and habits (Ball, 1994). But the power of texts for transmitting unfamiliar dispositions and effecting social change is limited, perhaps more so than many governments realize.

The teachers I spoke with often talked of their teaching challenges in terms of what was lacking: students' lack of understanding, lack of funds for activities, and lack of time to cover the content of the course. But my observations point to a different conclusion: the issue was not a lack of anything in particular, but rather teachers' possession of certain ingrained ways of thinking and behaving regarding the purpose of schools, their own roles as teachers, and regarding knowledge itself—arguably the same doxa and dispositions as those held by the curriculum developers who created Rwanda's first O-level curriculum, for both groups were drawn from essentially the same community of practice.[22]

Just as the National Curriculum Development Centre's learner-centered instructions to curriculum developers produced uneven results, there was no guarantee that either teachers or students would interpret the O-level and A-level curricula in the way Rwandan government leaders intended. The observations presented in this chapter illustrate the ways in which teachers reinterpreted the entrepreneurship curriculum through their own established doxa and dispositions, in the process unintentionally subverting many of the postdevelopmental goals of Rwanda's entrepreneurship education policy.

This analysis of what happened, however, poses the danger of presenting teachers as some sort of victims of their own habitus. It may be more accurate, instead, to view teachers as knowledgeable and skilled actors in a field of schooling that happens to reward particular examination- and credential-oriented competencies. The conceptual framework of negotiated social learning developed earlier in this book suggests that these teachers' attempt to position themselves favorably in Rwanda's field of schooling involves maneuvers that, while perhaps not conscious, are nonetheless strategic.

Successful practice in a social field, such as the field of schooling in Rwanda, involves developing the appropriate dispositions that signal one's mastery of that context. This cultural capital is connected to both tangible and symbolic rewards—economic power in terms of money and resources, social power in terms of networks of relationships, and symbolic power in terms of status and prestige (Bourdieu, 1986). Teachers' efforts to fit into "school culture" in Rwanda, in other words, are linked to important consequences for them—including their ability to find and retain employment, but also many more subtle dynamics beyond that.

Vavrus (2009) has written an illuminating article on how these considerations affect teacher pedagogy. As Vavrus attempted to introduce constructivist methodologies to future teachers at a Tanzanian teachers' college, she writes, her students began to raise a number of questions about the implications of these approaches for their own future social status in the schools and communities where they would work:

Although my students' initial reaction was positive, I quickly started to notice how often they began questions directed at me with the phrase "But Madam. . . ." [. . .] "But Madam, if we start a lesson by asking students what they already know about a topic, they will think we don't know anything about it ourselves." "But Madam, how can we have our students doing group work when the noise from their discussions will disturb our fellow teachers?" "But Madam, students don't actually read the novels in the syllabus because they only have to memorize the main ideas for the national exam. Why should we use class time to act out scenes from these stories when we could be drilling our students on relevant characters, plots, and themes?" (Vavrus, 2009, p. 303)

These future Tanzanian teachers knew from experience that part of a teacher's ability to maintain a learning environment in the classroom, at least in their context, depended upon establishing a form of authority in which students defer to teachers' expertise.

Teachers in traditionally structured schools are, in fact, engaged in a constant negotiation of authority with their students, and they must construct their role sufficiently convincingly to win students' consent. In the seminal work *Learning to Labor*, an ethnography of working-class student resistance, Willis (1977) argued that the mark of experienced teachers is the ability to use their own individual teaching practices to reinforce a more general "teacher paradigm" in which the teacher's authority is understood as legitimate and, for students, largely beyond question:

It is the *idea* of the teacher, not the individual [teacher], which is legitimized and commands obedience. This idea concerns teaching as a fair exchange—most basically of knowledge for respect, of guidance for control. Since knowledge is the rarer commodity this gives the teacher his moral superiority. This is the dominant educational paradigm which stands outside particular teachers but enables them to exert control legitimately upon the children. It is legitimated in general because it provides equivalents which can enter into other successive exchanges which are to the advantage of the individual. The most important chain of exchanges is, of course, that of knowledge for qualifications, qualified activity for high pay, and pay for goods and services. The educational is, therefore, the key to many other exchanges. (p. 64)

Teachers' legitimacy, in other words, traditionally rests upon their role as the quintessential master practitioners in the school community of practice and on the embeddedness of schooling within a broader field of livelihoods. As students apprentice themselves to the teacher, they hope to gain the knowledge and dispositions that will translate into cultural capital in the search for employment and socioeconomic mobility.

The teachers of Rwanda's entrepreneurship course that I observed throughout 2010 were therefore, in an important sense, modeling excellent teaching. By demonstrating their role as the central arbiters of knowledge on difficult terms and concepts, teachers achieved a stable relationship with their students that did not require struggling for legitimacy and authority day in and day out. And by doing a good job helping students prepare for their most important goal—good performance on the national examinations—teachers earned students' approval and appreciation.[23] This final "reward" has its altruistic dimension, of course: many teachers sincerely want to help their students advance through high performance on their examinations, and they would measure the effectiveness of their own teaching practice in that light. But ensuring students' approval is also crucial in making teachers' jobs *bearable* from day to day.

Chalking Up Contradictions to the Post-Developmental State

The teachers' behavior in these entrepreneurship classes may, upon reflection, seem understandable and rational, but it has contradictory implications for the goals of the post-developmental state. Even while the neoliberal underpinning of post-developmentalism requires a fundamental change in teacher pedagogy, the parallel need for a strong-state disciplinary orientation can be brought about only when teachers maintain their authoritative role.

This contradiction can be illustrated by examining the vast differences between the type of thinking promoted in traditional classrooms, in contrast to the creativity that is required for proposing new entrepreneurial ventures. As teachers spend day after day writing definitions and notes on the board, and students dutifully copy them down, it is not difficult to imagine the processes by which these repeated classroom experiences become incorporated into students' doxa and dispositions and, from there, influence how young Rwandans imagine the business possibilities open to them. Traditional schooling, after all, places strong constraints on students' imaginations and on their practical interpretations and analyses of the world around them.

In School A, for example, the Senior 3 students learned that there are three sectors of production, each involving a specific set of activities. Their notes for each category, in turn, involved a list of examples to be copied down and learned for examination questions, such as the following ones from their second trimester examination: "What are the types of professional fishing?" and "What is the difference between extensive animal husbandry and intensive animal husbandry?"[24] The codified approach to knowledge featured in lessons like the one described here is rational and perhaps appropriate as a first stage in learning about the economy. But if it is never opened up to require students to analyze the complex social and economic realities around them, it tends to cultivate an understanding of the world as involving preset categories and predetermined possibilities. It does not seem a far stretch from lessons like this one to a reasoning process in which young people decide that their business options are essentially limited to the types of enterprises already established in their immediate context.

During our interviews with these students, many hinted at just such a chain of reasoning when they explained why they planned to start a type of business for which there were already numerous identical examples nearby. "I want to open a hardware store," one young graduate—Marvin—explained to me, "because I heard that is a good way to earn money, better than other businesses in terms of what you earn after taxes." He had done some independent investigation to arrive at this judgment, but it was an investigation among the three or four types of business that already existed in his neighborhood.

It is quite a leap from this thought process to one in which students analyze their economic environment in terms of what is missing or yet to be improved. Having learned over the course of several years in school that most of what is worth thinking about has already been thought, categorized, and defined by others, it makes sense that young Rwandans would come up with business ideas that are essentially similar to what is already being done. In the process, however, the post-developmental goals of promoting self-employment and economic development of the nation may never come about—after all, the market can support only so many identical hardware, stationery, and corner grocery shops.

There is, however, a strong synergy between the teacher's traditional role as the central arbiter of knowledge, and the post-developmental state objectives of instilling regulations and controls. Beyond just their specific lessons on registration, taxation, and commercial law, the teachers in all of these class-rooms were teaching students to be orderly citizens in many other ways. As they acted out their traditional teaching role in the center of classroom activity, the relationship of these teachers to their students arguably became a meta-phor for the appropriate role of the Rwandan state in relation to citizens. The teachers did their best to play the part of a benevolent and authoritative source of knowledge and instructions, constantly keeping their students' future best interests in mind—just as the developmental state must take on the parental role of authoritatively informing citizens about their conditions, needs, and appropriate behavior. And by maintaining an orderly and disciplined, quiet classroom, teachers earned students' respect and were thus able to pursue the important goal of preparing students for examinations—just as the post-developmental state must actively cultivate citizens' willingness to pursue na-tional development goals in an orderly way.

Orderliness and teacher authority in the classroom, in other words, strongly support state authority and the ability of the state to accomplish its developmental goals. But students are not passive observers, even in tradi-tional classrooms. They must accept the teachers' authority for orderliness to be maintained. This suggests that the very targets of Rwanda's entrepreneurship course—students—may hold a great deal of power over the ultimate form that this post-developmental policy will take. In Chapter 6, we see how that power took shape over the course of the year.

Chapter 6

Students Question the Course

JACQUES, THE ENTREPRENEURSHIP teacher from School A, walked into his Senior 3 classroom one day late in the school year and greeted the students more brusquely than usual. Turning to face the class, he announced:

T: Prepare your entrepreneurship notebooks. I want to see your notes!

SS: [*Panicking, whispering to one another*] Eh! Eh! We're going to be dismissed this time . . .

T: You. Go to the front. You. You. You![1]

Circulating around the room to look at notebooks, he sent to the front of the room every student who had not been taking notes in entrepreneurship. Within minutes, about half of the class was standing sheepishly in front of the blackboard:

T: And as for you who don't even have your notebooks, get out! [*Five students, looking worried, reluctantly shift toward the door and leave the room*]. I know all your secrets. Please, when you are studying, do it for knowledge, not because you are doing tests or examinations![2]

. . .

These young Rwandan students were very interested in going into business, but one would never have known it from observing their entrepreneurship classes. When my research assistant, Flora, and I asked students how the Rwandan government could help reduce youth unemployment, one of the most common responses was "Teach us to create our own jobs!" Nearly everyone had friends or family members who were self-employed or had some sort of trading activity, and they pictured themselves going into business too. More than 90 percent of the students in this study thought they would become self-employed sometime in the future; and just before graduation, 57 percent said they planned to start their first business within the following three years. In contrast, the average rate of short-term intended business start-up in the rest of the world, for the same age group, is only about 20 percent.[3]

Notwithstanding these students' interest in going into business, they seemed singularly uninterested in the course that was supposed to help them do just that. Despite the disciplinary orientation of their teachers' pedagogical style, within just a few weeks from the beginning of the school year, increasing numbers of students were daydreaming and talking through their entrepreneurship courses. Not long after, when it was announced that entrepreneurship would not after all be tested on that year's national examinations, students' rebellion became more generalized.[4] Some continued to passively follow along, surreptitiously avoiding taking notes, while others vocally complained to teachers and administration that the scheduled number of class hours for entrepreneurship should be reduced. Finally, many students—especially in Senior 6—simply stopped attending class. Their neglect was especially noticeable when compared to the generally high degree of discipline and effort they demonstrated during the rest of the school day.

This chapter is about that paradox, between students' interest in the practice of entrepreneurship and their perplexing neglect of the course that was intended to teach them how to become entrepreneurs. It is also about the power of students to shape teacher practice and ultimately their power to shape the significance of educational policies themselves. Just as the Rwandan government was attempting to move citizens' expectations regarding the purpose of education in a more neoliberal and post-developmental direction, students appeared to be pushing back, doing their best to hold on to the—real or imagined—promise held out by conventional schooling.

Opposing Entrepreneurship?

As illustrated in Chapter 5, the entrepreneurship teachers that we observed in five different Rwandan schools often chose to use conventional chalk-and-talk methods in their courses, resulting in a pedagogical approach that was more successful at teaching "orderliness" than any sort of entrepreneurialism. In part, I have argued, this was because of teachers' ingrained habits and beliefs about schooling. But at some level this approach may have also represented a strategic choice, as teachers strove to maintain a mutually accepted relationship of authority with their students. The dynamics of that relationship, I have suggested, mean that students, and not just teachers, have the power to shape the implementation of any given educational policy.

This chapter substantiates that argument about students' power to influence policy by exploring what happened over the course of the year as students practiced many subtle and not-so-subtle techniques for communicating the relatively low esteem in which they held their entrepreneurship course. Students' "silence" in traditional classrooms, it turns out, is often much more active than it first appears (Stambach, 1994).

Rwandan students' resistance to the new entrepreneurship course has some historical precedent. Starting from before independence, East African parents and students have objected to attempts to shift the foundational logic of schooling through "ruralization" and "vocationalization" reforms (Foster, 1965; Lugumba & Ssekamwa, 1973; Mattee, 1983; Mwiria, 1990, 1991; Ssekamwa, 1997; Ssekamwa & Lugumba, 2002). In Rwanda's own history, successive waves of school reforms in the decades following independence, aiming to reorient the majority of students toward the more "appropriate" and "relevant" areas of agriculture and vocational skills, were also poorly received (Erny, 2003). In each case, resistance to reform has sprung out of demands for equality—if current elites attained their elevated status via participation in a certain kind of schooling, parents have argued, then their own children deserve access to exactly the same sort of education. Educational quality, in this sense, has often been popularly defined not in reference to one or another pedagogical theory but in terms of concrete evidence of status advancement.

Despite this resemblance to earlier instances of protest against school reform, however, student resistance to Rwanda's entrepreneurship course today poses something of a paradox. The reforms attempted in the twentieth century were linked to relatively low-status activities like agriculture and handicrafts; in contrast, "entrepreneurship" [*kwihangira imirimo*] is widely seen in Rwanda as positive, among parents and students alike. Furthermore, while parents' objections to earlier types of school reform have been quite vocal at various points in Rwanda's history, there is no such outright resistance to entrepreneurship education today. And the survey data cited earlier amply illustrate how interested students are in undertaking entrepreneurial activities themselves someday. How are we to understand, then, the fact that students so clearly rebelled against their entrepreneurship course?

While the teachers I described in the previous chapter may have relied on teacher-centered and examinations-focused practices to maintain order within the classroom, students appeared more interested in a different aspect of the conventional logic of schooling: its apparent assurance of a predictable connection between educational credentials and individual mobility, within a rationalized social and economic structure. Because students saw the entrepreneurship course as having little instrumental value in relation to that—to their mind—primary function of schooling, they resisted and rebelled against it. In other words, students resisted the course largely because of its very neoliberal-influenced characteristics: its attempted emphasis on student-centered inquiry and its implied delinking of schooling from educational credentials and employment.

Though they were not necessarily consciously aware of the intended differences between the entrepreneurship course and their other classes, and they were certainly not aware of the way in which it was linked to such a thing as neoliberal governmentality or the post-developmental state, students nonetheless sensed that something about their entrepreneurship course just did not fit with their own understanding of the purpose of schooling. Their resistance against this mismatch, as I show in the rest of this chapter, cemented the entrepreneurship course's deviation from Rwanda's post-developmental goals.

Questioning Legitimacy

In the previous chapter, I painted a portrait of the entrepreneurship classes as largely disciplined and organized, with the teacher in an authoritative role as the dispenser of knowledge and students mostly passively waiting to receive their lessons. This was, by and large, what the entrepreneurship classes were like—but not always. Particularly in the Senior 6 classrooms, I was sometimes shocked by how openly the students disparaged their entrepreneurship teachers and lessons. From the beginning of the year, some Senior 6 students poked fun at the entrepreneurship teachers, laughing—sometimes behind their hands and sometimes openly—at the teacher's comments, ignoring the teacher's questions, and refusing to be called to order.

Yet this was not the norm for the rest of the school day in these very same classrooms.[5] When another teacher entered the room, there could be a complete change of mood. In School E one day, for example, I watched the entrepreneurship teacher Eugene quietly slip into his Senior 6 classroom. The students, chatting in small groups, barely noticed his arrival and did not look up.

T: [*Speaking to a girl student*] Erase the board.
S(f):   [*Reluctantly brings the eraser to the front of the room and then moves back to her seat.*]
T: Come back and clean it.
S(f):   [*Pretending not to hear, as the other students look on to see what will happen*]
S(m):   I'll do it.
SS: Eh! Eh! [*Objecting, as if their fellow student has ruined their plan of avoiding the day's entrepreneurship notes.*]

As this classroom "traitor" went to clean the board, Eugene handed his notebook to another student, who reluctantly took it and moved at a snail's pace to pick up a piece of chalk. Settling down to observe the process of copying notes, the teacher seemed oblivious to the fact that most of the students were actually studying chemistry and mathematics, surreptitiously reading notebooks hidden under their tables.

After half an hour of copying notes with a constant undercurrent of talking, Eugene moved to the front of the room again:

T: Do you follow?
SS: [*Chatting in low voices, heads together in small groups. No one looks up.*]
T: Is there any question?
SS: [*Continuing to ignore the teacher*]

Eugene began commenting on the notes, often speaking inaudibly. Only a few students from the front desks made eye contact with him. No one seemed to notice when, ten minutes before the class was supposed to end, Eugene gathered his things and left the room.

The chatting continued.

Suddenly, another teacher walked through the door. A wave of silence passed through the room and within a few moments everyone was quiet. All rose to their feet, as if saluting. The teacher, there to deliver a lesson in biology, gave them an indulgent nod and motioned for them to sit. Within seconds, the desks were cleared of everything but biology notebooks, as the students waited for the teacher to begin his lesson.[6]

The students' reactions to these two teachers undoubtedly differed in part because of their different styles of teaching. Eugene, though knowledgeable and experienced in the topic of entrepreneurship—among other things, he and his wife had been running their own shop for years—was quiet by nature and had trouble capturing his students' attention. He also, like several of the entrepreneurship teachers observed in this research, sometimes seemed unsure about how exactly to formulate and explain some key point in the syllabus—an understandable difficulty, given that the National Curriculum Development Centre had not yet been able to gather together the budget necessary for teacher training. Comments about teachers' limited grasp of the entrepreneurship subject matter sometimes came up in our focus group discussions, such as the following remark from Clarisse, a student in School C:

This entrepreneurship course, even if it was put there [by the government]; it's not well liked. I should speak for myself—in fact, it's a good course, no problem, but again, the problem is that those who teach it to us don't know anything themselves. I mean, they teach us, trying to get by as if they understand, but in reality it's like putting the geography professor in entrepreneurship. It's an obstacle, they don't show you the path very clearly; they don't even know it themselves.

The biology teacher introduced in the previous vignette, by contrast, exuded authoritative knowledge from every pore, with his upright posture accentuated by a long white laboratory coat and a deep voice that easily reached to the back corners of the room. The biology teacher looked and spoke like a master of his subject, in other words, while with the entrepreneurship teacher, no one was quite sure.

The classes offered by these two teachers were also different in another respect. The biology teacher was obviously initiating students into a specialized world of expertise, with scientific terms and difficult concepts that could be grasped only by the brightest among them, and even then often only with some significant effort. In contrast, Eugene sometimes seemed to be making a big deal about things that were simply common sense—such as his efforts to offer precise definitions for *plan* and *project* in the previous chapter. Faced with their entrepreneurship lessons, the students often seemed to be projecting one question: is entrepreneurship a "real" academic course? On the basis of the available evidence available, they usually arrived at a negative conclusion. You could not, after all, obtain a university degree in entrepreneurship—as a number of students from different schools commented to me, accurately or otherwise. So what was it doing in their A-level program, as they prepared themselves for university entrance examinations?

This juxtaposition of disrespect toward the entrepreneurship class, sandwiched on either side of the schedule by evident deference and respect for other teachers, was repeated to varying degrees in all of the Senior 6 classes we observed for this research. This reaction seemed intimately tied to these students' anxieties about their examinations. While the Senior 3 students, younger and still in a more generalized phase of their education with ten compulsory subjects, simply seemed to accept the addition of entrepreneurship to their schedule, the Senior 6 students did not. Many of them protested openly that entrepreneurship should not be given the same weight—seven hours a week— as their three other principal academic subjects. "Yes, we might want to run our own businesses in the future," they seemed to be saying, "but *school* isn't supposed to teach us how to do that."

Objecting to Active Pedagogy

Although they were well intentioned, the entrepreneurship teachers observed for this research were hardly the most skilled teachers I have met. Yet these teachers' pedagogical abilities were roughly the same as those of the majority of other teachers we observed in each school. It was especially interesting to note, therefore, that students' uncooperative reactions to their entrepreneurship teachers seemed exacerbated whenever a teacher attempted some of the activities in the curriculum that were intended to promote a more active student-centered pedagogical approach. Just as Vavrus's (2009) study, cited in the previous chapter, suggested might happen, students often appeared to see these student-centered activities themselves as academically illegitimate

DEMANDING DEFINITIONS

I first noticed this resistance to student-centered pedagogy in the School C Senior 6 classroom right at the beginning of the year. This classroom's entrepreneurship teacher, Paul, clearly loved his topic and tried to an unusual degree to carry out all of the student-centered activities recommended in the A-level syllabus. This classroom was also, however, the site of the most explicit case of student resistance we observed in the course of this research. The tension revolved around the teacher's insistence that answers come from the students themselves, through group discussion and homework assignments involving interviews and observations. Paul argued that to become entrepreneurs, students needed to be able to engage in independent search for information and analysis of their own ideas. Students, however, protested that it was the teacher's job—not theirs—to provide the information they would need for examinations.

One day near the beginning of the school year, I had been sitting in class for two hours, watching the students independently copy history notes from their teacher's notebook onto the board and then back to their own notebooks, when the entrepreneurship teacher walked into the room and greeted the class. This was my first opportunity to see Paul teach the course—he had just been hired a week earlier, about a month after classes began.[7]

But from the very beginning, it was evident that Paul did not have the same expectations as his students regarding an appropriate way to teach entrepreneurship. It all began with a group discussion and a demand for definitions:

T: Last time . . . we did a group work. It was [*writing on the board*]:

1. Identify the types of work.

Before, we had classified work; the way that you can classify types of work. But after, we saw the types in general and then [. . .] we were supposed to make a table with six columns. First identify the types of work, then [*writing, with student input*]:

2. Contribution of this work to society

3. Does this type of work exist in our locality?

4. Do we need this type of work?

5. Talents/knowledge necessary for this type of work?

6. How do you prepare for this work?

T: I had divided you into six groups to do this assignment. Because entrepreneurship doesn't exist on its own! We take the ideas from students, like brainstorming: questions—responses.

S(m):   What is brainstorming?

T: It means to collect different ideas. We will get a lot of ideas and then we
     will see what sounds best.[8]

Paul was guiding his Senior 6 class in the first lesson of the A-level entrepreneurship curriculum.[9] There, the syllabus proposed that students should
begin the course with a series of independent research activities intended to
help them analyze the opportunities for introducing new products and services as entrepreneurs. They were supposed to observe their environment and
carry out some interviews to record a comprehensive list in their notebooks
(again, independently of the teacher) of types of work being done in the
locality.

From a teacher's perspective, the assignment would arguably be helpful
both for building understanding of a foundational topic and for practicing
some of the independent information-searching capacities that these young
people would undoubtedly have to exercise as entrepreneurs. But the activity
did not go quite as planned:

T: You are going to have to do this in the notebook; you need to write a
     table in your notebook. Is it necessary for me to show you that table?
SS: It's necessary! It's necessary!
T: Erase the board and I will show you. You will then put down what you
     already discussed in groups, and I will add—
SS: Prof! Do we copy, prof? Excuse me, prof, is this notes?

The students seemed unsure about whether they should be copying down everything the teacher was saying, as they usually would for a dictation of class
notes. Paul responded:

T: This is a reminder of what you talked about; you will have to have it
     written in your notebooks, but more in detail with your own ideas. This
     is what is required in the syllabus.

The students looked unconvinced by this explanation, and I could hear some
complaints spreading out in muttered waves around the room:

S(m): [*Looking frustrated*] I want to know if we have already studied the
       first chapter [of this course]? And second, I want to know what is the
       definition of that word—*entrepreneurship*—first.

T: You're supposed to know that already.

S(m): We studied it in fifth year, but in English. What I think is that when you start a level, you have to start with definitions, so that the others can follow too.

Still in a mild tone of voice, Paul replied:

T: What I think is that definitions are not so important.

SS: [*All at once, shouting and objecting*] What?! Not important?!

T: [*Surprised, relenting a little*] I will give you the definitions—

SS: [*Call out their approval*]

T: But what I want from you doesn't require the definition. That system of giving and copying the definitions doesn't do much—in the end, does knowing the definition help you a lot?

S(m): If you don't give the definition, it's like skipping a step!

Speaking with me later about this interaction with his students, Paul reasoned that the students' objections were simply a reflection of their different levels of background knowledge in entrepreneurship. "You see," he explained to me, "I have some problems with the group, because some students studied entrepreneurship last year while others did not. So sometimes I have to go back and explain."

I had sensed, however, that this was not the only issue. Students also seemed confused about the teacher's unfamiliar student-centered approach. At first, they were willing to go along with the teacher, even if the group activity he had proposed confusingly fell outside the bounds of the two class activities— copying notes and listening to explanations—they were more familiar with. But when the teacher denied what, to the students, must have seemed like a perfectly reasonable request for a definition, they were completely nonplussed.

By the next week, seven entrepreneurship class hours later, that bewilderment had transformed into anger.[10] As Paul continued to facilitate discussions rather than present the conventional notes to be copied, the students became increasingly convinced that their teacher had no idea how to teach effectively and was completely unknowledgeable about his topic—despite the fact that he in fact held a second job in an organization that advised disadvantaged populations on how to start and grow their businesses. Because Paul spent most of the class time asking them questions, they reasoned, he must not know the answers himself.

As I soon learned, the students had even already complained to the school administration about their teacher's methods:

T: [*Entering the classroom one day, in a frustrated mood*] Go back to your seats or I will send you to the Prefect! I have given you many things, but the only thing that you have found to say, is to go to the Dean and say that I am giving you disorganized notes!

SS: [*Several laugh and others shout out defiantly*] Yes! It's true!

T: [*Angry, he sends out two of the students who laughed. Then he turns back to the board, attempting to move on; this time actually beginning to dictate notes in the typical fashion*] Let's see the second point. Write down "Point 1.2."

The students, sensing that they had achieved some new power over their teacher, pressed him for further concessions.

SS: [*Several shouting out*] Write on the board!

T: That's a bad habit for students who are already in Senior 6! [*But as the students continue to object, he moves to the board anyway and begins to write*]

1.2: Beliefs and Values of Work.

Already the teacher's behavior was being shaped by his students' reactions, as Paul shifted toward a more formalized style of delivery, and even paused to discuss the definitions of *beliefs* and *values*.

But Paul soon resumed trying to encourage student input—a move that only served to anger students even further. As he struggled to get students to give examples of beliefs about work in Rwanda, the volume of background talking in the classroom gradually rose until it was nearly at a shouting level.

Out of the fray rose a few distinctly audible voices, complaining to one another that the teacher was still not giving them real notes. Paul turned to them, finally frustrated beyond the boiling point at their lack of cooperation, and replied in Kinyarwanda:

T: I'm not going to give you any notes! What's important is that you understand. If you continue to fool around, it's not my problem. If you fail the exams, what will you have gained?

SS: [*Shouting even louder, criticizing the teacher for mixing English and Kinyarwanda, rather than just using French in their Francophone classroom*]

As the bell rang for the end of class, the students rose from their desks in a swarm and congregated in small groups, their continued complaints buzzing from around the edges of the room like the wasps that had made homes in the classroom's rafters.

The class head boy separated himself from the crowd and politely approached the teacher, clearly intent on pursuing his classmates' arguments for a more conventional style of teaching:[11]

S(chief): Prof, will you give us some notes? [. . .]

      T: No, we will discuss, and after you have understood we will do a synthesis. This is to help you! You are in Senior 6 now. I will never give you notes just to memorize, no. It's a bad habit from those Congolese teachers. He comes and speaks his French to you and just gives you some notes to memorize.

S(chief): [*Diplomatically agreeing*] And after the exam, you forget.

      T: [*Sarcastically*] Yeah, your notebook becomes more intelligent than you are!

Paul clearly had the national examinations in mind and was aware of their power to motivate students to cooperate—but this was not his only objective. He genuinely felt that by encouraging students to be more active in learning for themselves, they would develop skills that were important to a practicing entrepreneur. Yet his students simply did not seem to want this sort of change in their school experience.

The activity he had intended to introduce—having students interview a few adults about their beliefs and values related to work—in fact never took off. "I tried to work on this [activity] with them," he explained later, "but they're not interested. They said 'Eh! What kind of course is this?! A course which makes us go and discuss, and we don't know French [. . .] What do you want us to do?!' [. . .] Me, I said they could do it in Kinyarwanda, because what we want in this course is for them to know. Once they have understood [the topic], they can also learn to express it in French. So, I sent them to interview people, then come back—But they go and they do it themselves: I discover they are themselves that answered the questions! And they say 'Oh! Teacher, we don't have time [to interview people]. At home, we are busy with other things.'"[12]

As the year progressed, these School C Senior 6 history, economics, and geography (HEG) students applied a variety of techniques of resistance to the entrepreneurship course. On the one hand, they continued to press for traditional notes and definitions, sometimes getting into further arguments with their teacher over this issue. On the other hand, the students continued to practice several different forms of disrespect, including criticizing the teacher to his face and skipping class. This classroom's reaction to their entrepreneurship teacher was so extreme, in fact—in a school where students were otherwise quite respectful of their teachers—that it eventually drove Paul out of the classroom, and then out of the school.

By September, eight months into the school year, the school administration had accepted Paul's resignation, replacing him with a new graduate fresh out of the Kigali Institute of Education.[13]

Not long before Paul was replaced, largely as a result of student complaints, he had given me his own evaluation of what was going on. To him, the fact that students rejected his teaching style was simply a symptom of the very reasons the government needed to introduce the course in the first place:

T: You see, MINEDUC [the Ministry of Education] introduced this course, because there was a huge need for it. As I have been explaining to you, people have a bad habit of learning—cramming! Eh? Emphasizing theory more than practice. That's why, when you go and you start exercising students in discussing, problem-solving and whatever, they don't like [it], because they are not used to doing that. They know that what they have to do is just to copy down notes. But with entrepreneurship, it is about practical things! It's about teaching somebody and transforming him into another [kind of] person! For example, if he's a student, he's used to having those theories, studying economics, macroeconomics and whatever—that's the theories invented by other people! But entrepreneurship, you should be creative. And being creative does not come just like that! Okay, theories from others could help you to get a start, but you are not supposed to concentrate only on those things. You have to learn through situations, examples, practice. [. . .] The objective of the government is to make students become creative and innovative. That's why the entrepreneurship program was put here.[14]

His students, however, did not want to spend their school time developing creativity by practicing independent research and analysis. They wanted to have the definitions and facts they would need for their examinations, and if their teacher would not cooperate with that objective, they were determined to make him change—or make him be exchanged for a new one who would.

STRATEGIC SILENCE

Though the Senior 6 classroom in School C represented an extreme case, milder forms of student resistance to the student-centered aspects of the entrepreneurship course were evident in every other school and classroom we observed. A more passive tactic of resistance many students employed might be called a strategic use of silence.

In a number of classrooms we observed, whenever teachers stepped out of their habitual call-and-response style of superficial "discussion" by asking students for some sort of genuine analysis relevant to the real world, students often simply waited them out. Looking blankly ahead or staring intently down at their notebooks, they settled back into their desks for the repeated questions that they knew would have to end, eventually, with the teacher providing the answer—just as we observed in the following Senior 3 lesson in School B, about how to reason through the best location for a particular business:[15]

T: Imagine we have one hundred kilos of sugarcane, how much sugar do we have? Imagine it's sixteen percent after processing. So we have sixteen kilos of sugar. Now the question is, where to put your enterprise: close to the client so you can transport the sugar to them, or close to the producers of sugarcane?

SS: [*Sitting silently, waiting for the teacher to continue*]

T: Who will respond? Give your reasons too . . .

SS: [*Still silent*]

T: [*Encouraging*] I'm coming to ask your advice, as real economists. What advice would you give?

SS: [*The students look back blankly, no one raising their hands*]

T: [*Patiently repeating her question while drawing on the board*]

| Sugarcane plantation | Clients |

You have sugarcane and you want to produce sugar. Where should you
put your sugar factory: close to the client, or close to the sugarcane
producers?

SS: [*Still no answer*]

  T: [*Becoming a little more impatient*] This is about the placement of
enterprises, we studied it in the notes. This is an example. Is it better to
have your sugar factory close to the plantation or to the clients?

S(f): [*The only one to raise her hand*] I would prefer to put it close to the
sugarcane plantation.

  T: Who can tell us why?

S(f): Because the elements are found in the enterprise?

  T: Is that the reason? [*Raising the volume of her voice in some frustration*]
The reason is easy: because it's easier to transport the sugar than the
sugarcane. Eh! A question so easy like that one! Are you there? You see
the price will be less because sugar is easy to transport. So you see the
importance of the location of the enterprise.

These students were not unusually obstinate, and they were not exactly being
deliberately insolent. They simply sat there and waited, giving the impression
that they did not know the answer and could not reason it out—or that they
just could not be bothered to think about and justify their own ideas when they
knew that the teacher would soon provide the correct answer for them.

Experiences like this one seemed to quickly influence the entrepreneurship teacher, Nadine, to reduce her expectations for the students. Some months
later, she commented to me:

The program was badly developed. It's as if it is for university level! They want students
of *this* age to learn how to plan a whole project?! Come on. What we can do is just adjust
this for their level. We can teach them the role of planning, and the definition, and that's
it. The rest is just maybe for those elite schools.[16]

Never mind the fact that the government's first purpose in introducing this
course was to enable students exactly like hers—most of whom were already
of legal working age, and many of whom might not be able to continue their
schooling[17]—to earn an income by starting their own small businesses. And
never mind that many of her students already had some business experience of
their own. These students had shown Nadine that they could not or would not

reason independently about business decisions—at least not while they were inside the classroom.

Nadine's interactions with her students thus simply reinforced what seemed in Chapter 5 to already be a widespread educational maxim: teachers have to give notes, definitions, answers, and explanations on students' behalf. In this outcome, subtly negotiated between teachers and students, it is of course the post-developmental values of self-reliance and initiative that lose out most of all.

PROTESTING AGAINST PROJECT PLANNING

One might argue that the examples of student resistance to learner-centered activities cited so far—avoiding an assignment to conduct out-of-school observations about types of work, refusal to interview people about working values, unwillingness to reason independently about the best location for a factory—involved issues that were simply uninteresting to students. After all, each activity was somewhat distant from students' most direct business interests and concerns. But similar dynamics were at play in even the most obviously useful activities, activities that might have a real impact on students' ability to achieve their goal of becoming self-employed one day, such as business planning.

The envisioning of a new enterprise and the detailed analysis of the requirements for start-up and initial growth are perhaps the most student centered and practically relevant of all the activities that the entrepreneurship teachers could have implemented in their classrooms. Yet only half of the entrepreneurship teachers observed actually asked students to plan their own business project, as required in the curriculum, and even these were in-class activities that did not allow for the kind of independent investigation and reflection that would be involved for real business planning. Most teachers may have reasoned, on the basis of the available evidence from their classroom interactions—like the teacher from School B—that their students simply were not capable of planning their own projects. But even in cases where teachers attempted to encourage project planning, their students' reaction was often not favorable, as the following vignette illustrates.

Only a few students were lingering outside the School D classroom when the entrepreneurship teacher, Samson, arrived one day for his scheduled class.[18] A bit perplexed by the low attendance, he greeted the students and they trickled in, filling only a few of the desks that packed the classroom from wall to wall.

For a class with almost fifty students, just twenty-three had found it worth their time to attend the entrepreneurship lesson that day:

> T: Morning! I can see that you are few today ... [*Pausing as if unsure what to do, he looked out at the students for a few moments without speaking*] Okay, today I am not going to teach; we are going just to discuss. I am going to give you some questions you can face during the examinations, and then you will discuss in groups of three.

The students listened quietly, their attention apparently captivated by the mention of examinations—the major preoccupation for most students in this final year of secondary school. But the mood in the room quickly changed upon Samson's next announcement:

> T: I am going to give you an assignment to make a project.
> SS: [*Many speaking at once*] Ah, ah, ah! No!
> S(m): Eh! *Birakomeye!* [*It's difficult*]
> T: [*Moving closer to one of the students who shouted out, challenging him mildly*] What? Ask me your question.
> S(m): It's too hard.
> T: [*Reassuring*] No, you are just going to discuss.

The students continued talking among themselves, complaining and protesting about having to do such an apparently demanding task. The teacher ignored them, beginning to dictate his question:

> T: "You intend to start a horticulture project"—
> SS: [*Many speaking at once*] Huh? What?
> T: This is the question. You can write it down if you want. [*Again switching into a dictation tone of voice, pausing to allow them to write. A few students pick up their pens, while others reluctantly listen.*] "You intend to start a horticulture project ... in your locality. ... Point A, describe the methods ... you would use ... to ensure production ... of quality products. ... Point B, explain how the project ... will benefit society ... Point C, suggest the measures you would take ... to reduce production costs." [*Pausing to allow them to complete their writing*] Now we will have eight groups of three. I want you to discuss!
> S(m): What is horticulture?

T: Where you are growing fruits, for example, oranges, apples, bananas, et cetera. You discuss and after you will have a presentation for each group.

Samson's suggestion of a "horticulture" project was not as unrealistic as it might seem—food production and distribution is a major economic activity in Rwanda, and many people in both rural and urban areas alike are involved in different parts of the chain of trade in avocados, tomatoes, oranges, bananas, plantains, and other fruits and vegetables.

With some grumbling, the students turned toward the two or three others seated nearest to them and apparently began to work. Through the low murmur, however, some comments stood out that made it clear that most groups were preoccupied with other topics entirely—an upcoming economics quiz, their favorite music, someone's wardrobe.

An hour later, the project presentations began. While a few of the groups actually tried to answer all of the questions, standing respectfully at the front of the room, the majority continued to express their annoyance at being forced to use their entrepreneurship class time to actually plan a business project. One student refused to stand up, muttering his group's answers inaudibly, much to his classmates' amusement. Another student rattled so quickly through his notes that no one could understand what he was saying, punctuating this performance with a loud "Thank you!" and sitting down before anyone could ask him any questions. As the presentations continued, the level of background chatting in the room rose to a roar that drowned out even the more serious presenters.

. . .

Students did not always object to their teachers' efforts to make the entrepreneurship course more practical. They especially loved the times when their teachers would give concrete—and often funny—anecdotes from their own lives about their business ideas and attempts to put them into action, about poor customer service they had experienced, about business failures they had witnessed, and sometimes even about ways of evading the law or cheating a little to save some money. Students in School A even cooperated with an in-class activity to plan business projects much like the one cited in the previous section (the teacher quipped, "The only project I won't accept is one for sorcery!"); later on, some students mentioned that activity as the inspiration for the chicken projects they hoped to start after graduation. But that experience in School A was an exception to the norm. Across all of the classrooms observed, students were rarely receptive to activities that demanded that they think for themselves rather than simply sitting back and listening to or copying down the teacher's ideas.

As I have said before, these teachers were not particularly skilled at attempting learner-centered activities, and perhaps they could have won more cooperation from their students if they had done a better job of bridging between these new methods and those students were more familiar with. For the time being, however, it seemed that these students would rather copy down a definition of the word *plan* than actually plan a business during class time. Whether it was through outright rebellion, strategic silence, or simply a begrudging sort of participation, students in both O-level and A-level alike made it clear that they were unconvinced by their teachers' attempts to introduce active learner-centered activities into their classrooms. Something about it just did not seem right to them, and they noticeably pushed back toward the more comfortable style of chalk and talk.

Examining Entrepreneurship

Students' resistance to the entrepreneurship course—silence in the face of questions, avoidance of assignments, chatting while the teacher was talking—was noticeable from almost the very beginning of the school year, especially in the Senior 6 classrooms. But if it was present in nascent form from the beginning, this resistance became much more overt and generalized a few months later, once it was announced that entrepreneurship would not be on the national examinations that year. From that point on, students saw little point in even taking notes in class. Even the rural and less privileged Senior 3 students in School A, who were generally fairly cooperative, increasingly avoided taking notes in their entrepreneurship class—as the anecdote that opened this chapter illustrated. The arguments between students and teacher increased in volume in School C, and many Senior 6 students, especially in Schools D and E, simply stopped attending their entrepreneurship classes, hanging out in their dormitories or in the school library until the teacher gave up and left, often long before the designated hours were over.

These tactics had noticeable effects on both teachers and administration. At the level of pedagogical style, teachers reacted in different ways—some becoming more stern and strict with their students, others passively accepting the situation, and one increasing his antics and anecdotes in an effort to at least win students' laughter. But the most common reaction by far, on the part of teachers, was avoidance: reducing the number of entrepreneurship class hours per week or even ceasing to teach the course entirely. In some cases, such as in School B, the teacher simply made an individual decision to replace some of the hours for entrepreneurship with a different course that she also taught. In other cases, such as in both Schools D and E, the reduction in class hours for entrepreneurship was sanctioned by the administration, which agreed that students should use the time to study the courses that would actually appear on the national exams.

Figure 9, using data from our weekly observations in each school, illustrates how the percentage of scheduled entrepreneurship courses that were actually taught became smaller and smaller as the year wore on.[19]

As Figure 9 shows, each trimester began (in February, May, and August) with some added efforts to teach the course. But that effort was lower each time and quickly declined until less than one-third of the scheduled entrepreneurship classes were actually being taught, by October, when the examinations period began. Though still an official requirement, the entrepreneurship course had effectively been almost erased from the school schedule by the end of its first full year of implementation.

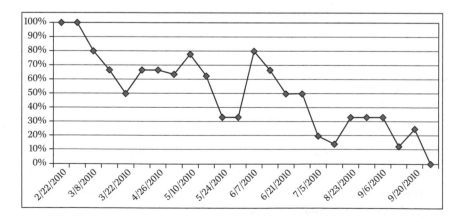

Figure 9   Percentage of scheduled entrepreneurship classes that were actually taught

This result, as the vignettes included in this chapter demonstrate, was not simply a matter of administrative decision making about how to use class time. Students' own disinterest in, and resistance to, the course also played a large role. These reactions are remarkable precisely because so many students were in fact interested in becoming practicing entrepreneurs later in life or already had their own business and self-employment activities. For reasons that I discuss further throughout the rest of this book, however, their entrepreneurship course simply did not strike them as practically useful for their lives. In other words—the entrepreneurship course might not have been slated for examination that year, but students put it to the test themselves, and it came up short.

Make It Practical by Giving Capital

Looking back over a year's worth of observations in ten classrooms,[20] some moments of which have been summarized in this chapter, there was a clear theme of students resisting many of the most "practical" aspects of the entrepreneurship course, insistently reinforcing a more traditional model of definitions- and facts-oriented teaching. When Flora and I spoke with students directly, both informally and in formal focus group discussions, we therefore not unreasonably expected them to complain about the course's unconventionally practical activities. Perhaps, we reasoned, they thought that the course was not serious enough, or that it did not seem to them like a "real" academic subject.

We were right in part, but this was not the full story. What these students told us about the entrepreneurship course prompts a reevaluation of students' thinking about schooling and of their capacity to influence even national education policy according to their own perceived interests. A significant number of students —including and even especially those who had resisted the sorts of practical activities discussed in this chapter—explained that they did not like the class because it was just "theoretical," not practical enough:

Adolphe: Me, what I see here in secondary school, I think that [the entrepreneurship course] is useless, because it has never helped anyone get anywhere. . . . Maybe if they increased the practical aspect, then you could say that it's useful somehow.

Charity: It [the entrepreneurship course] is a good idea, but for us [. . .] we just have the idea of entrepreneurship in theory, but we don't do any practice. We're not that interested; it could help, but right now the course is just not practically useful.[21]

This sort of opinion, explicitly mentioned by at least some students in every school, seemed paradoxical. On the one hand, the National Curriculum Development Centre had gone out of its way to develop an entrepreneurship curriculum that was intended to be far more practical than the standard academic courses, especially at the A-level. But it was precisely these sorts of student-centered, practically relevant, pedagogical innovations that students seemed to most strongly resist—including such activities as business planning and field visits to speak with practicing entrepreneurs. If this was not practical, we wondered, then what was?

The key to understanding this reaction, it turned out, hinged again on a question of definitions: to these students, the word *practical* simply did not mean the same thing as it did to the curriculum experts at the National Curriculum Development Centre. Specifically, *practical* did not mean providing contrived opportunities to practice ideas from the course, but rather providing the practical resources they needed to create real viable income-generating activities. Sharon, a student from School D, for example, reflected:

For me, this course—we study it, it's true. And we assimilate the lessons. But then, putting all of that into practice—that could be a problem because of lacking what you need to start. You have already understood [the ideas], but putting it into practice to start is a problem. It [the course] maybe just gives you the path, so that once you have money, you can do something—but if you don't find the money, you'll just have the knowledge without knowing how to put it into practice.

A number of students from the same School C classroom introduced earlier pursued the same train of thought in a focus group discussion:

Ibrahim: The entrepreneurship [course] will really just add on to the ideas of those who have means. It teaches people who have money how to put their ideas into practice. Ordinary poor people like me; it won't do anything for us. Where would I find money to apply what I learned? But if someone had capital, after your studies, you would use these ideas.

Hipolite: Me too, what I want to add is: even at the beginning of this course, I saw that this is something that's already in us, but we just didn't know that this is what it was called—"entrepreneurship." That was the only problem, in fact. [. . .] But now what is the problem? It has

come to fill us up with lots of [ideas for] projects, so that we can find
something to do. But the obstacle is this: where to find the means?
Even if you say you want to start some project, even a simple one
like raising chickens, where will you find the money for that? Everything becomes a problem for us. This course is actually good, but it
would be much better if we had something in our pockets—if you
have some cash!

Without capital, these students argued, the entrepreneurship course would be
of little benefit to them.

The majority of students in each school included in this research insisted
that their ultimate preference was to become self-employed. But they were
convinced that they would have to find their own start-up capital to accomplish this goal. Their families, they said, were too poor to have extra money to
lend to them for capital—and even if they did, it might lead to family conflict if
their business failed and they were unable to repay the loan. As for banks, they
laughed, no bank would ever lend to young people like them, with no proven
experience and even less collateral.

Some of these students offered a specific alternative proposal: that instead
of paying teachers to teach them things that they considered common knowledge, the government should instead direct those resources toward giving students capital to finance their business ideas:

Leo: Even if I had just studied the other normal courses, in my head there
       is something; I mean, I would do [entrepreneurship] no matter what
       happens. It's not because of the course; even before, I wanted to do it.
       To the contrary, me, what I would accept is a person who comes to say
       that he's going to actually support you to start your business, and all
       you have to do is tell him the project you want to do, nothing else.
Aimé: The state could create cooperatives for students who are finishing
       their studies, or help them find their first employment, so that
       students could get their own financing rather than going to look
       for loans from banks or businesspeople. Because, first of all, they
       don't have jobs and they don't have any other collateral to reimburse
       the bank in case of failure. It's the state's job to plan how to create
       employment for youth. Or rather, I mean to say, it should be the youth

who create the jobs for themselves, but it's the state's role to intervene
and give them access to the money they need in order to start work—
even if it's to be reimbursed afterwards, but at least having that start
would help them develop.

Odette: For me, instead of teaching, the best would be to give money—for
example, to establish student associations [and give them capital] to
create jobs, rather than taking a teacher and paying him to teach this
course. If you have money, you can ask anyone about the procedure
for going into business and he will give you advice to help you start.

For these students, the only way to truly make the entrepreneurship course
"practical" was by giving them capital. As long as the entrepreneurship course
remained theoretical—even if that "theory" involved the National Curriculum
Development Centre's ideas of practical learner-centered pedagogy—it was
simply a waste of their time. They already knew about entrepreneurship, they
asserted; after all, people all around them practiced entrepreneurship every day,
starting any activity they could, often simply in order to survive. These students
did not want a course to help them become interested in entrepreneurship and
develop their ideas. They wanted an initiative that would help them put entrepreneurial ideas—ideas they already had—into action.

And if the government was not going to give them start-up capital, then
they would have to earn it themselves. This was a path that required absolutely
playing by the rules of the conventional school game: earning enough to save up
some business capital meant getting a "good job," which required an advanced
diploma, which in turn meant performing well enough on their examinations
at each stage to get access to scholarships and public schools with lower fees.
Good performance on examinations, in turn, required good teaching—"good
teaching" of a certain kind. The most practical entrepreneurship teacher,
therefore, was one who would prepare them very well for their examinations
by making sure they memorized the appropriate facts and definitions—and if
entrepreneurship was not going to be examined on the way to their diplomas,
then the best entrepreneurship teacher was one who would get out of the way
and let them focus their time on the classes that really counted.

The difference between the official policy perspective and students' perspective regarding the route to entrepreneurship was quite stark—as Figure 10
illustrates.

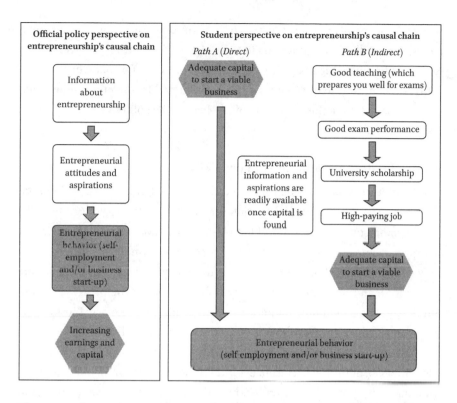

Figure 10   Contrasting government and student perspectives on entrepreneurship

While policy makers seemed to see the entrepreneurship course—and the knowledge it would convey—as the principal catalyst for entrepreneurial activity, eventually leading to an increase in personal earnings, students perceived things the opposite way. For them, entrepreneurial knowledge was already a given, widely available to them from family and friends who already had businesses. The problem, rather, was capital. If they did not have access to capital directly—and most did not, given the circumstances of their families—they would need a job to get some. And jobs, they all assumed, did not come without educational credentials.

These students thus had a fairly explicitly instrumental understanding of the purpose of schools. They did not really expect or even want their classes to help them develop creativity, problem solving, or other practical skills. Even the information and understanding to be gained through attending classes seemed largely tangential to their conceptualization of school's purpose. What counted for them, crucially, was school's role in preparing them for examinations, the hurdle they had to pass in their objective of getting a university degree and finding a high-paying job. Ironically, however, for many of them, all of this was in service of the ultimate goal promoted by the entrepreneurship course itself, despite their rejection of it—having the ability to finally become self-employed.

Understanding Student Resistance

Students, it turns out, can play a powerful role in determining the interpretations and significance of even national education policies, with potentially far-reaching consequences—in this case—for the Rwandan government's attempt to achieve a post-developmental state transformation. Over the past few decades, a large body of research has developed showing how policies are influenced, and often even completely reshaped, during the processes of operationalization and implementation (see, e.g., Hill & Hupe, 2009; Lipsky, 1980; Shore & Wright, 1997; Shore, Wright, & Peró, 2011). A significant subset of this research has examined teachers' practices as on-the-ground policy makers (Honig, 2006; Sutton & Levinson, 2001; Vavrus & Bartlett, 2013), but less attention has been given to the ways in which the apparently passive recipients of these policies—students—also play a decisive role. Across the eleven classrooms observed for this research, and apparently without ever discussing or deliberately coordinating their actions, students succeeded in shifting the entrepreneurship course's pedagogy back toward a conventional authoritarian structure of teacher-centered knowledge. They also succeeded in making life miserable enough for some of their teachers, and in insisting that their valuable class time be focused on their examinable courses, that only a third or less of the scheduled entrepreneurship classes were actually being taught by six months into the school year.

If these sorts of trends held true in other schools around the country, then students arguably transformed the Rwandan government's entrepreneurship education policy, at least in its first full year of implementation. From a course that was intended to cultivate a generation of "orderly entrepreneurs," the entrepreneurship education policy became something that, instead, seemed to incite students to relatively disorderly conduct in their efforts to ensure the norm of an orderly form of information transfer—with entrepreneurial creativity nowhere in sight, at least not in the classroom.

Even this relatively diffuse form of student resistance to the entrepreneurship course thus presents a potentially significant barrier to the Rwandan government's post-developmental goal of constructing state-guided economic development on a foundation of individual entrepreneurship. But it would be ridiculous to claim that students are deliberately protesting against "post-developmental" goals or "neoliberal" interpretations of the linkage between education and the labor market. Given that students were apparently unaware of the larger political implications of their actions, how can this student resistance be understood? And what does it say about any regime's efforts—in Rwanda or elsewhere—to shift a country's rationality of governance, using schools to transform an entire population's conceptualization of itself as citizens?

Shifts in rationalities of governance can be seen as educational processes because they require people to learn new ways of thinking and behaving, new doxa and dispositions (Bourdieu, 1972, 1977, 1990). But the vignettes highlighted in this chapter show yet again that this governmental teaching involves negotiation rather than straightforward processes of transmission. New approaches to governance necessarily take shape, at the micro-level, within multiple interacting communities of practice (Lave & Wenger, 1991; Sewell, 2005), each characterized by its own set of shared dispositions or group culture—which may counter in numerous subtle ways the dominant government narrative.

In the particular case of the entrepreneurship course's first full year of implementation, students and teachers alike belonged to a community of practice—defined by their shared participation in formal Rwandan schools—that emphasized certain roles for teachers and students, rewarded certain ways of behaving, and held a particular understanding of knowledge and its purpose. Yet teachers were also linked to a second community of practice, via the entrepreneurship curriculum, that had more direct exposure to new state ideas about pedagogy, the purpose of schooling, and the relationship between education and the labor market. Accordingly, some entrepreneurship teachers picked up on the possibility of practicing new ways of thinking and behaving in the classroom, ways that were intimately linked with the Rwandan government's neoliberal and post-developmental state goals—such as advocating student-centered activities, treating the entrepreneurship class as valuable whether or not it would be examined, and attempting to delink schooling from employment by encouraging direct business start-up.

As teachers brought these new ideas to their classrooms, however, students felt that something just did not quite fit with their own school culture. Having invested years in an education system that they hoped would promise them significant advancement in socioeconomic status—often involving major struggles to pass exams and pay school fees—they were not about to let an "incompetent" teacher ruin their chances by attempting to merely facilitate discussions and assign independent research rather than deliver proper notes. And they were not about to waste their time on a course that, as it turned out, would not in fact help them to earn their coveted diplomas. Students understood that the purpose of the course was to encourage them to start their own businesses, but they argued that it was resources, not knowledge, that they lacked. If they did not already have capital, as a shortcut to viable entrepreneurial activity, then the conventional school route appeared to be their only other option.

In the previous chapter, I recalled Willis's (1977) famous study of student resistance, *Learning to Labor*, as offering an insightful perspective into the ways in which teacher practice depends on the consent of students. As Willis observed, teachers in traditionally structured schools—like Rwanda's—are engaged in a constant negotiation of authority with their students, and must construct their role sufficiently convincingly to win students' consent. In Willis's description, the teacher's typical relationship of "legitimate" authority rests on some of the very factors that neoliberal and post-developmental reforms attempt to transform. By democratizing the teacher-student relationship, student-centered pedagogies begin to deprive teachers of their specialized position as sole possessors of that "rarer commodity"—absolute and codified knowledge—which is the source of their authority. In turn, neoliberal approaches such as entrepreneurship education and flexible specialization, which delink credentials from predictable careers, attack the very foundation of the exchange—knowledge for diplomas, and diplomas for jobs—at the base of teachers' legitimacy.

It is therefore not surprising that when students came in contact with the more neoliberal persuasions of the entrepreneurship course and their teacher, something just did not "feel right." In a mirror image of the "lads" in Willis's (1977) study of working-class student rebellion, the Rwandan students featured in this chapter noticed a disconnect between their own cultural expectations and those of their entrepreneurship teachers.[22] In this case, however, it was the students who wanted to conform to dominant school culture and the entrepreneurship teachers and their course who somehow seemed set against it.

Without having to analyze or understand at a deeper level the nature of this cultural mismatch, and without ever actively coordinating with their peers, these Rwandan students were able to act strategically and in concert, in ways that resulted in a changing of the entrepreneurship education policy—at least within their own classrooms and schools. Youth clearly have agency here, but it is something quite different from the blunt and purposeful agency that is usually imagined, such as the categories discussed in Abbink and Kessel's (2005) *Vanguard or Vandals* profiling youth in politics and protest movements, youth in conflict, and youth as a potentially dangerous marginalized class in Africa. There are some parallels: these Rwandan students were constructing a "symbolic counter-discourse" by questioning the value of their entrepreneurship course, acting on an alternative perspective that "challenges society in a moral and political sense and indicates alternatives" (Abbink & Kessel, 2005, p. 25). Yet they were not really doing so intentionally, and they did not position themselves as opponents to government plans. Indeed, in most other respects they described themselves as proud of Rwanda's governing regime and the progress it had achieved.

What happened during this first full year of implementing the entrepreneurship course can be better understood by recalling that students have diverse social repertoires at their disposal. While schooling has by and large taught them to be obedient, other social experiences have provided them with tools of irony, passive disobedience, resistance, and even defiance. These students were able to draw on the dispositions in their personal repertoire that would cause teacher discomfort and ultimately result in a reintegration of the entrepreneurship course back into a more familiar school mode.

This dynamic of student resistance is full of implications for educational policy making in contemporary post-developmental states, and for shifts in governmental rationalities more generally. Even if curriculum developers and teachers were able to more uniformly reflect post-developmental dispositions themselves, there would still be no guarantee that such a transformation would ultimately be cultivated within classroom settings. Students themselves may push back against unfamiliar teaching practices, unless the overall structure of access to the rewards they care about also changes at the same time—a point I take up further in Part IV of this book.

Part IV

Youth Entrepreneurship in Rwanda

Figure 11 Young self-employed market porters (*abakarani*) in their cooperative
uniforms

Source: Copyright Chris Honeyman, used by permission.

Chapter 7

The Creative Enterprise of Earning Credentials

TEN YOUNG PEOPLE were waiting for us outside their classroom. Shading themselves from the sun, they had all squeezed onto the narrow strip of concrete between the building's rough brick walls and the line of pruned bushes bordering the school yard. They looked out of place in the empty school, especially those who had rejected their now-obsolete school uniform in favor of the fashionable secondhand clothing you could find at any of the city's outdoor markets. Filing together into the cooler, dark classroom, we arranged the heavy wooden desks in a circle and sat down.

These Senior 3 graduates had been randomly chosen a few weeks earlier to stay in contact with me and my research assistant, Flora, for the following six months, part of an overall sample of 110 graduates from eleven classrooms and five schools. They had come back to school that day, after the end of classes and exams, to talk with us about their plans. The graduate to my right began.

"I didn't even get half the points in English," he said conversationally, "so I'm going to study English during the vacations. I'm going to be in some other deals too, doing some mechanics stuff, helping some mechanics so I can earn a bit of money."

The next boy spoke more quietly: "I'm going home, I'll help my parents with the cows and cultivating."

"At home, we do business," the next girl explained after a bit of prompting. "I'm going to help. But before, I'll go on vacation, visit some people in the family for a bit. After, I'll come back to help."

"What about your plans for school?" I asked.

"For school, I'm going to succeed [the exams] and continue afterwards." She paused, thinking: "Because if I don't succeed in January, I don't have the money to pay for a private school." She glanced down at her hands clasped on the desk, then at the next boy on her right.

"I'm going to try to look for money," he said emphatically, "look for any kind of job possible that could give me some money. I've tried some electrical work, helping others while trying to learn. In January, if I succeed I can study . . . If not, it will depend on the will of God. It's difficult."[1]

And we continued around the circle, hearing the first hints of what the next few months would be like for these new graduates from lower secondary school.

•   •   •

At the conclusion of the 2010 academic year, the Senior 3 and Senior 6 graduates in this study faced a number of choices. In the eyes of the Rwandan labor law, they were already independent economic actors—or they soon would be, in the case of those who had not quite yet turned sixteen.[2] Some accordingly started to look for work. But others, in their own eyes, were still just students, waiting for the next round of classes to begin. Either way, nearly everyone had their eyes set on somehow reaching the next phase of their education, many with the hopes of moving beyond their own parents' station in life. This Part IV of the book is about what these young Rwandans chose to do after graduation, and why, completing the last scene in our sketch of the landscape of youth entrepreneurship in Rwanda's post-developmental state.

Counting and Encountering Entrepreneurs

The thousands of lower- and upper-secondary school students from around Rwanda who earned their O-level and A-level diplomas in November 2010 represented the first cohort to be exposed to a full year of formal entrepreneurship classes in their schools. Yet it would be a mistake to label these young Rwandans a straightforward "test group," one capable of indicating the success or failure of the policy on its own terms. Rather, they are part of the process of the policy's developing significance: exposed to only a portion of the intended course, studying at the same time as the policy—and the school system—itself was changing, and in turn bringing their own priorities and assumptions to bear on the policy's significance outside of schools.

If Part III of this book explored one contradiction at the heart of these students' interactions with the entrepreneurship education policy—near-universal agreement on the value of entrepreneurship, combined with widespread disregard of the course intended to teach it—then this Part IV presents a no less perplexing paradox beyond school walls. Here, surveying a panorama of young Rwandan graduates' activities, the challenging climb of diploma seeking takes shape as an entrepreneurial venture, even as the footholds for ascent from the lowest levels of socioeconomic standing are increasingly being cordoned off. This landscape has arisen out of the complex set of social interactions going on as the Rwandan government tries both to develop creativity and to bring it under certain standards of control, in a context where credentials are still seen as the surest path to "good jobs" and socioeconomic advancement.

As we follow graduates into their lives beyond school walls, it becomes apparent that most manifestations of youth entrepreneurship in Rwanda that go beyond mere survival in fact represent the *means* by which students attain an education rather than its result. These students, we discover, regard school credentials as an essential prerequisite for attaining the higher social, cultural, and economic capital that would enable them to move from a subsistence level of forced self-employment to a level at which they could become high-earning entrepreneurs by choice.

These insights about entrepreneurial practice among young Rwandans come from interactions with a sample of graduates, ten students drawn randomly from each of the eleven classrooms included in this study.[3] Over the course of a three-year tracer study, my research assistant, Flora, and I were able to contact 101 of these 110 selected graduates at least once, and we spoke to the majority of the graduates on four separate occasions.[4] During the first six months after graduation, this contact included one in-depth interview—often conducted at the graduate's own home—and two brief updates by telephone. Three years after graduation, in late 2013, we were able to gather updated information on the schooling, jobs, and businesses of 67 of the original 110 students.

Our phone calls and interviews with graduates in their own homes during the months immediately following their graduation from Senior 3 and Senior 6 included casual discussions of their lives, priorities, dreams, and struggles, as well as updates on each stage of their efforts to carry out their plans for schooling and work. Several of the schools in this study, like many Rwandan secondary schools, were set up as boarding schools to accommodate the students assigned to them from all over the country; as a result, the graduates we spoke to and visited included many from rural villages or towns outside of Kigali city. This sample, though not strictly representative of the entire population of recent Rwandan graduates, thus enabled us to come in contact with young people from quite a range of circumstances and to get a sense of common patterns of perspectives and experiences.

All of these encounters with graduates also made it possible to do some counting of youth entrepreneurs. Defining entrepreneurship as any activity in which the graduate was directly responsible for investing capital and attracting a clientele in order to earn an income,[5] we found that a little less than one-fifth (17 percent) of our whole sample of graduates had gained some experience with entrepreneurship by six months after graduation or before.[6] Their activities included selling school snacks, live chickens, telephone airtime, shoes, prepaid electricity, and regionally imported goods; running a shop; working as a broker to locate goods or property for a customer; organizing filming and dance groups at weddings; and teaching tennis and English.

As a point of comparison, just over two-fifths of the graduates (41 percent) had gained experience with short-term jobs or salaried employment during the same period. These jobs were located on commercial farms and food-processing stations, construction sites, small corner shops, large supermarkets, hair salons, schools, hotels, garages, and in government projects, among others. Figure 12 shows these overall figures, as well as the breakdown of the same data according to educational level, sex, rural versus urban residence, presence or absence of parents, and family's economic circumstances.

These summary statistics hint at some basic trends regarding youth entrepreneurship in Rwanda. Two-thirds (66 percent) of the sample could be considered economically active in the six months following their graduation, in that they were interested in looking for ways to earn some income. Older graduates were more economically active than their younger counterparts, as were males in comparison to females. Overall, the Senior 6 graduates sampled had a slightly higher rate of experience with entrepreneurial activity, and much higher rates of employment, than did their younger peers graduating from Senior 3. Graduates originally from both rural and urban areas were roughly equal in terms of both entrepreneurship and employment—though most entrepreneurs of rural origins actually started their business activities in towns, and virtually the only available rural employment was as teachers in primary and secondary schools. Significantly, the highest rates of entrepreneurship and employment were among orphaned or abandoned graduates and those from the poorest backgrounds.

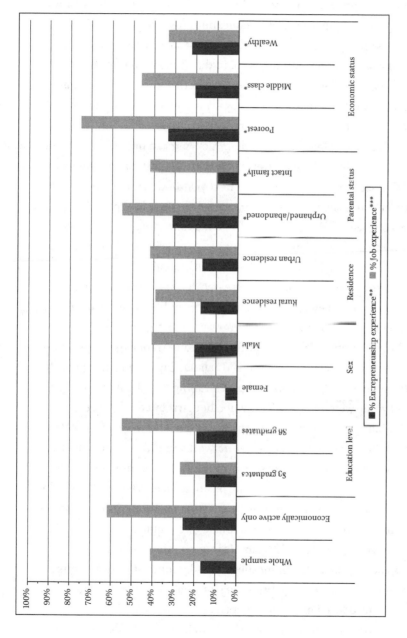

Figure 12 Percentage of sample with entrepreneurship or job experience by six months after graduation

*These categories could be determined only for those graduates who were interviewed in person; percentages are calculated accordingly.
**Entrepreneurship experience indicates any activity in which the graduate was directly responsible for investing capital and attracting a clientele to earn an income.
***Job experience indicates that the graduate has worked for another person for wages. This does not include assisting his or her family in farming or other economic activities, as the interviews showed that such work is rarely remunerated.

The central story line that emerges through the details of these graduates' lives is one of strategies for achieving status advancement. As secondary students during an era when access to this level of schooling in Rwanda was just beginning to open up, the level of education these students had already achieved marked them, or their families, as at least somewhat upwardly aspirational—and at least somewhat successful in that pursuit. In this respect, the young Rwandans included in this study are distinctive from another segment of the Rwandan youth population who may have largely given up on schooling (Sommers, 2012). Some of the young people included in this study were at risk of joining that category—sure that their luck had run out at Senior 3 and that they would have little chance of getting further. The vast majority, however, had their sights set firmly on attaining the next year of their education. As the previous two chapters suggest, these young people believed in schooling as offering them a chance at a desirable future, one that often involved some sort of dreams of eventual business ownership, but at a far higher level of capitalization than the survival-level businesses they saw all around them.

The graduates interviewed for this research fell into three main groups, divided largely by their perception of how they would be able to advance to the next level of education. In the first group were those graduates (primarily, but not exclusively, from O-level) whose future studies were largely ensured—either by parental means or by a guaranteed scholarship—and who spent the months after graduation "just sitting at home" waiting for school to start again. In the second group were some students who, though they could not be entirely sure of their ability to continue on to Senior 4 or university, were fortunate to have extensive and well-connected social networks to draw upon, which enabled them to find employment and save up a bit for future studies even while continuing to dream of future high-earning business ideas. The third group, by contrast, had no assurance of their future education and no well-placed social networks to draw upon. Some of these graduates were quickly discouraged by their situation, giving up when their first idea for a job or a business did not materialize as hoped. But a significant subset was, by contrast, very determined and resourceful—and had been so beginning long before the entrepreneurship course was first introduced into their schools.

After graduation, just as during much of their previous educational history, this last set of graduates from both Senior 3 and Senior 6 took on all sorts of jobs and exercised entrepreneurialism in all sorts of settings, just to ensure that they would be able to study for one more trimester or one more year. The kinds of entrepreneurship these young Rwandans practiced, however, included not only self-employment and small business activities but also the exercise of entrepreneurial creativity and initiative in finding ways—often ways around the established rules—to study each semester. *This* was the reality of youth entrepreneurship in Rwanda as the new technologies and structures of the post-developmental state were gradually being erected. These students did not attend class to learn about becoming entrepreneurs, as the government's entrepreneurship education policy assumed. They *were* entrepreneurs, in order to attend class.

Just Sitting at Home

After their examinations were completed, from time to time we would see graduates around town or call them on the phone just to find out how they were doing. But asking them, "What's up?" (*Amakuru yawe?* or *Quelles nouvelles?*) did not always lead to a long response about their plans and activities.

> "I'm not doing anything special, just cultivating and resting in the afternoon."

> "I'm just waiting at home for the exam results to see if I succeeded."

> "Nothing's new; I'm just sitting at home."

As one graduate explained to us, "I'm not even thinking about work. I'm really not obliged to, I'm still young. And then, if I start to work today and touch money, I think I won't be capable of concentrating well on my studies. I still have time; I prefer to study first."

The statements and choices of many of the participants in this study implicitly gave the sense that studying and working were mutually exclusive categories of activity.[7] Our survey of students at the beginning, middle, and end of the 2010 academic year showed that at any given point, only about 12 percent of students were engaged in any sort of income-earning activity while studying.[8] Though a slightly higher percentage of Senior 6 than Senior 3 students worked, the difference was not large during the school year. Even after graduation, many acted as if they were just on another school vacation—especially those who had only completed Senior 3. They bided their time, occupying themselves with watching films and listening to the radio, helping out around the house or farm, and perhaps even preparing for further studies by attending special computer or English courses—but they did not pursue work independently.

Many of these graduates seemed to believe that they were too young to work; that studying was their job for the moment. Even if they were technically already of legal working age, they were simply uninterested in working—especially if their next level of studies seemed ensured. For these young Rwandans, the kinds of jobs that were available at their level of education were so undesirable that they seemed beyond consideration—even, in some sense, invisible. Wasting their time on that kind of activity seemed nonsensical to them, given that their schooling would quickly move them—they assumed—into a higher category of social and economic status with access to what they considered "real jobs." Our interview with Pacifique, a Senior 3 graduate from School A, helped us understand this perspective.

We met Pacifique in a bustling little town with shops, petrol stations, and a busy outdoor bus station lining the main paved road. His house, on one of the many neighborhood streets tucked behind that commercial avenue, had a large garden and was spacious and in good condition, if not overly fancy. The interior of the house was dark, with unpainted walls and a gray concrete floor, but bits of luxury here and there—several overstuffed chairs, a television—suggested a stable family economy.

Pacifique's sister and aunt were mixing a big pitcher of sugary juice as we entered the house, and they poured each of us a glass as we talked.

"What have you been doing during vacation?" I asked.

"Nothing . . ." Pacifique replied, leaning back in his chair. "Just staying at home, watching some DVDs with music videos." He gestured at the television.

"You had said on your questionnaire that you might like to do a business with food products. Do you think you'll start that soon?" I wondered.

"No, that's not for now. I'll do it later. I want to study first." His sister and aunt made some noises of approval.

"What about work? Do you think you'll find some here?" Flora continued.

"No, I don't think so," he shook his head again. "Here, the kind of work they offer is only for people who have at least finished [upper] secondary."

This comment struck me as interesting, given that many of the young people we had observed working during our walk through the town may not have even begun secondary school, much less completed Senior 6. Sure that there must be some kinds of work accessible to those who had lower levels of schooling, I pressed him on this point: "So what do they do, the people who have only finished Senior 3?"

He thought for a moment, then replied: "I guess they have bicycle taxis, or they work as *aide-maçons* [carrying cement and bricks on construction sites]."

These two kinds of jobs in fact filled the streets all around him. But Pacifique's first reply revealed something of how he, and many of his peers, regarded this kind of work. Graduates referred variously to these low-paying and/or temporary jobs as an *ikiraka*, a *petit boulot*, or even (though in a much more cheerful tone than its ordinary implication in English) a *f—ing job*. This sort of unskilled or temporary labor, Pacifique seemed to imply, is not really legitimate work, or at least not the kind that someone would choose unless they had no other options. For someone who was reasonably sure of improving their life chances through furthering their studies, these jobs were not even part of the visible range of possibilities for using their time.

This ordering of priorities—focusing their energy toward studies rather than seeking even temporary employment—was true of even some of the poorest graduates we interviewed. But in every case, if a poor student was not trying to earn an income, it was because he or she was already fairly sure that the next year's school fees had been guaranteed from another source. Working was not necessary, in other words, as long as the graduate had enough capital of some kind to draw on in order to guarantee his or her next level of studies.

Cedric and his sister, for example, lived only with their mother, who was partially blind. Although they lived in a small town, their conditions of living were closer to the rural norm: their house had a hard-packed dirt floor and seemed to double as a stable for their goats at night. Cedric's older sister worked on odd jobs here and there to earn her school fees and transport money, but Cedric had no such work experience—he was assured of continued assistance from an organization called Compassion to continue his education after Senior 3.

And Jean Claude, who lost his father in the 1994 genocide, planned to follow a course in dance and music offered at one of the city's youth centers rather than looking for work after finishing Senior 6. Though his family's economic situation did not look very stable—he lived with his mother in a subdivided room, one of four rented rooms strung one next to another in a simple building—he was not particularly aware of the work that his mother did as a clothes seller in the nearby market. Regarding his studies, he explained that the National Assistance Fund for Needy Survivors of Genocide (FARG) had always paid his school fees. "I'm not really worried about the scholarships," he told us, "because if I don't get one from the government, FARG can always give me a sponsorship. I'm sure I'll be able to study what I want."

As these comments show, the low level of employment among students in Rwanda is not simply the result of labor market saturation, or even of the admittedly difficult logistical implications of combining school and work. There is also, and perhaps more fundamentally, a question of identity. These young people saw themselves as students, not workers, even after they had completed the stage of schooling that the Rwandan government had defined as a sufficient "basic education" for entering into the working world. They had cultivated a particular habitus, a "schooled identity" (Cheney, 2007; Levinson, Foley, & Holland, 1996), in which certain styles of dress, language, and activities set them apart from the uneducated. By "just sitting at home," they were, in effect, signaling the relative certainty of their aspirations for upward socioeconomic mobility.

Seeking Work, Dreaming of Business

Not everyone, of course, took such a relaxed view of the time after graduation. One-third of the Senior 3 graduates in our sample, and nearly all of the Senior 6 graduates, walked out of school on the last day of examinations with the intention of seeking some sort of work. By six months after graduation, 62 percent of these had met their goal. Like any entrepreneur, these job-seeking graduates knew that to earn money, you need to start with capital. But for these graduates, the capital that counted couldn't necessarily *be* counted. It was the social capital of their networks of friends, relatives, and acquaintances that they exploited in order to earn the "profit" of a job and a salary. For these graduates, though they might still dream of starting a big business in the future, a formal job was enough for the moment—it provided a regular occupation and a steady source of income, and it allowed many of them to save up for their next year of studies.

With friends in the right places, it almost always seemed possible to find a job—especially if the graduate also showed personal initiative in exploiting his or her social networks to the fullest. A friendly young Senior 6 graduate from a public boarding school, Diane was one of the most open in her class about discussing her plans after graduation, in the process drawing many comments from her classmates. "I think if I get a job, I will do it," she explained, "either RwandAir or MTN. I have some personal connections to help." At this, another student near her muttered, "Nepotism!" under his breath. This earned a laugh from Diane and others in the circle. "But if I'm not successful, I will go home in the village and I will cook in my father's restaurant," she went on.

About a month later, on the day scheduled for her interview, Diane told us by telephone that she had been delayed at a certain large hotel where she was pursuing a job opportunity. A receptionist at the hotel was planning to leave her job to go to university, she explained, and it looked like Diane would be offered her place. We were surprised that it could be so easy to find a job and planned to ask for more details once we arrived.

As we entered Diane's home and sat down on the couches an hour later, Diane told us how she had begun her job search with her brother, but apparently she had had to quickly change strategy. "My brother is a manager in RwandAir—he has a master's in business from M—— University. But he told me he can help me get any job *except* one in RwandAir!" Diane laughed. "He said, 'RwandAir wants to employ people in February, but *not* relatives of their employees!' They even investigate who you hire and if they find you are related, you can be punished!"

RwandAir is a national airline in which the government holds majority ownership. It seemed that the Rwandan government's ongoing public drive to eliminate corruption in public offices had extended to the airline's hiring practices.[9] However, this unexpected obstacle to her original plans did not quash Diane's enthusiasm for looking for other jobs, and such strict attitudes against hiring relatives and friends turned out to be the exception rather than the rule.

Diane began to describe the other places she had looked for work: "I was trying many places. I tried in H—— Hotel, I even have the manager's phone number [. . .] It's another friend from school last year who is working there and connected me. I also tried D—— it's near Kisimenti. Someone connected me there. They want people to do marketing, but they're not yet ready. And then there's a kind of restaurant and supermarket, N—— I'm supposed to come on the third of January for an interview. So I will just see which job works out first."

As this was the first place Diane had mentioned where she did not already have a contact, I asked: "Did you know someone there too?"

She laughed. "I didn't know anyone, I thought! But I heard that some students were working there and would soon go back to university. And when I got there, I found two boys that I know working there!"

We asked her to tell us more about the opportunity she had found at the large city hotel. "A friend from [my school] worked there for one year," Diane explained. "Now she's going to university, so she called me to replace her."

"Is it that easy?" I asked. "She can just choose you?"

"The boss is easy, he asked for a [school] certificate and then there will be one other simple interview. Though it's like I already did an interview, because I talked with the boss, and it's as if he has accepted me . . . It's just a simple job. It's to be a receptionist, not giving rooms. For example, directing people who come about where they can find the restaurant, the toilets, et cetera."

Diane set about arranging how to get a copy of her school certificate that very day, calling the headmaster while we ate lunch together—rice, avocados, and beans mixed with some ghee made from their own cows' milk at her parents' rural home. A few weeks later, Diane called to tell us that she was offered the position at the hotel and had begun her training.

When we met again, three months after graduation, Diane was happy with her job. "They have given me a job of receiving calls from Rwanda and outside. I think it's good. They pay me good money too, 150,000 [$250 per month]!"[10] She was clearly proud of her good fortune, joking: "I think that's enough!" Through her contacts, Diane was lucky to have gotten a "real job" with a guaranteed salary that many Rwandans her age could only dream of. "If I get money to invest in it," she commented, "I might start a restaurant like my father one day"—but for the moment, her job and her plans for university seemed like plenty to satisfy her.

Nearly every graduate in our sample who succeeded in finding what these youth called a "good job" drew on their extensive social networks to do so, even as many of them also continued dreaming about the high-earning businesses they would start one day. Allen, a Senior 3 graduate from School C, found work painting houses, then as a bus conductor, and finally as sales staff in one of the city's largest all-purpose stores—all through connections with friends and a little "creative" enhancement of his résumé—even as he dreamed of creating his own painting business in the future. John, a Senior 6 graduate from School D contacted the director of his local school as soon as he got home, and was soon rewarded with a teaching job—all the while insisting to us that his ultimate preference was to become self-employed. And Michael, a Senior 6 graduate from School E, was bursting with business ideas—he had already earned some money in school selling snacks during break times, he wanted to invest in a popcorn machine at a time when they were still rare in Kigali, and he planned to use earnings from that business to gradually save up to start a restaurant in a university town in the Eastern Province. He had also joined up with a few of his friends at school to create a savings group; their future business dreams ranged from selling prepaid electricity units to starting a textbook-import business, to creating a workshop for fabricating paper packaging in response to Rwanda's ban on plastic bags. But for the time being, even Michael was most focused on using his social connections to find a good job, eventually obtaining a position as a waiter at a large Kigali hotel where his aunt also worked.

Through their contacts, these graduates were able to find just the sort of stable employment that many students aspired to as the first step on the road to eventually saving enough capital to start their own businesses. For the time being, however, these business ideas remained little more than dreams.

The Creative Enterprise of Earning Credentials

The two broad categories of graduates discussed in the previous sections— those who were happy "just sitting at home" and waiting for school to begin again, and those who were able to use their social connections to find employment—were mostly relatively privileged Rwandan youth. But our sample also contained a significant percentage of youth who were less privileged, in terms of their possession of social, cultural, and economic capital (Bourdieu, 1986). These students may have belonged to the same school community of practice (Lave & Wenger, 1991) as their peers, but their relatively disadvantaged position in Rwanda's broader fields of power and resources constrained their social experience in a variety of ways.

By and large, the graduates who had little money and were uncertain of their prospects for further education were also the least well-connected socially. They had no aunts or uncles who could pull some strings in order to give them their first jobs. They had fewer friends who participated in the word-of-mouth networks that would give them information about prospective job opportunities. They also had less knowledge of how to present themselves in order to seem capable and fit in with the culture of the working world. They had, in short, little chance of finding formal employment. Some of these graduates, we found, were quickly discouraged by their situation and resigned themselves to "just sitting at home"—though much more uneasily than their peers who were simply on school vacation.

Others, though, managed to find work anyway. It was these sorts of young Rwandans, in fact—poorer, less well connected, but still strongly determined to achieve a better life—who made up the majority of the actual entrepreneurs in our sample of graduates. While their more privileged peers preserved their special student status by relaxing at home, or by getting the kinds of real jobs that suited an educated person, for these graduates, the *ikiraka* represented the only way of achieving that coveted "schooled identity" (Cheney, 2007; Levinson et al., 1996) in the first place. As they took on a series of unstable temporary jobs and scratched together enough to start informal microenterprises, these students demonstrated that, in Rwanda, earning a credential is itself often approached as an entrepreneurial endeavor.

We found Ben—a Senior 6 graduate from School C—where he worked, in a small building facing a dirt road. The outside walls were the same color as the dust that rose in clouds from the street, but the inside was painted a brilliant green. Two clients sat in plastic chairs in the small hair salon, looking into broken bits of mirror on the wall as an electric razor buzzed over each of their scalps.

Seeing us at the door, Ben passed his razor to the other barber and came out to meet us. Around the back of the building, we found some chairs and took a seat. At first, we spent several minutes talking about his experience working as a barber, learning by watching in his rural village, then working on his own for a time, then joining this small business in the city. He was planning, he told us, to start his own barbershop or some other type of business as soon as he could save up enough capital—and his savings were already well under way.

Then, Ben began to tell us about his parents and his siblings, a rural family who relied for income only on their small plots of farmland. "If you don't mind," I said, interrupting his story after a few minutes, "how were your parents able to [send you to school]? Usually, for parents who are farmers, it is very difficult to find enough money to pay school fees . . . Are they the ones who paid for you?"

"You want to know how I studied?" Ben laughed quietly, leaning back in his chair and making himself more comfortable. "That's a really long story . . ."[11]

The "long story" that many graduates recounted to us when we asked them to tell us about their educational history included innumerable examples of ways they had found to earn, obtain, or even bargain down their school fees. Their efforts often began with a search in their own extended family and contacts for some form of assistance. If that was not forthcoming, they looked for organizations or government agencies that could assist them—a quest that often required a number of entrepreneurially relevant skills, such as independent search for information, delivering a convincing presentation, perseverance, and sometimes a little "creative" invention. Others bargained with their school institutions directly to achieve a reduction in their school fees. At the same time, they exercised their initiative and resourcefulness, searching for work or starting up their own small-scale income-generating activities—all with the goal of earning not just their own survival but also their school fees.[12]

In this section, I introduce the experiences of five young Rwandans—Innocent, Charles, Sylvia, Wilson, and Leo—to illustrate this theme. Innocent, Charles, and Sylvia were all Senior 3 graduates; Innocent from School A, in a rural area outside of Kigali, and Charles and Sylvia from School B, a public secondary school situated just outside the ring of Kigali's urban neighborhoods.[13] Wilson and Leo, however, were both Senior 6 graduates from School C, an urban private secondary school whose comparatively low school fees attracted many less privileged students. Together, the schooling histories of these five students illustrate the many ways in which Rwandan youth already practice entrepreneurial qualities in the "enterprise" of earning school credentials.

INNOCENT: CHICKENS AND AN *IKIRAKA*

Innocent, it seemed, was already a man on his own at nineteen years old. Not having visited his mother since finishing Senior 3 a few months before, he hosted us at his friend's house in a rural town, where he stayed whenever he found a job there. "I'm looking for something to do if I find capital," he had told us in the last week of school. "If the money I get is enough, I will have capital for a business and for going to school—at least, if I can get into a public school."

Innocent's mother was a widow with eight children. Depending only on her farming for an income, she was never able to support her children's school fees by herself. In his childhood, Innocent had studied in three different primary schools, in different parts of the country, as one family member or another took him under charge. By secondary school, he needed to be able to meet most of his needs by himself, and he rose to the challenge.

When he first told us his plans for the months after graduation, he was very specific. He had the modest goal of finding an *ikiraka* after school to save up enough capital to start a chicken-selling business. "I've already done this business, two years ago, and I know that it pays," he explained. "I can earn at least

500 francs [$0.83] per chicken. If I find the capital—at least 30,000 francs [$50], I will start it up again. With that much money, I can buy at least twenty chickens—each chicken costs 1,500 francs [$2.50], and I can resell them at 2,500 francs [$4.15] if I'm lucky!"

This idea had its origin in the class that was a precursor to the entrepreneurship education policy—a course called Initiation to Economics. "In Senior 1," Innocent explained, "we were studying Initiation to Economics and the teacher liked to tell us that we should try to do little businesses with our friends. So I proposed this idea of buying and selling chickens to my friends at home. We were four and they had some money; they agreed. We started with a capital of 70,000 francs [$117] and we had a profit . . . I don't know exactly how much because often we had to 'eat' it, but I know that we never lost money, we always earned something."

After graduation, Innocent was hoping to get a job in a carpentry workshop to save up for his chicken business. But these plans fell through; "I didn't have the tools right away," he said, "so they gave the job to someone else."

"Now all I have," he continued, "is a f—in' job," and it's going to be finished in a few days. "But, anyway, at least it allows me to buy some things for school, to get around, and to buy some clothes when I need them."

Demonstrating once again his resourcefulness, he ended the phone call by telling us that he had found someone who agreed to pay his school fees for him to do one year of training in mechanics at a vocational school in another province.

CHARLES: VARIETY AND PERSEVERANCE

During the last days of school, Charles had told us about his plans after graduation, saying: "I look for money using my intelligence, like being an *umukomisi-yoneri* [a broker arranging sales] of houses, bicycles, telephones . . . That gives me some money. I also repair telephones." Meeting one day on a cobblestone road just past one of Kigali's permanent open-air markets, Charles ushered us through a rusted-over metal gate and into a room that was well maintained on the inside, with a large central rug and attractive ceiling light fixtures. As Charles sat down on one of the chairs, his face and bearing looked much older than his seventeen years.

Charles was born in the Southern Province of Rwanda, in a rural area. When his parents died in the 1994 genocide, he and his sister went to live with relatives;

his sister was still staying with an aunt in the same sector where they were born, while Charles had been living in Kigali since the fourth year of primary school. When we met him, he was staying with the family of his cousin. He alternated his stay there with longer terms spent at a friend's house, apparently in order to not become too much of a burden to either one. Though he may have accepted their help with lodging and perhaps some food, Charles was proud of his independence in managing the costs of his studies.

"Since I started secondary school," he told us, "I've managed on my own to pay the school fees. When I was in Senior 1, I rented a motorcycle after school, and that allowed me to pay the school fees and school supplies." Motorcycle taxis constitute a particular type of business in Rwanda, in which the driver rents the motorcycle from its owner for a certain fixed fee each day, which the driver must then earn back through fares from passengers. We asked Charles how he had learned to drive a motorcycle, and at such a young age, since he must have been about fourteen years old when he began. "When I was a kid, I liked to go to the K—— market," he explained. "There was a field where people learned to drive motorcycles. I asked the owners to lend theirs to me: that's how I learned."

Charles also began his work as an *umukomisiyoneri* at about the same age. "As an *umukomisiyoneri*," he explained, "we make an agreement with the two sides, the one that wants something or the one that wants a client, each one pays me." This work, like driving a motorcycle taxi, depends on skills rather than capital. Not a small amount of effort in searching for buyers and clients is also involved, and Charles's work as an *umukomisiyoneri* was successful enough at one time to allow him to become a vehicle owner himself, though on the lower tier of bicycle taxis. "I looked for bicycles for people," he explained. "I was also able to buy my own bicycle at 25,000 francs [$42]. I gave it to another kid to rent, and one trip around the field cost 20 francs [$0.03]. He gave me 1,000 francs [$1.67] per day. He might have earned even more than 2,000 francs [$3.33] because a lot of people wanted to learn to ride a bicycle! But with me, he agreed to pay 1,000 francs per day."

Through these activities, Charles was able to pay his school fees for Senior 1 and the beginning of Senior 2. But in 2008, when Charles was in the second trimester of Senior 2, he had a motorcycle accident and seriously broke his arm. "I had to stop going to school for the rest of the year," he told us, adding that he also stopped driving the motorcycle. "When I went back the next year, I couldn't pay the school fees anymore." Like many students we spoke to, however, his school's administration was willing to consider his case and make exceptions. "I had to talk to the director," he continued, "and she allowed me to continue studying without paying."

In this way, Charles was able to complete Senior 3 in 2010, even while he continued trying to do work here and there to support himself. But when we left our first interview with Charles, he was still in a state of doubt about whether he would be able to continue his studies in upper-secondary school. He told us that he wanted to study electronics and telecommunications, and he seemed determined to keep looking for ways to earn money for school fees.

In early 2011, Charles got the disappointing news that he had "failed" the national exams, meaning that he had not scored high enough to earn a place in a public secondary school. "Now I really don't have any hope of continuing," he told us. "But still, I'll come back to Kigali to try to find a way to pay for [my studies]. But if that doesn't work, I'll look for something else, because I can't just stay sitting . . . I failed, but not because I didn't try."

Despite the disappointment, Charles must have persevered, because when we spoke again in April 2011, he was back in school. "I found someone, an *umusaza* [old man], who accepted to pay my school fees for me," he told us. "Even though I don't know how long he'll keep on helping me," he added as an afterthought.

Not one to be discouraged by the minor obstacle of doubt about his future, Charles paused for only a moment before continuing: "But for now I'm studying accounting," he continued, "and I want to do economics if I get the chance to go to university."

SYLVIA: TELEPHONE AIRTIME AND PRAYERS

Sylvia had a similar story of perseverance against extraordinary odds. Of the graduates in our sample who had some early entrepreneurship experience, only one in seven were girls—a proportion that is roughly reflected in the gender balance of the selected cases featured here. This fact seemed intimately linked with young women's paths to education and with the barriers that many encountered along the way. Overall, most of the young women in the secondary schools featured in this study were fairly well supported by their families; the mirror image of this fact, by implication, is that girls who did not receive family support were much less likely than boys to find independent ways of attending school.[14] Yet Sylvia was an exception.

When we met her one day, following her directions over rutted roads in the pouring rain, we found ourselves in one of the hidden rural valleys that somehow still exist in pockets between other heavily populated neighborhoods of Kigali city. Contrasting with the brilliant green of the valley grass, there was mud everywhere else—even Sylvia's house was made of rough mud bricks; unprotected by cement plaster, the house itself looked like it might one day melt in the rain.

Offering us her dimpled smile somewhat shyly, Sylvia invited us into a tiny dark room that seemed to double as a kitchen, and we made ourselves comfortable on a rough bench and an overturned bucket. The dirt floor was covered with an old blue tarpaulin, and dim light shone through a few pinholes in the metal roof sheets, illuminating the commercial posters of smiling couples that were tacked onto the mud-brick walls. Crowded around us, on the floor and a small table, was a sack of charcoal, a pile of a few kitchen utensils and plates, and two cases of beer and soda bottles. From one corner of the small room we heard some rustling noises, and Sylvia lifted out a rabbit for us to admire, explaining that she and her sister raised them for food.

Born in 1991, Sylvia and her two other sisters had lost their mother in 1999 and then their father in 2004, when Sylvia was in Primary 4. Before his death, their father had built the small house where she and one sister were now staying, together with the sister's young son. For a time, Sylvia's aunt had been able to pay her school fees for her, and Sylvia did well enough on her primary school exams to earn a place at a government boarding school. But after Senior 1 and 2, her aunt could no longer pay, and Sylvia had to stop her schooling for a year. When we first met her, she had been able to restart Senior 3 at a local school, supporting herself in a variety of ways: "I sell telephone airtime," she explained to us, "and since I live with my older sister who sells beer, I help her too."

Selling airtime for Rwanda's major telephone company, MTN, was a common form of self-employment in Kigali, if one that brought little profit. At every major intersection in Kigali and around the country, these businessmen and businesswomen were visible with their bright yellow smocks. Though they were registered with the telephone company, they were individual operators, dependent on a good location, on perceptiveness and speed in reaching prospective customers, and on their ability to attract a regular clientele.

Explaining the economics of the business to us, Sylvia remarked: "There's not really much you can earn, but it's better than nothing. There are different sorts of cards you can buy [to sell airtime to other people]. For the one that costs 12,075 francs [$20], they send you 12,500 francs and so you earn 425 [$0.71]. There is one for 14,500 francs [$24] and they send you 15,000 so you earn 500 francs [$0.83], et cetera. Me, I use the one for 12,075 francs." Though Sylvia was operating at the lowest tier of the business, it could still take her a month or more to earn a profit equivalent to her start-up capital. "If you have a big clientele," she continued, "you could buy and sell as many as three cards per day. But for me, when I've really worked well, it takes one day and then I can buy another card the next morning. And if I sell badly, I could even stay with one card for two full days." In this way, Sylvia earned on average around $0.50 per day. When she stopped selling during exams and they had to use her meager savings for their expenses, Sylvia had to wait until her sister could save up some more money from selling beer for her to start selling airtime again.

Because Sylvia was not a genocide survivor, she could not access the FARG funds that helped a number of other orphans we had interviewed, and she was very worried about not being able to continue her studies in upper-secondary school. We asked if there were any other government projects to help students like her. "There is MINALOC [the Ministry of Local Government]," she replied, "but they give very little money—only 10,000 francs [$17] per trimester. That's really very little for a poor student like me who has no other sources of funds. Even if they offered that to me, I couldn't study. I don't have any other means. [. . .] Boarding schools are really expensive. Here in Kigali, you pay 70,000 francs [$117] per trimester for A-levels, and in the provinces it's around 35,000 francs [$58]. I don't have any way of finding money like that. [. . .] There are other projects, but you know the problem here is that there's favoritism for choosing who is really poor. They know that we are poor, but to choose us, well . . ." She trailed off.

I asked her to tell us more about what she had done during the year she had missed school, and how she was able to restart Senior 3. "I worked at X——," she began, "It's an association that works with coffee. I did the work of cleaning the coffee beans and removing the leaves and things that couldn't be used. It was casual work. We went there every morning, and the bosses came to choose. If you were lucky, they chose you; if not, you went back home."

Sylvia was clearly academically talented, because when we talked a few months later we learned that she had performed high enough on her O-level examinations to earn a coveted place in a government school in a rural district.

Again through her own initiative, she was able to find a way to pay the first trimester's school fees, even though the time she spent searching meant a delay in starting the school year.

"I was finally able to start," she told us by telephone during a school break. "After I saw that neither I nor my family could pay, I went to the district office to ask for assistance. The Director in charge of education recommended me to the sector office because I had good grades, and told them to find a way to pay for me. At the sector, they gave me the school fees for the first trimester, so I went to school! It's going very well there, except that it's very cold. And I succeeded in the first trimester with one of the best grades in my class. But I'm still worried about what's going to happen in the second trimester, because now they said that they don't have any more money for me and they sent me back to the district."

She told us that she was trying to follow up on her case at each government office. "I have to study, no matter what happens," she said. "I will not stop here. By the will of God, I will continue. Please pray for me."

WILSON: DETERMINATION AND NEGOTIATION

A number of Senior 6 graduates we spoke to had also combined casual work and self-employment with an unusual degree of assertiveness toward their school administration and local authorities. Wilson, for example, spoke of how his early experiences had made him not want to depend on anyone for assistance, even as he asserted his rights under school regulations. "I already told you that my life is a long story," Wilson began, visiting me in my own home shortly after the birth of my first child. "In fact, I was born in the DRC, in Uvira. In 1995, I came with the family of my paternal uncle, leaving my parents in Congo. I did primary school here in Rwanda."

"During those years," he explained later, "when I was still in primary, I used to sell grilled maize. I would buy it from Nyabugogo [market] and then take it someplace where I would cook it and sell it out on the road. From primary school, that helped me to be able to buy my notebooks and some other things that I needed."

He frowned. "But when I got to secondary school, my uncle only paid for me for one trimester, and then he just let me go. It was family stuff, his wife didn't really want me around; they mistreated me and I left. I lived with friends, just like that, and I started to cope for myself, looking for work in order to live. I didn't want to complain. I said to myself, 'If I ask for money, I'm going to just consume it, and then it will be gone. But if I ask for work, I'll learn how to earn money and that way also be aware of its value. I was even a *kadogo* for some time."

Wanting to be sure that I had understood him correctly, I asked whether that meant that he was a child soldier.

"Yes," he continued, "during the war in Congo, for three years. I saw children die, ones that I knew. Hundreds of them—they're all dead. After, I built my own life without counting on anyone. My uncle, who had brought me to Rwanda, had abandoned me. [...] So I continued my life. If there's something in this world that changes a lot, it's a person's life, and you forget bad experiences quickly."

Leaving the Congo for the second time around 2003, Wilson came back to Rwanda and decided that he would find his own way to study in secondary school. "I started to look for jobs starting in Senior 1, because I had to pay my school fees by myself. I worked every school break in order to find those fees—little jobs here and there that helped me learn some skills and get some acquaintances."

Wilson continued by explaining some of his personal philosophy, displaying many entrepreneurial values in the process. "Even if I *have* a problem, I know that *I* am not one. Me and the problem that I have are different. My job is not to confuse myself with my problem. Rather, I try to be the solution to my problem. If I'm hungry today, tomorrow I'll eat. You can't just withdraw into yourself! [...] I have some principles that have helped me in life: determination, acceptance of myself, to be just, faithful, to be content with what one has. People have problems because they don't accept themselves as they are. They can't be content with the life that they have, so they become frustrated."

But in an important sense, Wilson was not simply content with what he had. He seemed to be constantly striving to move ahead, and he even told us at one point that he had decided to call 2011 "the year of planning and objectives," because he intended to accomplish four important things: get a driving permit in order to become self-employed as a driver, learn English, learn to use a computer, and start university. It was this initiative and determination to achieve his own plans that allowed him to complete his A-levels despite often not being able to pay his school fees.

"In Senior 6," he explained, "I almost didn't study because of the lack of school fees. I came for some time, and then they sent me away [for not paying].

The new director [who came partway through the year] even tried to prevent me from registering for the national exams! He said that he didn't know me, that I wasn't one of his students, that he had never seen me at school. I explained to him that it was because of the school fees, but he refused. Finally, I went to look for the District Education Inspector to plead my case. I got his number, and I called him. I asked if it's really true that students who don't have money are not allowed to do the national exam, explaining to him that the school had refused me the right to register myself.

"The Inspector told me that they don't have the right to refuse. Because if I have a debt, I can do the exam, but afterwards they can't give me the diploma until I have finished paying my debt. So the Inspector telephoned the Director to ask him to put me on the list. It was just the night before the national exams! There were even other students who were in the same situation as me and benefited from that call too. Later, the Director called me to ask why I went to say something like that directly to the Inspector, when he could have arranged something personally with me. [. . .] So I went the next day to take the exam, all stressed out, really afraid. But after the first exam I felt a little more at ease."

"And I succeeded," he concluded his story. "I did well, even for someone who hadn't studied [. . .] and there are those who failed even though they studied every day. The Director even called me to congratulate me. Of course I still have that debt of 80,000 francs [$133] . . ."

From what he had told us about his various prospects for work, however, it seemed that he would not be in debt for long—unless he simply decided he had more important things to do with his money than paying his school for an education he had already received.

LEO: FROM CARTON TO CORNER SHOP

We met Leo in the corner shop he owned in Kigali, just a few weeks after he had opened for business. His was the last door on a small cement-floored building that contained several other similar shops, facing a dirt road in a populated neighborhood. Inside, he had squeezed a stool and a small bench for customers. Behind the simple wooden counter were shelves stocked full of the typical goods always found in these sorts of neighborhood shops: small sacks of sugar, salt, and two types of flour, cooking oil, bottled water, toilet paper, laundry detergent, skin lotion, sodas, beer, candies, cookies, cigarettes, matches, condoms, straws, toothbrushes, toothpicks, superglue, peanuts, pens, and many other small items.

Seating ourselves facing the shop counter, we asked how he had come to start this business. "I studied upper secondary school in K—— in humanities, up to Senior 5," Leo explained. "But then I had to stop because I didn't have the school fees. I wasn't a student anymore, but I didn't just stay sitting." In his rural home, he was able to find some day labor preparing land for farming. "I tried to join an *ikimina*," he explained, "and little by little I learned to save."

It was Leo's early participation in that *ikimina* (a group savings system, in which each member makes regular payments into a common fund, the balance of which is paid to each person in turn) that had enabled him to reach this point, a Senior 6 graduate with enough capital to establish his own formal business.

"With my savings from the *ikimina*," he explained, "I started a little *ikarito* [carton] business." This formerly common—but now illegal—activity for young men with few job prospects involved vending small goods like candies, peanuts, tissues, and cookies from a box that could be picked up and carried around in search of customers.

"The money I gained from that," Leo continued, "I invested [back] in the *ikimina*. Little by little I got enough money to start a little shop, and I had that for two years before deciding to go back to school." With his earnings from the shop in his home village, informally run from his parents' home, Leo had been able to pay for his last year of secondary school and still have enough money left over to start up another small shop—this time in Kigali.

As Leo told us the story of his business, a customer came in and purchased a tiny amount of cooking oil—two little tomato-paste cans' worth, poured into an old plastic bottle, for 200 francs ($0.33).

"I came here [Kigali] three weeks ago, the twenty-seventh of January I think..." Leo continued after the customer left. "First, I looked for the place, and I paid two months' rent for 50,000 francs [$83]. I bought the shelves and also the counter, and installed them—that cost me 30,000 francs [$50]. Then I went to look for the merchandise. I used maybe 150,000 francs [$250]. I think I used around 250,000 francs [$417] to install everything."

Despite the steady stream of traffic in the shop—I counted twenty-six clients over the approximately two hours' time that we spent visiting and chatting—and despite the fact that he had just begun his business less than a month earlier, Leo already seemed discouraged. "I don't think that I'm going to continue this business and make it my future," he remarked. "It can't take me anywhere."

Though he was not keeping any formal accounting books, the expression on his face clearly showed the sum of his informal calculations: taking into account the prices of goods, along with rent, taxes, and fees, the shop simply would not be as profitable as he had hoped.

"I wanted to continue my studies," he went on, "but with this store it's just not possible right now." Looking back at his shelves of merchandise, he added as an afterthought, "Maybe if I manage to find a job."

In a sense, Leo's comment brings this research full circle. Young people want to complete secondary school and get "good jobs." Good jobs can provide capital to start businesses. But this young Rwandan businessperson felt that his only possibility for advancement lay in becoming a job seeker again so that he could earn enough to continue his education—which is important because it presumably opens access to even "better" jobs. Even the young Rwandans who have already proved themselves to be entrepreneurs hope that school credentials can give them a route to higher economic status and stability.

Student Identities and Status Advancement

The stories of Innocent, Charles, Sylvia, Wilson, and Leo illustrate how, in Rwanda, the practice of youth entrepreneurship—in all senses of the term—is often a matter of both survival and the pursuit of status advancement. By deciding to use their meager earnings for school fees, these students exhibited "educational resourcefulness"—the struggle to "maintain a schooled identity" precisely by becoming what their peers considered to be its opposite—a wage earner (Cheney, 2007, p. 99). While their classmates largely rejected informal work in favor of the higher status afforded by being a student and the promise of future formal employment, these disadvantaged youth relied on their informal jobs and microenterprises to stay in school from year to year.

The divergent lives of these graduates outside of school illustrate once again that policies acquire their meaning through complex social negotiations inside particular communities of practice (Lave & Wenger, 1991), which are in turn shaped by their relative positions within broader social fields (Bourdieu, 1993). Even in a single school, students' maps of social belonging are diverse, and their habituses have been shaped differently by larger social and economic dynamics. On the one hand, there are students who belong to a larger community of practice with a reliable supply of economic, social, and cultural capital, helping them maintain a schooled identity and gain access to "real jobs." On the other hand, there are students whose social connections have very little economic and social capital, and very little knowledge of how to find job opportunities in the formal economy. As a national policy applicable to all secondary school students, Rwanda's entrepreneurship course had the difficult task of being relevant for young people from these two vastly differing categories of social and economic experience.[15]

Ironically, as Part III showed, at least in the first year of implementation the policy did not convince either group. For the well-connected students, the course seemed unnecessary because they had other means of attaining their goal of socioeconomic advancement that did not immediately depend on starting a business. For the disadvantaged students, the entrepreneurship course seemed unnecessary because their larger community of practice already possessed significant knowledge and experience of how to run a typical microenterprise. Of course, that knowledge may not have included successful techniques for growing a business beyond survival mode. But in their eyes, it was really capital and not knowledge that was the deciding factor for growth, and better access to capital could come only through education and employment. A formal academic education was their stepladder, in other words, between two levels of entrepreneurship—the kind that earns little profit beyond mere survival and the kind that could provide them with a decent income and hope for continued opportunities for advancement over time. School represented one of their only opportunities to develop the social networks, dispositions, and credentials that would allow them to gain access to higher-status work, and therefore economic capital, later on. No wonder the students in this study had such strong opinions about their entrepreneurship course and its implications.

Regardless of the personal agency these young people exercised inside the classroom and in their search for work beyond school walls, they were still constrained by the broader structure of Rwanda's social and economic environment. To reach their dreams of a decent livelihood, many of these students first had to practice just the sort of informal economic activity that is progressively being regulated out of existence in Rwanda. It was their ability to start earning a living by investing little more than a few thousand francs, which allowed them to get a foothold in the world of schooling in the first place and—in a number of cases—to grow their earnings little by little over the years.

In the following final chapter, I turn more directly to the regulatory environment that now surrounds these young Rwandan entrepreneurs and the implications for the next generation of Rwandan youth who hope to move from mere survival to a life of some status and stability.

Chapter 8

We Will Help the State, but Will the State Help Us?

It is very difficult in Rwanda. I have lived in other countries where everything is possible with whatever amount of money. But here in Rwanda, you can't do something with just a little money. Either they tell you that it's dirty, or they say it's disorderly. It is really difficult . . . especially for youth who don't have a lot of means.

There aren't really any laws that are particularly difficult for youth. Everyone has the right to do business—as long as he has the capital and he pays his taxes too.

Here in Rwanda, if you have just a little bit of money, there's nothing you can do.
—Interviews with Rwandan youth, three years after graduation

IN THE PREVIOUS CHAPTER, I argued that entrepreneurial creativity among youth in Rwanda is often practiced in order to obtain educational credentials, rather than as a result of any particular course studied in school. As many of the most disadvantaged young Rwandans in this study pursued their goal of finding or evading the school fees needed to study each trimester, they invested capital—often in tiny amounts—and employed the entrepreneurial qualities of creative problem solving, resourcefulness, perseverance, and skillful negotiation in all sorts of settings. Some of their entrepreneurial "creativity," in fact, involved forms of bending the rules that—while never maliciously intended—seem hardly in line with the Rwandan government's objective of regulating the practice of entrepreneurship.

In this chapter, I therefore turn to a direct consideration of the tensions inherent in the Rwandan government's dual objective of promoting entrepreneurial creativity while retaining it under strict controls. For, even as the government is attempting to facilitate business activity in Rwanda by extolling self-employment and streamlining the business procedures measured by institutions like the World Bank, Rwanda's overall regulatory regime is being extended deep into daily life—and compliance is enforced ever more effectively day by day. As graduates struggle to master the start-up procedures that increasingly apply to even micro-level business activities—registration, licensing and permits, local fees and taxes, and the need to maintain fixed and "orderly" business premises—many have begun raising questions about the business regulations they face. "We are willing to help the state by paying our taxes," they seem to be saying, "but will the state help us create our businesses so that we *have* something to pay with?"

Their perspective on the Rwandan government's responsibility to help them create their own jobs amounts to a subtle transformation of the government's post-developmental logic, retaining elements of Rwanda's long-standing patron-client social structure just as the Rwandan government is attempting to move away from a rhetoric of dependence. Graduates understood that the government could not solve youth unemployment through some simple magical solution; ultimately, they agreed that much depended on their own hard work and entrepreneurial efforts. But if the government was not going to act as their patron—by providing them directly with jobs, or with the capital they needed to start their businesses—then they argued that it should at least fulfill the role of a partner by guaranteeing the conditions that would allow them to start their businesses with limited means. Failing that, they explained, they would not be able to earn a livelihood or contribute to the country's development—for, as one young graduate remarked, "Here in Rwanda, they want orderly business, they don't want disorder; you can't just do whatever you want with the little money you have."[1]

Patrons, Clients, and the Post-Developmental State

From the beginning of this book, I have described contemporary Rwandan governance as a reimagining of the state along East Asian post-developmental lines, a fundamental kind of governmental transformation made possible in the wake of the massive civil and institutional destruction of the 1994 Genocide against the Tutsi. However, no social institution can ever truly start from scratch and embark in an entirely new direction. A number of authors have argued that Rwandan governance today continues to exhibit certain institutional characteristics present at other times in Rwandan history (see, e.g., Newbury, 2011). One such line of continuity, I would argue, is the way in which Rwanda's shifting rationalities of governance throughout the twentieth century and into the twenty-first have all been layered over a logic of patron-client relations that arguably persists in Rwandan doxa and dispositions up to the present day—inevitably influencing, in the final analysis, even Rwanda's post-developmental policy of entrepreneurship education.

Precolonial Rwanda, like a wide variety of societies around the world, was characterized by a system of patron-client relations, a broad category of social structures that involve "asymmetric but mutually-beneficial and open-ended transactions" (Hamzeh, 2001, p. 167). Patron-client relationships are mutually beneficial because both parties make contributions to the exchange, such as labor in return for protection. But they are also asymmetric: the patron ultimately has power over the client, and it is rare for them to change their relative positions.

In Rwanda, different forms of clientship had been practiced for hundreds of years. There were many facets of this system, but one basic form was *ubugabire*:

> [*Ubugabire*] consisted in the loan of any good, but especially of cattle. After a client so-licited him, the patron would entrust him with one or several cows. In return, the client would return one calf of the first calving to his patron and some more calves later on at regular intervals. But he was expected above all to aid his patron and come to work for him when the need arose. (Vansina, 2004, p. 33)

Whether or not Rwanda's historic patron-client relationships allowed for some socioeconomic mobility remains a topic of significant controversy in Rwanda (Prunier, 1995). There were, however, undoubtedly responsibilities for assistance placed on both parties.

The client bore the brunt of these obligations, including offering tax dues, gifts, labor, and spying on behalf of the patron (Erny, 2005; Pottier, 2002; Vansina, 2004). But the patron also had social duties: "the 'sovereign' owed his 'vassal' financial and legal protection, which translated into assistance in cases of misfortune, sickness, conflict or judicial proceeding" (Erny, 2005, p. 66). The client relationship also offered the important improvement in quality of life represented by the loaning of cattle themselves, which were valuable both as a status symbol and for the nutritional supplement that their milk products could offer.

Writing from an educational perspective, Erny (2005) has asserted that Rwanda's various forms of clientelism had a psychological effect that permeated many other aspects of Rwandan life in a lasting way:

> The system applied in its most rigid sense, which was more and more widespread, led to this important psychological influence: that dependence became desired, sought after, entreated by everyone, no matter what their status. Within the clientship pyramid, every *shebuya* [patron] had himself another more powerful *shebuya*, all the way up to the divine king. In the intermediary level between the monarchy and the ordinary population,

everyone was at the same time supplicant and benefactor, inferior and superior, pro-
tected and protector. (Erny, 2005, p. 68, my translation)

Being in a position of dependence, in short, was not necessarily regarded as a
negative sign of weakness: it was also a desired status, signifying that—*if* the
patron met his recognized social obligations—the client had some recourse in
times of trouble, and potentially even some opportunity to better his family's
circumstances over time.

Colonialism, not surprisingly, brought with it a number of changes to clientelism in Rwanda. In particular, systems of taxation and forced labor were
intensified, primarily to the detriment of the peasant population, even as they
were brought under bureaucratic rather than personal control (Pottier, 2002).
The Belgian colonial administration did little of public benefit with these taxes,
as their overall investment in the country was minimal (see, for example, the
unfavorable estimation of colonial government investment in education, in
Jesse Jones, 1923). Colonial insistence that peasants grow cash crops, partly in
order to be able to pay taxes, also entailed the expansion of a monetary economy and increased opportunities for gaining wealth and status that were not
solely tied to cattle in the patron-client relationship (Mamdani, 2001). The colonial regime also played a role in convincing King Mutara to abolish hereditary
forms of clientship in 1954.

Nonetheless, many authors have argued that patron-client structures do not
simply disappear with the introduction of contemporary bureaucratic institutions
(see, e.g., Booth & Golooba-Mutebi, 2012; Kitschelt & Wilkinson, 2007; Piattoni,
2001; Roniger & Günes-Ayata, 1994). Rwanda's postindependence government arguably carried forward its own forms of patronage. In particular, under the Habyari
mana regime of 1973 to 1994, clientelism at the government level, as opposed to
more informal types of clientelism that likely continued to be practiced throughout the population, involved widespread "regional favoritism" and "nepotism,"
which benefited only a small elite (Fujii, 2009; Mosko & Damon, 2005), particularly
in relation to the jockeying for access to state revenues from taxation as well as
to funds from international development aid programs (Uvin, 1998). In addition,
educational advancement under the Habyarimana regime was heavily influenced
by patronage and regional favoritism, and those who were lucky enough to obtain
a secondary education were virtually guaranteed a job within the government or
the few private enterprises owned by members of the political elite.

Government discourse on clientelism and patronage, however, has significantly changed since the 1994 genocide, as these practices have been increasingly categorized negatively as dependence and corruption. First, the current Rwandan government has worked quite strenuously to cultivate a clean international image by acting against ethnic and regional favoritism,[2] as well as by pursuing extensive and public efforts to counter nepotism and other forms of corruption. As I pointed out in Chapter 1, these efforts have been met with international acclaim, including studies proclaiming "Rwanda has negligible corruption" (2010) and is the "least corrupt among East African countries" (Karinganire, 2011). Green (2011) argues that patronage continues to influence the upper echelons of power in Rwanda, as in other countries in the region. Yet he also acknowledges that the current regime has "reduced the amount of patronage in the periphery" by drastically cutting the number of middle- and local-level government jobs, while noting that patronage promises were completely absent in recent election cycles (Green, 2011, p. 430).

At the same time, current Rwandan government rhetoric also portrays one of Rwanda's greatest contemporary challenges as a fight against an attitude of dependency. The entrepreneurship education policy that is the focus of this book is, in many ways, central to that endeavor. In the interviews I first introduced in Chapter 2, Rwandan policy makers described the typical young Rwandan as expecting to automatically get a job after graduation, preferably in the government, through the intervention of more influential relatives or other social connections. The government official who first proposed the idea of teaching entrepreneurship to young Rwandans explained, in turn, "I expect them to be enlightened, that we can create a job ourselves. Also changing minds—changing that idea that we always need someone to help us. [. . .] This dependence needs to change."[3] Dependency is thus portrayed in contemporary political rhetoric as a key challenge to overcome at the level of individual Rwandans' mind-set and habits.

Furthermore, the current government has also described the efforts of young Rwandans to create their own jobs as key to the nation's ability to overcome international aid dependence. This connection depends upon citizens' willingness to "pay taxes, build Rwanda, be proud!" as one ubiquitous Rwandan Revenue Authority (RRA) billboard puts it, with the hope that internal revenues will supplant reliance on donor funds (see Figure 13). The Rwandan government

Figure 13 Rwanda Revenue Authority billboard

Source: Photo by author.

has in fact made a significant effort to increase taxpayer awareness and compliance, including streamlining business registration procedures at the national level, as well as increasing surveillance and penalties for noncompliance (RRA, 2012). With this tax revenue, the government has already demonstrated its significant commitment to creating a context conducive to development, implementing effective infrastructure improvements, subsidizing health insurance, and expanding access to public schooling—without, however, entering into any substantial regime of social protections, such as promising assistance for the unemployed.

Rwanda's contemporary post-developmental approach to governance thus entails, among other things, yet another transformation in the historic role of the powerful as "patrons." Post-developmental logic argues that those in power do not have a responsibility of direct assistance towards the disadvantaged. Instead, the post-developmental state promises sweeping structural plans and improvements in which increased individual mobility should be possible, at least for those who make an entrepreneurial effort and follow the rules. The question of whether the Rwandan population will accept this conceptualization of the state's responsibilities, however, is yet to be determined.

In the following sections, I turn to the question of students' own perspectives on the issue of government assistance and government regulations, showing that, while many accepted the government's legitimate right to demand payment of taxes and even felt proud that they might be able to help their country advance, they were also perplexed by the state's apparent unwillingness to extend them much of a helping hand. Young Rwandans' reactions to today's entrepreneurship policies and regulations seem like a cry for, if not a patron state, then at least a partner state, a state that will fulfill its position of power by promising to assist its subordinates. It is this issue, finally, that may determine the nature of post-developmental governance in Rwanda and the place of young Rwandans as they search for their own role in Rwandan society and economy.

My exploration of this issue, in this final chapter of the book, begins with students' perspectives on government regulations while still in school and extends through their experiences over the three years following graduation.

Happy to Contribute . . . A Reasonable Amount

Sitting in a classroom with a small group of students, just after the last class bell had rung in the middle of the 2010 academic year, my research assistant, Flora, posed a question that we had begun to ask at all of the schools involved in this study. "There's a phrase that people often like to say," she began. "'When you do business, the most important thing is to earn a big profit for yourself.' Do you agree with this? Or do you think that there are other objectives you should have in business?"

With so many students interested in going into business sometime in the future, we had become curious about how they thought about the business profits they would earn—were they interested mostly in individual gain, or did they have their families in mind too? Did they have any ambitions along the lines of corporate social responsibility, orienting their businesses toward some sort of broader contributions to their local communities? All of these, it turned out, were on their minds to some extent. But, to my surprise, students also often talked about the usefulness of profits for paying taxes. In their own words, one of the benefits of running their own business was the ability to contribute to the country's development through their contributions to national revenue.

On the day in question, the students in School A answered Flora with exactly this line of reasoning:

Rachel.   In addition to money profit, you should also look at the benefit of your business for people who live in the country—I mean the country's profit in relationship to your business. You wouldn't only look for money benefits for yourself.

Arlette: Me too, I think that you wouldn't only go after profit for yourself without thinking of that of others. You can, in fact, work so that the country gains from you too. If you work for yourself only and the country doesn't gain, then how will you be developing it? It will stay low, always begging [funds] from other countries.

Louise: Me, I think that there will be profit for you, but also profit for others—or rather, profit for the state. [. . .] Your profit is first, but without reducing that of the others, because they all need to gain from that revenue.

Delphine: Because when you work well and earn money, you give tax to the state.

This perspective, focusing on how business activities could benefit the country through tax payments, did not only occur in School A. As we moved from school to school, at least some students always echoed this theme.

It is perhaps not so surprising, after all, that many students saw government regulations, taxation, and development programs in a positive light. After all, in Rwanda, many development programs actually work—with visible results in the form of an expanding network of paved roads, increased access to electricity, and programs intended to provide jobs through public works in the country's poorest sectors (MINALOC, 2009). In Parts II and III of this book, I also argued that the credentialist orientation of Rwandan schools can in many ways reinforce government goals of promulgating a strong regime of regulations and controls. As teachers worked their way through the content of the entrepreneurship syllabus, lecturing and delivering their notes, they almost always passed on messages that were supportive of the state's guiding role in establishing and enforcing laws in pursuit of national development. Students in Senior 3 had heard these messages most often, and seemed especially receptive to them, but even Senior 6 students saw themselves as future contributors to national development.

Overall, it was clear that students held fairly strong beliefs about business's responsibility to obey the law and safeguard against negative effects on society and the environment. In their anonymous questionnaire responses, for example, students overwhelmingly disagreed with the suggestion that business profits are more important than social responsibility.[4] In response to a statement arguing, "Entrepreneurs should focus on earning a big profit, and not worry about their business's effects on society—it's up to the customers to decide whether what the business offers is good for them or not," 69 percent of the students in this study disagreed. And a full 80 percent contradicted the assertion, "It is okay to 'bend the rules' as much as possible in order to make sure your business earns a decent profit, even if that means being dishonest sometimes."[5]

The students in this study seemed to feel that business owners have definite social obligations, and this extended to the notion that they could contribute to the country's development by providing employment and paying taxes. But some of these students also suggested that their acceptance of taxation was not simply voluntary benevolence: they were well aware of the stiff penalties for those who did not follow the law. A classmate of the above students, for example, remarked:

Christian: If I can add to what my colleagues have said, business is not just
            about looking for money [for yourself]. Because if you go after

money here . . . in fact, when you are going to start a business, first
you have to prepare your project that you are going to do, and after,
not only go after money—because if you only think about that,
there are a lot of traps you could fall into here. No, first you have to
pay the taxes, because when you do business without paying taxes,
they can lock you up and you will lose your business. You will pay
the taxes, and *then* put the rest of your energy into developing your
business.

Thus, while some students clearly believed in paying taxes in order to contribute to the country's development, others simply pointed out that there would be serious consequences if they did not comply.

Many students, in fact—especially those from more resource-constrained economic backgrounds—thought that the existing Rwandan tax regime and other regulations posed an obstacle to business activities, and by extension also an obstacle to resolving Rwanda's problem of youth unemployment. In their end-of-year questionnaires, 53 percent of the students agreed that "taxes are too high in Rwanda for most new entrepreneurs to survive," and 61 percent agreed that "in Rwanda, government regulations on businesses make it hard for poor people to earn a living." At the same time, 62 percent agreed that "the government should take responsibility for helping people find employment and improving the situation of the poor, and not expect individuals to solve our country's economic problems on their own." In the latter two cases, these responses directly correlated with students' own socioeconomic status: the poorer the student, the more likely he or she was to feel that government regulations placed heavy burdens on the poor, and the more likely to wish that government would help.[6]

Rwanda's business regulations are all targeted explicitly toward national development goals. But ironically, they often seemed to shut out the very people who most need to benefit from that process of development. As Axel from School C commented at the time, "Rwanda is raising itself up to be comparable to America—which is not really that possible. We are an underdeveloped country that wants hygiene and order everywhere, as if we have already arrived. Whereas, if they were flexible, people could start with a little tiny business—like in Uganda, you see that there, business is easy, it's easy to work there. They sell on the road: tea, chapattis . . . earning a living there is really possible. But to start a shop here in Rwanda! You find out that it requires a lot of money. This is our problem."[7]

Regulations and Requirements

As of the time of writing, anyone who wants to start a business activity that is regular enough to be visible to local authorities—and since the Rwandan government has functional subdivisions of authority down to the level of approximately one hundred households (the *umudugudu*), a large proportion of activities fit in that category—has to follow a number of formal requirements.

First, all businesses are legally required to register at the national Office of the Registrar General, which also automatically leads to registration with the Rwanda Revenue Authority and the Rwanda Social Security Board. Even microscale businesses are subject to a specific law that requires them to register nationally (Ministry of Trade and Industry, 2009), although in practice national registration is not yet widespread for the smallest businesses.

Second, businesses must have a fixed location, along with the attendant requirement of paying rent. The Rwandan government has outlawed mobile trading and required these businesses to move into newly constructed formal markets, one strategy in the effort to clean up the streets and bring some order to previously informal activities. Individuals in the transport sector—such as motorcycle or bicycle taxis and market porters (*abakarani*)—must belong to registered cooperatives and wear uniforms. Though some Rwandans still practice roadside and ambulant forms of business, they are now constantly under the threat of police detention and confiscation of their merchandise (Abbott, 2010; Education Development Center, 2009; Sommers, 2012). Businesses of all sizes also have to pay various taxes and fees. At the local level, these costs include paying a yearly business license and monthly taxes that vary slightly by category of activity. To this are added regular fees for neighborhood security and garbage collection, plus occasional mandatory contributions for local education funds and special events. All but the very tiniest businesses are also legally required to pay national taxes, and even these are required to file a statement of earnings.

Many of these taxes and fees are payable upon business start-up, meaning that before someone in the Kigali area has even begun earning an income, he or she must use at least $65 of capital for taxes and fees, in addition to the requirement of paying rent for a fixed place of business.[8] This may not seem like a large amount, but given some leaders' views that Rwandan youth should be willing to "start from peanuts" (see Chapter 2), and given that most young Rwandans would indeed have significant trouble gathering even $30 of capital to start a business, these start-up costs are steep indeed (Abbott, 2010; Education Development Center, 2013).

This is, in brief, the regulatory context that strongly shaped the lives of the young Rwandans included in our sample of graduates. By three years after graduation, 19 percent of the Senior 3 graduates and 36 percent of the Senior 6 graduates had gained at least one experience running a microbusiness activity.[9] In the following sections, I present excerpts from interviews with these graduates, many of whom are attempting to become the "orderly entrepreneurs" that the Rwandan government seems to want them to be. As they planned the types of businesses they wanted to start, filled out business registration forms, set up their businesses as taxpaying entities, and otherwise adjusted their activities to obey the law, they demonstrated goodwill about following the rules.

But at the same time, their experiences suggest the price of trying to organize and formalize every form of entrepreneurial activity—especially for the poor and those just above poverty. As their flexibility is reduced, so are the openings that allow people with few resources to engage in bootstrapping resourcefulness, creating their own employment from whatever is available at hand. The result only seems to reinforce young people's impression that their best route out of poverty is an educational credential that will allow them to get a "real job," sometime in the future, only aspiring to rejoin the ranks of the country's entrepreneurs once they have already managed—they hope—to move into a higher social and economic status.

DESIGNATING APPROPRIATE ACTIVITIES

One of the most important decisions of an entrepreneur is, in theory, the very choice of what sort of activity to undertake. But some of the Rwandan government's policies channel people into (or out of) particular, predesignated areas of business activity, regardless of their own entrepreneurial judgments. These policies are often explicitly aimed towards promoting entrepreneurship in areas where the vast majority of the population still depends on farming—a legitimate development goal in a context where most people have only tiny plots of land with dwindling productivity. By trying to rationalize rural activities according to a particular mold conceived in government offices, however, such policies may in fact be blocking people's very entrepreneurial instincts.

In the rice-growing region where one of the graduates in our sample lived, for example, some of the farmers I spoke with described what was—to them— an illogical and frustrating government policy. Where these farmers had been accustomed to cleaning and processing their own small quantities of rice for sale, they told me that the government had recently forbidden them from following that practice, now requiring them to sell their unprocessed rice to someone they called "the entrepreneur" (*rwiyemezamirimo*) or "the investor" (*umushoramari*) for factory processing.

A newspaper article from the *New Times* reported on the new regulation as a move to help the region reach standards high enough to allow for rice exportation:

RUSIZI—The Ministry of Trade and Industry has announced a new set of rules and regulations to boost rice farming in the country. The new guidelines require the rice supply chain from traders, rice processors, distributors, wholesalers and retailers to hold a valid certificate of registration issued by the Rwanda Development Board (RDB) and an authorised permit issued by MINICOM. [. . .] Under the new move, rice farmers and traders are also required to keep sale/purchase records, acquire warehouses for wholesalers, including subjecting their rice to quality control by the Rwanda Bureau of Standards. Additionally, processors must also adopt a new standardised approach of packaging in bags of smaller quantities ranging from 2 kgs to 25 kgs and 50kgs.

"Unless we perfect the selling and processing of rice, we will not reach the exporting standards, yet the government is putting additional efforts in rice farming," warned Kanimba. [. . .] He warned illegal rice millers to seek licenses to avoid being penalised. [. . .] It is understood the proposal is expected to ensure quality and quantity rice, stabilise prices and increase profits across the supply chain. (Nakayima, 2011)

While the objectives of the policy seem logical, according to those I interviewed it also resulted in a significant reduction in income for the rural farmer-entrepreneurs who formerly did their own rice milling: not only were they being required to sell a lower-value unprocessed product, but the price of their raw rice was also strongly controlled by the oligopoly the policy had created. In the process of trying to formalize existing practices into a more quality-controlled and growth-oriented form, in other words, the government seemed to have pushed a large number of rural entrepreneurs out of business.

If the rice policy was an example of telling some entrepreneurs what they could not do, we also encountered a rural development policy that instructed farmers on one kind of business activity they must do. During our visit to Didier's home, a clean but simple mud-brick structure surrounded by fields, Didier told us that he had been helping his parents cultivate since he was thirteen years old, especially with their planting and harvest of sweet potatoes. Having heard some news about the government's efforts to increase cash-crop farming in rural areas, we asked Didier's parents whether they were still allowed to cultivate any crops they wanted to.

"No," Didier's father replied, "each *umudugudu* is supposed to specialize in a certain crop. For us, it's coffee. If you have a big field, it's possible to cultivate one part of it for what the state wants you to do, and on the other part cultivate what you need to eat. But those who don't have big lands are obliged to cultivate what the state wants, because there is a minimum surface area you have to devote to that, and then they have to go to the market to buy what they need to eat."[10]

A recent newspaper article on the effects of a similar policy elsewhere in the country, the government's Crop Intensification Program intended to promote intensive farming of staple foods, remarked on the sometimes controversial nature of these reforms:

"The population in the area resisted to planting maize and Irish potatoes which was the chosen crop for the area. They wanted to plant sorghum as they were used to—they are very attached to it," he says, adding that sorghum is popular because it is used to make beer that plays an important role in many social functions. After the switch, people had to resort to importing sorghum at rather high prices, something which they obviously aren't happy about. (Nsanzimana, 2012)

In Didier's own village, the requirement to produce coffee amounted to an effort to move farmers more fully into the cash economy rather than relying on the type of subsistence farming that was becoming increasingly precarious year by year. But by obeying the requirement to plant a single specified cash crop on a minimum amount of land, farmers could no longer exercise independent judgment about the types of crops that were best for that season's weather, had the best prospects for sale in the market, or would most adequately ensure a good living standard for their families. While the government was trying to convert farmers into entrepreneurs, it seems, the policy was simultaneously removing their right to act entrepreneurially.

REGISTERING

Whether in rural or urban areas, many of Rwanda's business regulations are primarily concerned with one development goal: becoming a self-financed government, no longer dependent on foreign aid, by achieving much more widespread participation in the national tax system. To accomplish this goal, businesses must be visible; they must have a known place of operation; they have to be accessible to tax enforcement. The Rwandan government, therefore, has begun systematically expanding its knowledge of business activities, beginning with an increasingly encompassing process of national registration.

All businesses of any size are legally required to register at the national level, through the Office of the Registrar General at the Rwanda Development Board (RDB) (Ministry of Trade and Industry, 2009). Visiting the RDB offices in 2012 to see for myself how the process worked, I found the business registration room completely full of people, some standing at the back to check over the posted list of categories of economic activity, others consulting the business name register or getting advice on how to fill out their forms, and another fifty or so occupying the chairs in front of the registration desks. As I watched them deal with what seemed like an unending stream of potential business founders, the RDB staff were impressively friendly and helpful, perhaps having been some of the first to benefit from the RDB's (2012) own recently launched national customer service campaign. If the lack of empty chairs at the registration office is any measure—I remember thinking at the time, while searching for a seat—Rwanda's business sector must be booming.

Of all the graduates in our sample, only a few contemplated going through the national registration procedure, however, and most of these were comparatively privileged students—members of the same savings group in School E that Michael, from the previous chapter, belonged to. Our interviews with several of the members of this group gave us a sense of the process they went through as they tried to formalize their activity under Rwandan regulations of business registration.

Oliver, the de facto group president, explained how they first realized that they would need to register at RDB. "We went to the bank to change our account," he began, "because it was in the name of Damascene; he's the treasurer. But the bank told us we have to register first so that we can own an account as a group. And to register, you have to make a constitution, make your things clear, and then go to register in RDB. So we tried to make a constitution; after that we will see how we can register."

The first step had been to decide on a name for their business group, ensuring that it was unique from all other names already in the business register. "We met last Tuesday," the treasurer of the group, Jean Damascene told us. "We're thinking of registering as T10—the Terrific Ten!"[11] He smiled broadly as he proclaimed the name with a flourish.

"Now," he continued, "we're gathering information about how to do that registration. Everything is with RDB, it all goes there," he explained.

"Is it easy to do? What do you have to do in order to register?" I asked, wanting to hear his own understanding of the procedures.

"It's somehow difficult," he replied, "but we will try. You have to have the constitution, members, pay 10,000 francs, even include the bylaws."

He and the others in the group were mistaken about the registration fee—which was actually 15,000 Rwf ($25), or free of charge if they could figure out how to do it online. This would not be an insurmountable setback for the group, which had already saved up more than 120,000 Rwf ($200) after more than a year's worth of monthly personal contributions. But in conjunction with the other start-up fees and costs, everything added up—especially considering the kinds of formal businesses they dreamed of starting.

Three years later, in fact, we found that the group was still saving up. The four members who had been included in our sample were all studying at university, three of them in economics and one of them in law. As one of them remarked, "We still have our savings group with the other members—you remember. We haven't done anything yet; we plan to do something after university. Now, it would just be too hard to combine with our studies." Just as we saw in the previous chapter, with their education guaranteed and all of them having found formal jobs at some point, business was still basically just a future dream, not an immediate necessity.

For some other graduates, however, the necessity of working did translate eventually into a formalized business—and the obligation to register at the national level. When we caught up with Innocent, three years after his attempts at earning money from chickens and an *ikiraka*, we found that he had put his business sense to good use, saving up and finally investing in a machine that would allow him to sell prepaid electricity units (called Cash Power) and become a transfer point for mobile money exchanges (TIGO Cash).

"I couldn't continue to upper-secondary school," Innocent told us one day recently, "but I didn't just sit and do nothing either. I registered for a training in auto-mechanics [. . .] for six months, and then I did a training with RDB called Akazi Kanoze for three months,[12] and then I found a way to learn how to use a computer. After that, someone hired me in his stationery shop, where I did printing and computer work, and also selling Cash Power."

He continued, clearly satisfied with the direction his life had taken, "I saved up, and afterwards me too—after having gotten some means—I created my own business. I sell Cash Power and also TIGO Cash. I don't live badly; it gives me a way to pay my rent, eat, pay my health insurance, and take care of some other problems in my daily life."

Innocent, unlike most of his peers, was actually registered in the national taxpayer system because of the type of business he had chosen. "I have a TIN number," he explained, "because when you want to start a TIGO Cash business, they ask for your TIN number and also your criminal record. And I'm registered at my sector too, so that I can pay for my business license."

When we asked what he thought of these requirements, Innocent reflected. "It all depends on the capital you have," he answered after a moment. "If you have some capital, it's easy. But it's also very difficult for someone who has little means. Really, it's very difficult."

LICENSING

In practice, only larger and more visible businesses tend to register nationally. At the local level, however, it is much harder to escape formal requirements. Certain types of licenses and regulations apply to the few sanctioned mobile activities, such as the bicycle, moped, and motorcycle taxis found clustered at every major intersection in Kigali and in towns throughout the country—each driver has to belong to an association, wear a uniform, hold a driving permit, and pay monthly taxes and a yearly business license fee. Fixed businesses must also hold a formal business license. For a typical one-room shop anywhere in Kigali province, big enough for the owner to stand behind a counter and serve clients from a few shelves of stock, the local business licensing fee is 40,000 Rwf ($67) per year, to be paid in the first month of business operation, in addition to the cost of rent, which can vary from $8 to $80 or more, depending on the size and location. Even those just renting a table at the market must have a license to operate, with correspondingly lower rates, but also lower profits. If you do not have a fixed table or a room—if you are just out on the street, selling what you can carry—you may not have to pay for a license, but you do pay in other ways, in terms of the constant stress of avoiding arrest and confiscation of your goods.

The comments of another student introduced in the previous chapter, Charles, illustrate how the government's increased attempts to formalize all of these sorts of micro-level businesses—though perhaps justified—nonetheless may exert a disproportionate burden on the poor.

Charles was one of the very disadvantaged students who had been able to pay for his own school fees only by dint of a great deal of hard work and entrepreneurial resourcefulness in finding small-scale self-employment as a motorcycle driver, renting out his bicycle, repairing telephones, and occasionally serving as an *umukomisiyoneri* (broker) for clients looking for a house or vehicle. All of these jobs, however, depended on a certain amount of anonymity and invisibility from government regulations, and those conditions were changing quickly, starting right around the time of his graduation from Senior 3.

We first learned about how these changes affected Charles's life in 2010, when we asked for news about his work repairing telephones. Discouraged, he told us that he had not been able to find repair work to do for some time. Thinking of the large number of pedestrians we had seen on the road just outside the house where he was staying, I asked: "Couldn't you put some kind of a sign in front of the gate to this house in order to attract some clients?"

"No, it's impossible!" Charles quickly replied. "They couldn't allow it, and plus then I would be obliged to pay taxes!"

As long as he did not advertise his business activities, he was invisible to the local authorities. But once he identified a particular place of business, he would become liable for the yearly business licensing fee and for local monthly taxes, a steep requirement for someone operating on essentially only his own human capital. But his alternative form of publicity, word of mouth, did not seem to be working well for him at the moment. "If it still doesn't work," he continued, "I'm going to go back to the motorcycle."

That did not seem like a very attractive option, given that just a year earlier he had broken his arm seriously in a motorcycle accident. But even that fallback plan seemed difficult to achieve, as he went on to say, "But I'll have to look first for a license."

"You didn't have a license before?" we asked, surprised. "How did you drive the motorcycle?"

"Before, it wasn't so difficult to hide," Charles replied. "But now the traffic police has become much stronger; it's not like it was in 2007. It's more serious."

When we spoke with Charles a few months later, he seemed to be up against insurmountable obstacles: "I don't know what has happened this year," he lamented. "Nothing is working! For the *umukomisiyoneri* and telephone repair work, I searched in vain. And about the motorcycle—I've already abandoned the idea. I still don't have a license and now it's dangerous to drive without a permit."

While it seems obviously important for drivers to have licenses in order to ensure some minimum safety standards, and local governments need to collect taxes in order to fund their activities, Charles's example illustrates how such regulations can make it difficult for the very poor to get by (also see Rollason, 2013). In a less regulated environment, Charles had been able to make use of essentially only his own intelligence and capacities to learn how to drive a motorcycle and repair telephones, and then attract clients to him in those and other forms of self-employment. As government control of these sorts of activities increased, however, his human capital was not enough—he would have to somehow acquire the financial capital necessary to pay the licensing fees required just to begin operating again under more formal conditions.

But Charles was persistent, as we saw in the previous chapter, and he was able to find his way. After chancing upon someone who was willing to pay for his A-level studies, he also managed to save up enough from his informal business ventures to eventually take his driving test. "I got category B," he reported happily to us some time later, "so I could actually teach people to drive a car and a motorcycle. With my friends, we decided to start a driving school. So whenever I'm not at school, I work with them, teaching people how to drive."

"Are you registered in your sector?" we asked him.

"Yes," he answered, and he went on, reminding us that many of the young people were proud of the idea that they might be able to contribute something to the country's development. "It's important to register, and plus that enables us to pay our taxes and work in an orderly way."

Echoing many of his peers, however, he added: "A lot of people want to do business, are looking for what they need to start, but they aren't able to find it. When you have means, though, then everything becomes easy."

PAYING TAXES AND FEES

Business registration and licensing, as Charles pointed out, bring a business to the attention of Rwanda's tax agencies, which exist at both the national and local levels.

National business registration automatically connects a business to the Rwanda Revenue Authority, where business taxes are payable quarterly. When I began this research, all businesses, regardless of income level, were legally liable for national taxation, at a rate of 4 percent of gross annual turnover for businesses earning less than 20 million Rwf ($33,000) per year, and at the standard corporate tax rate of 30 percent on net profits for all businesses earning above that amount. But as part of the Rwandan government's ongoing efforts to facilitate business activities and encourage investors, while simultaneously bringing more taxpayers into the internal revenue system, a new 2012 law introduced low flat taxation rates for businesses with gross earnings between 2 million and 12 million Rwf ($3,300–$20,000) per year, and reduced the tax rate of businesses earning between 12 million and 50 million Rwf ($20,000–$83,000) to 3 percent of annual turnover. At the same time, this new law eliminated all taxation requirements at the national level for businesses earning less than 2 million Rwf ($3,300), although they are still required to file an annual statement of earnings to avoid penalties. These initiatives have been undertaken with the explicit objective of reducing tax evasion by small businesses, and thereby increasing government revenues (Ngarambe, 2012; Ojulu, 2012).

There have not yet, however, been any reforms to the local structure of taxes and fees. On top of the cost of obtaining the local license, businesses are obliged to pay monthly local taxes ranging from 1,000 Rwf ($1.67) to 5,000 Rwf ($8.30), and sometimes more, depending the type of business and its location. There are also fees for security and sanitation, as well as for different local-level funds and activities, amounting to 3,000 Rwf ($5) or more per month. Businesses usually have to pay each of these taxes and fees within their first month of operation, often before they have earned any money at all.

Leo, the young man who had grown his business from an *ikarito* to a corner shop, helped us understand further the relative cost of these local taxes, together with the yearly licensing fee, on a small business that is just being established. He had used 250,000 Rwf ($417) to pay two months' rent, install some rough wooden shelves, and pay for some basic merchandise. But he also had to consider local taxes as part of his start-up costs.

"On top of my expenses," Leo told us, "I paid 40,000 francs [$67] for the license, and I need to set aside some money for the taxes. They are really high. I think that the government doesn't really help out people who want to start in the business world [. . .] I haven't gone yet to pay; probably I'll go next month. But if you delay, you have to pay a fine. They do a follow-up of businesses, and if they find that you don't have a receipt proving that you have already paid, then it's your problem."

"But it's not fair," he continued, "that everyone pays the same amount at the Sector. Whether you have a boutique worth 200,000 or 1 million francs [$330–$1,700], if you're in the same neighborhood, you pay the same fixed amount. Maybe they should establish some different rates of payment, so that those who gain a certain amount pay a certain amount. That would be more flexible." These fees seemed to have contributed to the discouraged look on his face, even as he made a steady stream of small sales during our visit, calculating his take at around 5–30 Rwf ($0.01–$0.05) per item. His profit margins after rent and taxes, he seemed to feel, would not really allow him to make much of the shop.

Three years later, however, he was still there. He had not been able to earn enough to go back to school, as he had originally hoped, but he seemed to have settled into his adult life. Married, with one child, he continued to make do.

The only businesses in our study that paid no local fees whatsoever were able to escape these requirements because of the very mobile nature of their work. One graduate, for example, had done a few tours using the ordinary bus system to transport tree tomatoes from his home province to the capital city for a client, and his activities were effectively invisible to authorities. But often even the most microscale entrepreneurs, operating on just a few dollars' worth of capital and with no formal location—like Sylvia's, from the previous chapter—fell under the net of local authorities.

Sylvia had not been as successful in attaining her objectives as some of the other graduates featured in this research, since the days when she was selling telephone airtime and on her way to continuing her secondary studies. "You know," she said when we last talked to her, "things haven't gone that well for me. I passed my Senior 3 examination and continued studying for a while, but after that I had the bad luck of getting pregnant, and I wasn't able to finish. Even though," she said, her tone brightening for a moment, "I managed to finish Senior 5 with a lot of points!"

"My son is now six months old," she went on. "I still live with my older sister and her son, and we have a difficult life. I couldn't continue selling M2U [mobile phone airtime] like I did before; I didn't have enough capital because we had to use it at home. We didn't have anything to eat, so I gave that money—I didn't have a choice, so I stopped. Now I'm just sitting at home."

She had tried to do something else in the meantime, but the fees she had to pay were too high to allow her to earn much of a profit at all. "I had started a little business of selling grilled maize. [. . .] But when you work for yourself, you pay a lot of taxes, higher than your own capital [. . .] For example, when I sold maize, at the place where we were, they came every evening to make us pay things. [Every month] we gave 1,000 Rwf [$1.67] for security, 500 Rwf [$0.83] for hygiene, and then every day we even had to pay 30 Rwf [$0.05] in taxes. But then, when we got home, we had to pay the same amount for security and hygiene there again."

"Don't you think," she asked, sounding upset, "that this is a lot of money? How much would you get as a profit—and at home you still have to eat, have something to wear, and raise your child? The taxes are really higher than your earnings."

Just like her peers, she said that everything would be easier if she just had more to work with. "I think it's easy [do to business in Rwanda]," she reflected, "as long as you have the capital and your idea; it's possible. But the laws that regulate taxes are really high. People pay taxes that are higher than their capital, so you discover that it's very difficult. These laws prevent young people from trying to do some kind of business; they are afraid of them."

Who Is Responsible for Solving Youth Unemployment?

In our series of focus group discussions with the more than four hundred young people participating in this study, we asked students to talk to us about what they thought caused youth unemployment in the country and who was responsible for solving the problem. Students told us that they thought the government could do some things to increase their chances for employment—make sure the country was secure and at peace, attract investors to create businesses with more jobs, require them to hire Rwandans rather than foreigners, enforce laws against corrupt hiring practices, and ask employers to give young people a chance to gain experience.[13] But they also gave credit to the government for already accomplishing, or at least working on, many of these objectives.

These young Rwandans did not expect the government to do everything for them—in discussion after discussion, they kept emphasizing that "it is us, the youth" or "us, the general population" who had to work and make an effort in order to get beyond Rwanda's challenge of youth unemployment. One discussion from School B illustrates the general trend of nearly every one of these conversations:

Researcher: From what you have said, it's clear that there is a problem of unemployment. But who is going to solve this problem of lack of work here in Rwanda or in Kigali?

Jean de Dieu: Me, I think that unless you create your own job, I mean, work without saying that you're trying to be employed—of course, if you have the chance, you could find a job somewhere, but if you say, "I'm the one that's going to create my own job, in order to employ other people"—that's when you'll find that finally a lot of people are able to get work.

Adolphe: What he just said is true. Creating a job for yourself so that others can get jobs too, because not everyone can find employment [...]

Lionel: Me, I think that finally it is us who are going to solve this problem.

These students believed, in a fundamental way, one of the primary messages of the entrepreneurship education policy—they were responsible for finding a way to earn their own livelihood.

But at the same time as they acknowledged the government's efforts to encourage youth to work for themselves, it would be hard to overlook the consistency in their perspective on Rwanda's regulations. "If you have capital, everything is fine," they said time after time. "But if you don't, there's nothing you can do." As one of the classmates of these students commented to his peers:

Arnaud: If the government says to each of us that we should create our own jobs—and me, for example, if I take my basket to go sell something, if I arrive in town, they will arrest me, even though that is just what I was able to do. That is really difficult.[14]

In other focus group discussions, the opinion was the same, and it surfaced again in the final updates for this research, three years after graduation:

Clarisse (School C):   Here in Rwanda, it's not permitted to do whatever you
want, in the sense of creating employment. Saying
"create your own job" here means that you need to
have a visible registered place, even though we have to
evolve from very low. Let's say that if, here in Kigali, I
have my 5,000 Rwf [$8.30]—I couldn't do anything. I
can't set up my little *ikarito* business—they'd give me
a kick on the rear and the police would take me away!
We can't live like that.[15]

Emmanuel (School D):   There are laws that prevent you from doing certain
types of business in a particular place; this makes it
difficult for a youth who doesn't have a lot of means,
and yet wanted to work in that area. Also, the fact of
obliging young people to join together in a cooperative
in order to do a certain type of business. This blocks
the person who wants to do a small business, and the
person who wants to work independently with just a
little capital. It's much easier for someone who has a
lot of capital.[16]

Thomas (School E):   There are laws that prevent you from doing informal
businesses. Here in Rwanda, they want orderly
business, they don't want disorder; as a result, you
can't just do whatever you are able to.[17]

Many young Rwandans thus feel caught in a double bind—they have few
chances at finding formal employment, but at the same time, it seems that they
will not be allowed to create for themselves the kinds of jobs that suit the means
actually at their disposal.

Finally, many said, the best thing the government could do would be to continue encouraging youth to create their own jobs—but at the same time, make
it possible for them to work for themselves. In Chapter 6, I highlighted some
students' arguments that the government should actually give them capital directly. But they were fair in their judgment of the likelihood of that scenario:

Ben (School C):   In fact, if you look at the situation carefully,
you will see that it is the population that has to
resolve the problem [of unemployment]. Because

> if you talk about "help from the state," the help
> that the state can give *comes from* the taxes given
> by the population. So if people don't work in
> order to help those who are still below, nothing will
> change, [. . .] because the state won't give any help
> if it has no money.

If the government could not directly give them jobs or capital, though, at least some students in every school argued, then it should provide them with loans in some form or another:[18]

Donatien (School A):	Even if the government cannot solve the problem of unemployment, it could at least give you a loan so that you could create your own job.
Thierry (School B):	Here in Rwanda, getting a bank loan is difficult. If [the government] could facilitate that a little bit, so that people could have money to create their projects, things would become easy.
James (School E):	I think that the government has its budget, and for someone who has done the work to organize his project, to prepare it, it would be correct for the government to help you. They shouldn't imagine that you have done nothing, that you are just sitting there! Just the fact of organizing yourself to do something, they should support that.

These youth did not necessarily want to start microenterprises with just a few dollars of capital. As we have seen in the past two chapters, their aspiration was to start higher-capital, viable businesses that could earn them a decent livelihood. They hoped that the government might find a way to loan them some money to start a more formalized business, or at least that the government would work on getting microfinance institutions and banks to loan to them more readily.

But if the government would not, or could not, secure start-up business loans for them, then these young Rwandans argued that it all came back to regulations again. The government had to loosen up its rules to enable them to start a business with whatever capital they could pull together themselves—no matter how little the amount.

Jacqueline (School C): The thing that I think could help get rid of unemployment is to give everyone the freedom to do whatever he thinks he is capable of doing in order to advance. It's the government [that has to decide this]. Because I have seen that in Uganda, it's a country that is visibly more developed than Rwanda, and I think that—even if people say that it's disorderly, disorganized—at least people are developed, because they are left in peace. Each one does what he can, whether it's selling chapattis in a public place, or whatever—he will do it. He can try anything, and in that way he evolves. On top of that, the government should reduce the taxes they require from small businesses.

These students were, in effect, arguing for the right to do business in a *disorderly* fashion at least until they could set aside enough money to create something more stable and formalized. Ultimately, they did not object to being "orderly" about their business activities by following government regulations—but, they argued, they had to be given a realistic chance to actually become entrepreneurs before they could follow all of these rules and contribute to the nation's development by paying taxes.

They wanted, in brief, a chance to follow an entrepreneurial path like that of Wilson, the former child soldier introduced in Chapter 7. "My life has really changed," Wilson exclaimed when we called him to hear his news three years after graduation. "Now I'm a big man, you wouldn't even recognize me! Now I've started a little cleaning business. I look for clients at construction sites where people are building their houses. I do house cleaning, carpets, and some garden landscaping."

After a rough start, Wilson had achieved something truly remarkable. "I have seven permanent employees," he explained, "but when I get a big job, I hire more and my employees supervise them. In each domain, I have one employee; they get a salary of 60,000 Rwf [$100] per month."

When we asked how he had achieved this, he explained, "I made some brochures and I went door to door; on the brochures I put the services I would be able to do. When I went door to door, I asked for people's telephone contacts, and later on I called to ask if they were interested in my services. [. . .] One day I had a client that really appreciated my work, and when he had to leave [the country] he even offered me a machine to vacuum carpets!"

A business with enough consistent revenue to pay regular salaries for eight people—this was something truly unusual. How much did he pay in taxes, we wondered?

"I don't have a license or anything," he went on. "I didn't have a fixed address before, but now I'm getting ready to register. Because now I am becoming stable, and I'm starting to have permanent contracts."

Technically, what Wilson was doing was illegal. But he did not think of it that way—he was just waiting to become stable enough to feel that registering made sense. Couldn't there be a middle way, many of our research participants wondered, that would allow them to grow their businesses from scratch like Wilson, and still become, in time, contributors to the development of the country?

Creativity and Controls Under a Partner State?

The stories of these youth—especially those living in severely resource-constrained conditions—highlight the strongest internal contradiction between creativity and controls in the post-developmental state. In the process of trying to control young people's entrepreneurial creativity, the government might just be discouraging their initiative before it even has a chance to take root.

Happily for the Rwandan government's post-developmental priorities, however, these Rwandan youth are not rejecting the government's guiding role. Instead, they simply want the government to redirect its regulatory powers toward the facilitation of their nascent entrepreneurship. The creation of a more formal business sector through registration and regulation would be fine, they suggest, as long as they do not have to pay taxes or meet unreasonable requirements before having a chance to become established. And they are enthusiastic about starting their own enterprises, if the state will only exercise some of its power to help them gain access to sufficient capital.

In the introduction to *Policy Worlds*, Shore and Wright (2011) remark, "Governments may try to use policy as an instrument to impose their ordering

principles upon those they seek to govern, but 'reflexive subjects' [. . .] sometimes 'answer back'" (p. 17). The Rwandan youth in this study are, indeed, an-
swering back—in their own rather nuanced way. The model of negotiated social
learning employed throughout this book illuminates how it is possible for these
youth to exercise such agency even in the face of strong structural forces: educational policy and institutions, business regulations, socioeconomic class, and
the very weight of Rwanda's complex history. Young people can never be completely constrained by the structures that surround them, because structure is
never completely encompassing: their participation in overlapping and often
contradictory communities of practice allows them to develop a repertoire—at
times conscious, at other times less so—of alternative perspectives and ideals
In this case, the youth perspectives shared in this book are not really part of a
conscious collective movement, and they do not seek outright rebellion or revolution. Theirs is a more subtle voice, acknowledging the Rwandan government's
overall wisdom, but hoping for a reconsideration of certain aspects of the post-
developmental approach.

The question that remains to be seen, therefore, is whether the educational
process of governance can really go two ways. Will young people's alternate perspectives be limited to changing their own classrooms and schools? Or will they
find ways of expressing themselves that will gradually carry their perspectives
back through a chain of interlinking communities of practice, until Rwandan
leaders themselves have learned a new way of seeing their partnership with
Rwandan youth?

In recent years, the Rwandan government has in fact begun to put into
place some of the very kinds of initiatives that students hoped for. In late 2011,
the Ministry of Trade and Industry began sponsoring a new project, Hanga
Umurimo (Create a Job), a business-plan competition targeted at women and
youth (MINICOM, 2011). In the first round of the competition, the authors of
fifty business plans in each of Rwanda's thirty administrative districts were selected for further training, after which ten plans from each district were chosen
to receive private financing, underwritten by a guarantee from the government's
new Business Development Fund (MINICOM, 2012).

Many young people, however, have the impression that Hanga Umurimo is
only for educated youth with larger-scale business ideas, like the business competitions that have been sponsored for many years by Rwanda's Private Sector
Federation (2014). There have also been some problems with organizing Hanga

Umurimo loans through the Business Development Fund, with initial reports that banks were reluctant to lend to youth, even with the fund guaranteeing 75 percent of the loan for approved projects (Bucyensenge, 2013; Nyamagabe, 2013; Nyesiga, 2012). The Ministry of Trade and Industry has continued to work on these issues, although difficulties remain (Esiara, 2014; Uwanziga, 2016).

In 2012, partly in response to concerns that Hanga Umurimo might not reach vulnerable youth, the government also announced the Kuremera program, intended to provide seed funding for young people who are just starting out with modest business ideas (MIFOTRA, 2013). For the moment, however, Kuremera does not have funding attached to it; initially, it has involved only a sensitization campaign to "donate freely [. . .] in order to help young people without capital start their own businesses" ("Kuremera should be premised," 2013).

At the same time, a national network of local savings and credit cooperatives (Umurenge SACCO) has been established in Rwanda—with the goal of vastly increasing access to financial services, sometimes somewhat forcibly, for the country's general population. Yet even here, significant obstacles remain for many youth: "Here in the countryside," a graduate from School D told us in our last interview, "people don't observe the laws given by the government, for example when you want to ask for a loan at the [Umurenge SACCO]. You may have a complete file and application, but they don't want to give you your loan." Experiences such as these seem widespread and certainly discourage young people from feeling confident that they can access financing from these institutions. Again, however, there are signs that the Rwandan government is aware of some of these challenges and is taking steps to improve SACCO management structures (National Bank of Rwanda, BNR, 2010).

Programs like Hanga Umurimo, Kuremera, the Business Development Fund, and Umurenge SACCO signal an important symbolic shift in Rwanda's post-developmental discourse, along the very lines that some of the youth in this research suggested. Earning a living, Rwanda's post-developmental government continues to insist, depends on young Rwandans' individual initiative. But these projects suggest that those who make an effort to plan and ask for assistance may just receive it—entering into a contemporary sort of patron-client relationship with the state by promising, in turn, to contribute to Rwanda's vision of orderly development.

The limitations of these programs in terms of scope and effectiveness, however, mean that this is not yet the kind of partnership of mutual assistance that the young Rwandans in this research most hoped for. Business capital is by no means guaranteed, and if they cannot gather together sufficient means on their own, disadvantaged young Rwandans are effectively still stuck. For the regulatory regime that prevents them from engaging in "disorderly" microscale and informal businesses is only becoming more extensive over time.

Conclusion

Figure 14   Rwandan youth on the move in a Kigali street scene

Source: Copyright Joanna Paola Honeyman.

Conclusion

The Orderly Entrepreneur in Rwanda and Beyond

RWANDAN YOUTH DREAM of going places, but the route may be a long one—following the predictable path of schooling if they are fortunate, or struggling to start a microenterprise amid an expanding regime of regulations if they are not; using credentials and social capital to search for jobs; and, for many, looking toward a horizon filled with dreams of starting a bigger business one day. This book has explored the Rwandan government's efforts to shape that landscape of schooling and youth livelihoods by introducing a required six-year course in entrepreneurship for all of Rwanda's secondary school students. Rwandan policy makers hope that this course will encourage more young people to initiate creative and growth-oriented enterprises, starting as small as necessary with whatever resources they have at hand. But no matter how small the enterprise, policy makers also envision these initiatives as part of the formal sector: organized, registered, stable, law-abiding, willing participants in government plans and programs, and contributing to national needs through regular payment of taxes. The Rwanda of the future, in short, is meant to be populated by a generation of orderly entrepreneurs.

Post-Developmental Landscapes

The ideal of the orderly entrepreneur is being promulgated throughout Rwandan life. In this book I have explored its manifestation in four particular settings: the national and international policy context that is today shaping a post-developmental style of governance in Rwanda, the offices and meeting rooms of Rwanda's National Curriculum Development Centre,[1] the classrooms of Rwanda's secondary schools, and Rwandan graduates' lives beyond school walls. Through detailed observation of these scenes, I have sketched a theory of governance as a negotiated process of social learning, which must occur within and across communities of practice at all levels of scope and scale. The resulting picture shows the complex and multilevel social interactions taking place—from the international circulation of ideas down to the most intimate economic decisions made within graduates' homes—and the often unexpected policy transformations that have occurred along the way.

I have also explored the implications of Rwanda's post-developmental approach to promoting an ethos of regulated self-reliance, illustrating the many internal paradoxes and contradictions with which the post-developmental state must contend while attempting both to cultivate creativity and to keep it under tight controls. One key paradox can be found in the credential-focused purposes of schooling. Even while the post-developmental state needs schools to instill traditional values of order and discipline, it simultaneously expects teachers to promote neoliberal values of self-reliance and creative independent thinking, potentially decentering the very teacher authority it relies on for the production of an orderly society. A second, even more significant paradox is presented by the effects of post-developmental state strategies on disadvantaged youth. While many young people dream of starting large-scale formal businesses with high earnings potential, disadvantaged youth have virtually no resources available to help them work toward that goal. In that context, each strategic regulation the state puts into place can become an added barrier to young people's very efforts to comply with the post-developmental ethos of earning a living through their own initiative.

This concluding chapter summarizes and connects these findings to broader considerations and suggests some concrete recommendations for policy makers and international development professionals trying to find their way through the complex social and economic landscapes facing young people today, both in Rwanda and beyond.[2]

Governing Dynamics of Social Learning and Negotiation

Rwanda's entrepreneurship education policy is the result of certain social dynamics being played out on the national and international scene today. Teaching entrepreneurship to youth may indeed respond to specific Rwandan national priorities. But beyond any particular needs assessment or baseline study—which, in fact, were never carried out in this case—the idea of teaching entrepreneurship to young people was adopted because it matched deeply held presuppositions, or doxa, of a key set of Rwandan policy makers. They held a fundamental shared belief, rooted in shared social experiences and strongly echoing neoliberal ideas, that such a course would help reduce perceived widespread attitudes of dependence, respond to problems of youth unemployment, and increase Rwanda's economic competitiveness and prestige internationally.

Yet they were not fully comfortable with the idea of an unpredictable and uncontrolled entrepreneurial path, organically taking shape in an unfettered market. Drawing on their own experiences of authority and hierarchy and on the iconic example of Singapore—itself rising significantly in international stature at the time—Rwandan policy makers resolved to regulate the country's entrepreneurial activity and channel it strategically toward the state's development needs. In effect, they created a set of entrepreneurship policies that represent a fusion of neoliberal and developmental approaches, part of a broader post-developmental style of governance that characterizes a growing number of states around the world today (Baildon, 2009; Ong, 2006; Park, 2007).

Part I of this book introduced an anthropological lens for analyzing these policy-making processes, gaining insight into the social dynamics through which policy ideas are understood—and often misunderstood and transformed (Rizvi & Lingard, 2010; Shore & Wright, 1997; Shore, Wright, & Peró, 2011; Stone, 2002; Sutton & Levinson, 2001). Foucault's (1982, 1991) work on power and governmentality and Bourdieu's (1972, 1990) theorizing of social practice have been particularly influential to interpretivist efforts to study policy—as they are throughout this book. But the conceptual elements developed by these two thinkers have not been fully satisfactory in clarifying the dynamics of influence, misunderstanding, reinterpretation, and resistance that ethnographic studies of policy witness from the supranational down to the most local levels. To explain how these dynamics have played out in the context of Rwanda's entrepreneurship education policy, I have introduced a new focus on the social learning and negotiations involved in policy making and governance.

In brief, the theoretical perspective I refer to as a model of negotiated social learning draws attention to the social effects of individuals' participation in widely varying constellations of social groups, or communities of practice (Lave & Wenger, 1991), which are themselves strongly shaped by the structure of rewards—economic, social, cultural, and symbolic capital—in surrounding social fields (Bourdieu, 1986, 1990). Participants in a given community of practice become proficient in that group's manner of seeing and behaving through long exposure and experience, developing an almost unthinking mastery of the ways of thinking and behaving that will be most intelligible and rewarded within that context. But, since we all have experience in multiple communities of practice, we in fact develop multifaceted repertoires of social habits and perspectives. To some extent, we exercise volition in playing up different aspects of our habitus according to what is appropriate within a given social setting, and in bringing our presuppositions from one community of practice into new social situations. All forms of social interaction—from the purely interpersonal to the act of governing a nation—therefore involve negotiating among and learning from diverse dispositions and presuppositions. This constellation of overlapping communities of practice serves as a potential reserve of nascent social indeterminacies and social change, from governor to the governed and back again.

Understanding governance in terms of negotiated social learning offers a great deal of insight for academics, policy makers, and professionals working in the field of social and economic development. As these actors go about their social lives, moving continuously among multiple communities of practice, they necessarily bring certain habits of thought and action from one social context into other domains. This is what makes it possible for policy makers to evaluate their own society from a seemingly external and critical perspective, just as the Rwandan policy makers who decided that their own national culture was not sufficiently entrepreneurial. The "deficiencies" policy makers may identify in this way are, however, more accurately described as recognition of social difference—different ways of approaching the world from those the policy makers have embraced as a result of their own social histories. In many cases, policies—especially those related to deliberately changing perceptions and actions—are fundamentally about creating likeness, about bringing the target population closer to policy makers' own norms of laudable thought and behavior. As Chapter 2 showed, this sometimes means that policy solutions are, in effect, chosen before the precise social problem they are intended to fix has been systematically explored.

Policy makers and other professionals in positions of public influence need to be aware that the transformations they propose may be based more on their own presuppositions and social experiences than on a real systematic understanding of the complex issues and perspectives involved. There is nothing necessarily wrong with this—it may just be a fact of human decision making. But an acknowledgment of this dynamic should highlight to decision makers in Rwanda and elsewhere the vital importance of trying to understand the perhaps very different perspectives of all those who will implement and be targeted by a given policy. Their perspectives are often based on unfamiliar practical and social experiences that may offer a fundamentally different interpretation, of both the current situation and the desired improvements, from that of decision makers' received ideas.

Under the confrontational style of democracy that prevails in many Western countries, it is often assumed—though this is debatable—that these diverse perspectives will come to the fore through public debate, the workings of the free press, and electoral processes. Such may not be the case under post-developmental styles of governance, however, where public discussion is much more likely to be supportive of government plans (Ingelaere, 2011; Leong, 2000; Tey, 2008). This raises an interesting dilemma for post-developmental state leaders who are genuinely interested in gaining a better understanding of how different populations understand and experience particular policies and problems.

In the context of this study, most young Rwandans agree with the government's goal of promoting job creation through entrepreneurship—but they do not have the same theories about how this goal can best be achieved. In response to the research presented here, policy makers could choose to initiate a review of the broad range of government policies currently intended to support youth employment and entrepreneurship in Rwanda, incorporating youth perspectives as valuable data to indicate which policies to scale up, scale down, or revise, and which new approaches may be needed (see, e.g., Hopma & Sergeant, 2015). Understanding those alternative perspectives, and their own legitimate roots in social experience, can help to create policies that more effectively respond to young people's lived realities and priorities, in the process contributing even more sustainably to the development goals that policy makers and youth hold in common.

Exploring Processes of Curriculum Development

Rwanda's entrepreneurship education policy was framed with very practical objectives in mind: build entrepreneurial attitudes and abilities, promote job creation among youth, and thereby contribute to broader national development goals. Despite this practical vision, however, when the O-level (grades 7–9) entrepreneurship curriculum development process began in 2008, the focus quickly turned towards codifying list after list of regulations and terminology, even turning creativity itself into little more than a word to be defined. Beginning just one year later, however, the A-level (grades 10–12) entrepreneurship curriculum development process took a turn in a very different direction. Featuring a wide range of activities that focused on independent investigation and reasoning on real-world issues while largely leaving the rules and definitions behind, this second curriculum reflected almost entirely neoliberal ideas. Neither curriculum, it seemed, reflected the hybrid post-developmental aims of the Rwandan state.

There are very few published ethnographic studies of curriculum development processes to draw upon in the attempt to explain this unexpected outcome.[3] Yet the study of educational policy making requires close attention to curriculum development; after all, curricula and textbooks are just as much educational policy statements as are the political decisions that call for them. It is crucial to understand the social dynamics involved in their production—dynamics that may, as in the Rwandan case, significantly transform initial stated policy goals.

Part II of this book analyzed Rwanda's entrepreneurship curriculum development process as an instance of negotiated social learning, offering some insights for those trying to coordinate or analyze curriculum development processes. Since the participants involved in the development of a curriculum constitute a community of practice—with a whole set of assumptions and procedures to negotiate among themselves as they proceed with their work—the social histories of the participants matter. Specifically, curriculum developers are very likely to produce the same kinds of curriculum, textbooks, and pedagogical recommendations that they experienced and were rewarded for mastering, as students and teachers themselves. This social experience has led to ingrained presuppositions and dispositions that strongly outweigh the influence of any alternate theories of curriculum or pedagogy they may have read about, but have never seen demonstrated, much less experienced or enacted themselves.[4] Guidelines and instructions alone, as desocialized "texts" divorced from their original social conditions, are very unlikely to be able to change ingrained assumptions and habits. For such microsocial transformations to occur, this study suggests, there needs to be sufficient interaction with people whose own social histories have caused them to embody these new ideas in an instinctive form of mastery. Even under those conditions, however, there may still be social translation problems between participants with very different social repertoires—misunderstandings and disagreements which have to be overcome through processes of social negotiation as new understandings are gradually learned or constructed through shared experience.

These observations of Rwanda's entrepreneurship curriculum development process also bolster arguments that rewards and incentives matter in processes of social change (Easterly, 2001), including in the very act of translating policy directives into specific programmatic detail. By rewards, I do not mean direct benefits offered to policy makers for taking certain actions, but rather policy makers' largely subconscious awareness of the general structure of rewards shaping the surrounding social field. Policy directives that do not match those broader incentives—such as the directive to implement student-centered approach to curriculum when examinations are still dependent on a very teacher-centered definition of knowledge—are very likely to be transformed along the way to implementation simply because policy actors cannot make sense of the disconnect.

These reflections suggest some ways for the Rwandan Ministry of Education to more effectively reach its goal of promoting constructivist student-centered pedagogy in its schools. To begin with, those who are involved in curriculum and materials development may need to see deeper evidence that independent and creative thinking will actually be rewarded in schools, in examinations, in the transition from school to work, and in broader Rwandan society. Furthermore, there may need to be a change in the composition of the panels that create new curricula and other educational guidelines. There is an understandable preference for the Rwandan curriculum to be written by people who have a deep understanding of Rwanda's realities—which often means involving Rwandan teachers who are steeped in the current culture and expectations of Rwanda's school system. But there should also be space to include at least some contributors who can demonstrate real personal and professional experience within education systems that take a more constructivist pedagogical approach.[5] Along with making a greater effort to consult a range of externally produced student-centered curricula as examples, it is this social presence that can help demonstrate new pedagogical possibilities while still remaining relevant to Rwanda's reality.

In 2014 and 2015, Rwanda in fact engaged in a national curriculum revision process intended to shift every school subject toward a more competence-based and student-centered approach. This process was led by a team of international consultants who emphasized a constructivist approach to learning, and in the beginning they faced strong resistance from a host of Rwandan teachers and curriculum developers who preferred a more traditional approach.[6] These new participants were in an influential position, however, and they embodied a mastery of constructivist presuppositions that was rooted in their own social histories. A preliminary exploration of the new entrepreneurship curriculum for both O- and A-level suggests, indeed, that their influence did in the end prevail in making the curriculum more focused on building students' abilities to analyze and innovate within their own reality (Rwanda Education Board, 2015a, 2015b). Yet even in the shift away from credentials toward creativity, the learning of state controls has still retained a prominent role in the new entrepreneurship course (Honeyman & Rutiyomba, 2015). Perhaps this is finally the hybrid post-developmental entrepreneurship curriculum that was so elusive during Rwanda's first attempts in 2008 and 2009.

Studying Policy with Teachers and Students

When Rwanda's original entrepreneurship curriculum was first introduced into schools in 2010, it had the potential to create two very different outcomes—a focus on credentials and controls in O-level and a focus on independent initiative and creative problem-solving in A-level. But once the course entered Rwandan schools for implementation, this curricular difference was erased. From school to school and classroom to classroom, almost every entrepreneurship teacher in this study took up a traditional role as the authoritative source of knowledge, spending each class dictating or writing notes up on the board—page after page of definitions and explanations for students to copy down and learn word for word, in preparation for their examinations. Surprisingly, this abstract academic style of teaching took shape despite the fact that the majority of these teachers were, outside of school, practicing entrepreneurs themselves.

This pedagogical outcome was due not only to teachers' own ingrained habits but also to an attempt to defend against students' reactions to the course. As the weeks went by, students increasingly treated their entrepreneurship teachers with less respect than the teachers of more traditional academic courses, resisted the practical elements of the course, and—especially once it was announced that entrepreneurship would not appear on that year's national examinations—simply stopped taking notes or, in some cases, even attending class.

These reactions stood in stark contrast to students' statements outside of class, where they amply demonstrated that they were personally interested in business as a likely future source of livelihood.

Part III of this book again employed a model of negotiated social learning to analyze why teachers and students reacted to the entrepreneurship course in the way that they did and to understand the implications of students' subtle and not-so-subtle forms of resistance. In the community of practice that the classroom represents, structured in a broader field of traditionally oriented authoritative schooling, teachers are almost unavoidably regarded as the master practitioners of academic ways of being and knowing. In the classroom, motivated students take on the role of novices—aspiring to master the game of schooling by following the guidance of their teachers and absorbing the knowledge they possess. A teacher who does not act in the authoritative way that students expect puts this entire social agreement into jeopardy, as students begin to feel that perhaps they know better than their teacher how schooling is supposed to work. To avoid the discomfort of such a role reversal—a real social danger, given some of our observations of the sort of disrespect students showed toward their teachers whose legitimacy they questioned—teachers do all they can to bolster their authoritative status, not surprisingly falling into the traditional teacher-centered mode of instruction in the process.

Beyond the dynamics of the teacher-student relationship, students also need evidence that the time they spend in school serves in their construction of a schooled identity and fits the structure of rewards that will shape their futures (Chency, 2007). From the beginning, especially in A-level, many students concluded that entrepreneurship simply was not an academically authentic course—in part because it seemed entirely outside of the primary purpose that they ascribed to schooling: earning credentials in order to have a better chance of finding a good job, which many of them dreamed might give them the capital to start a real viable business one day. This was the structure of rewards in Rwanda's fields of schooling and employment, as they understood it, and any aspect of schooling that did not relate to those rewards was extraneous at best and at worst a waste of time that could be better used in studying for their exams.

Far from policy makers' typical conceptualization of students as passive recipients of educational policy, this research shows that students have definite opinions about what happens inside their classrooms. Policy makers should recognize this reality and value the perspectives of students as representing a legitimate perspective to be understood rather than just overcome. The importance of this observation stands out in light of recent discussion around the obstacles to achieving universal education for Africa's youth, given that many young people actually choose to drop out of school because of the poor quality of the education they are receiving, and its apparent lack of utility for their lives (Inoue, di Gropello, Taylor, & Gresham, 2015, pp. 10–11). In the more limited context of this study, many Rwandan students were clearly saying that the entrepreneurship course did not match what they expected from school. If it is truly an important goal to teach students entrepreneurial attitudes and abilities, then policy makers need to ask themselves what can be done to meet students halfway.

One way of better aligning entrepreneurship education with students' expectations for schooling is to accept the central role that examinations play in the traditional school system and radically change the examinations themselves in order to change teacher practice and student expectations (Wiggins, 1989). If the entrepreneurship examinations can be reformulated to more profoundly assess the complexities of entrepreneurial abilities, students and teachers alike will soon understand that the teaching of entrepreneurship needs to change as well. Entrepreneurship has already been introduced as a new subject on the national examinations at both O- and A-levels, a development that has surely gone partway toward helping students give greater value to the course. But there is still much more that could be done to align the entrepreneurship examinations with the actual abilities that students will need if they decide to start their own businesses.

Furthermore, the entrepreneurship examinations could also be linked to rewards that are more directly associated with entrepreneurial behavior, so that students will have more of a reason to put some effort into their entrepreneurship courses in the first place. A major part of students' examinations, for example, could require them to present a detailed business plan to be accomplished for a fixed amount of money. Students from each sector or district presenting the most original and viable plans could be awarded that money, as a grant or guaranteed loan, for their top examination performance. In this way, though the entrepreneurship course does not fit the typical reward structure of examinations-credential-job that is still most emphasized in the Rwandan field of schooling, it could reward entrepreneurially oriented students with an alternate route to economic opportunity.

Another response to students' perspectives would be to provide more extensive teacher training and institutional support to entrepreneurship teachers. In the first years of this entrepreneurship education policy, there was no budget for widespread teacher training. No wonder teachers sometimes had difficulty explaining difficult concepts or struggled with the course's unfamiliar student-centered pedagogy. Teachers clearly need further support in understanding the basic material, and in learning how to create a more learner-centered interaction in their classrooms—through observation, role play, and guided experience, not just through lectures on active pedagogy. But even this will not be enough. Educational policy makers and teachers also need to find ways to help students move from their teacher-centered expectations toward a more active student role. Teachers need to learn an approach for meeting students where they are—when, for example, they "demand a definition"—and gradually building students' understanding of how to carry out activities that require more independent thought and practical engagement.

Finally, school leaders can go a long way toward supporting these changes in schooled behaviors. Teachers take real risks when they try out new pedagogical styles, and school administrators can support them by reinforcing the message that this, too, is a legitimate way to teach. Schools also need to find ways to help students practice their entrepreneurial abilities at a small scale, in an environment that encourages learning from experience. There are many reasons schools are reluctant to allow small-scale business activities on school grounds—among them the concern about avoiding accusations of child labor, and the legitimate worry that introducing money into the school environment can create divisions among students from different socioeconomic backgrounds. Yet despite the widespread feeling in Rwanda that working and studying do not mix, it is when young people are still students that they have the luxury of being able to learn about work without—in most cases—being directly responsible for earning their whole family's livelihood. Rwanda's Ministry of Education could explore options, and experiment with them on a small scale, for introducing activities such as savings-and-loan groups, entrepreneurship clubs, business-plan competitions, and temporary income-generating activities into schools, to add a much more practical dimension to students' entrepreneurship lessons.

Understanding Youth Perspectives on Employment and Entrepreneurship

The immediate objective of Rwanda's six-year entrepreneurship course, arguably, is to convince more young Rwandans to create their own businesses. This study has demonstrated that the dream of starting and owning a business is in fact very widespread among Rwandan youth. But at least in the first few years of this policy's implementation, there was not such a direct causal connection between entrepreneurship education and entrepreneurial behavior as policy makers may have originally imagined. After the school year was over, most O-level graduates simply spent their free time "sitting at home," waiting for the next school year to begin. And many A-level graduates, even as they mentally nurtured their business ideas for the future, focused their most immediate efforts on using their social connections to find employment.

The more disadvantaged students, in contrast, turned the policy's linear logic on its head: they were not going to school in order to become entrepreneurial; they were entrepreneurs in order to go to school. These young Rwandans, in a context where many other disadvantaged youth had already given up on school (Sommers, 2012), had persevered with their education through great personal effort and sacrifice over the years. They were virtually the only truly practicing youth entrepreneurs in this study's random sample of graduates. And they had by and large started their businesses with almost nothing, at a time when Rwanda's business regulations were not yet very strictly enforced. Often with less than $35 of capital, they had sold chickens, maize, and telephone airtime; circulated on the streets with handheld cartons of sweets and cookies; worked as brokers arranging sales; repaired telephones; and done innumerable other *ibiraka* (little jobs). With their small earnings, they had paid for notebooks and school uniforms, covered their school fees, and contributed a little to their households' very limited income—and some of them, over time, had managed to grow their activities into something much more established and formalized.

There has been a great deal of enthusiasm internationally about the idea of teaching youth about entrepreneurship (see, e.g., Salzano, Bahri, & Haftendorn, 2006). Rwanda's entrepreneurship education policy is one of the first experiences globally in introducing such a course as a mainstream requirement of formal schooling. On balance, however, this research suggests that young Rwandans, and other youth in similar circumstances, will not be fully persuaded by entrepreneurship education until its claims become more fully reflected by the realities of economic life they see around them (also see Pells, Pontalti, & Williams, 2014). Schooling, examinations, credentials, and employment were centrally important to the Rwandan students in this study because they continued to represent—especially in the observations and experience of less advantaged youth—virtually the only available path from barely subsistence-level farming and self-employment, toward the capital accumulation that might eventually afford them higher social status and economic security.

One way the entrepreneurship course could better reflect the economic realities facing young Rwandans is to treat more seriously their concern with the issue of capital. Since finding capital is a problem, the course could explicitly teach about different sources of capital in the Rwandan context, including practical advice about how to gradually build some personal savings if young people are able to find even a low-wage job. The course could also focus more on the question of how to grow a business from a very low-capital microenterprise to something more stable and profitable. Education policy makers could take advantage of the growing body of research on youth livelihoods in the African context that acknowledges the need to work with youth to learn how self-employment could become a better "pathway out of poverty" (MasterCard Foundation, 2015; also see Abbott, 2010; African Economic Outlook, 2012; Education Development Center, 2009).

Important changes are also happening in the fields of schooling and livelihoods surrounding these youth—on the one hand weakening the link between school credentials and finding employment, yet on the other hand making it increasingly difficult to start a business without significant capital. During my research, the Rwandan government announced that access to O-levels would be vastly expanded, in principal becoming universal, through the Nine Years Basic Education program. Not long after, this policy idea was extended to a new Twelve Years Basic Education policy, with the goal of giving all school aged youth access either to academic A-levels, or to technical and vocational education (Rwirahira, 2012). Given the strongly hierarchical pyramid structure of educational access in Rwanda's history, discussed in Chapter 3, these policies amount to an educational revolution—for the first time, all Rwandans are considered to have a right to a full primary and secondary education, even if the remaining costs of uniforms, school materials, and mandatory parental contributions continue to make attendance unaffordable for some children and youth (Williams, 2013;

Williams, Abbott, & Mupenzi, 2014). These policies imply a significant change in the meaning and importance of Rwanda's national examinations, as they no longer absolutely determine access to the next education level.[7]

At the end of the secondary school cycle, the significance of the A-level examinations has also begun to change significantly. Previously most graduates with a decent score on their A-level examinations were virtually guaranteed a university scholarship, and until around the year 2000 a university diploma in many disciplines still promised high hopes for finding employment. Now, however, a policy of offering scholarships only to the highest-scoring and most disadvantaged students has come into force across the board (Kamugisha, 2008). At the same time, Rwanda has experienced an increase from approximately four thousand university students in 1994 to the current figure of more than forty thousand (Ministry of Education, 2014), without a comparable increase in white-collar jobs. University entrance is still dependent on receiving at least a minimum examination score, but in all other ways passing the A-level examinations no longer represents the guarantee of higher education and increased access to employment opportunities that it once did.

Rwanda's field of employment and livelihoods is also changing. With ambulatory businesses now illegal in law and in practice, and with the increased effectiveness of oversight on issues such as business registration, licensing, and taxation, it has become much more difficult to start a microscale activity with little capital. Yet the very same young people who cannot afford to pay school fees and costs also cannot gather together enough capital to start a formalized business. "What are we to do?" they might justifiably wonder. The available paths for socioeconomic mobility seem to be increasingly closed off to those at the bottom.

In all fairness, teaching about entrepreneurship is not the only effort the Rwandan government is making to address the difficulties of youth unemployment. The government's efforts to cultivate an "orderly" image for the country is just one part of a larger strategy to increase business investment in Rwanda, in hopes of more large-scale employers offering both skilled and unskilled jobs. The Rwandan government has also initiated the Vision Umurenge public works program, which is intended to give an infusion of jobs and income to the poorest sectors in the country (MINALOC, 2009). These are highly laudable efforts and should make a real difference for the situation of some youth. Yet these strategies cannot be expected to reach all disadvantaged youth, at least not in the short or medium terms. It is crucial, then, to consider how to extend further options to the young people who have a desire to entrepreneurially earn an income but who have very few resources at their disposal to get started.

There are several things that the Rwandan government—and governments in other developing countries that wish to promote youth entrepreneurship—can do. First, they can take seriously students' argument that they need resources, not just information, in order to become entrepreneurs (Abbott, 2010; Education Development Center, 2009; MasterCard Foundation, 2015; and Triki & Faye, 2013). There is a need to understand in much greater depth whether disadvantaged youth—not just the well educated and well informed—can truly access funding from the array of programs (such as, in Rwanda's case, programs like Hanga Umurimo, Kuremera, COOJAD, and the Umurenge SACCOs) that are currently being developed to meet this need. Where difficulties and obstacles are found, it should be possible to adjust these programs and propose additional approaches that may help to meet unfulfilled needs. One possibility, already mentioned, is to link students' final entrepreneurship examinations to the awarding of small business loans. Alternatively, small-scale savings-and-loan groups seem to have been successful in helping young Rwandans gradually learn how to save, invest, and collaborate—they may, in fact, be an important prerequisite for successful efforts to create cooperatives, another one of the Rwandan government's policy ideas for promoting orderly youth entrepreneurship (Education Development Center, 2013). Perhaps some further thought should be put into how to support the formation and effective operation of these groups among youth who already have at least some source of income. Finally, serious consideration should be given to the possibility of establishing a fund for small business grants with a "pay-it-forward" structure (Banerjee, 2011), in which disadvantaged youth would receive small seed capital and guidance, and would be encouraged to pass on a portion of their profits for start-up financing to other youth, rather than paying back interest on a loan.

Parallel to this, the Rwandan government needs to carefully consider the effects of its increasing array of rationalized business regulations on disadvantaged youth and adults. The World Bank and other influential development organizations have been criticized in the past for romanticizing the informal economy in the context of neoliberal reforms—as Elyachar (2005) rightly points out, the poor's "talent for self-help" should not be used as an excuse to leave disadvantaged populations on their own, euphemistically labeling them entrepreneurs when in reality they produce little more than "survival itself" (p. 9). Some schools of thought have advocated for the formalization of these businesses as a way to boost their productivity and growth (see, e.g., World Bank, 2011). But doing away with the informal economy is not, in itself, the answer to this critique. After all, the flexibility offered by an unregulated informal economy is important to those who have little capital at their disposal. This study shows that the push to formalize every aspect of economic activity—making every self-employed person and microenterprise registered, visible, organized, and regulated—can shut out hardworking and self-reliant young people from many opportunities to earn a livelihood and even from the very possibility of going to school and bettering their life chances.

It is not the purpose of this study to critique the post-developmental desire for an orderly and regulated economic environment. There are significant advantages to a strong regulatory regime in terms of consumer safety, labor protections, and the state's ability to finance important development goals. But there could be ways to maintain these key goals while reducing the burden of regulations on the poor.

To begin with, the Rwandan government could greatly reduce or eliminate start-up taxes and fees for at least the first year of business operation. Mandatory local monthly fees that become payable after obtaining a business license—for security, sanitation, local political parties, local fund-raising efforts (e.g., school construction), and special events—add up to a significant amount (Abbott, 2010; Education Development Center, 2013). A larger-scale study could be carried out to determine the start-up and running costs that Rwanda's current regulations and fees pose for businesses—from the national level down to the neighborhood, including the transport required to visit government offices and other incidental costs—to determine whether, indeed, these regulations add up to an insurmountable barrier for the poor and to study what adjustments could be made. Businesses could still be required to register, for example, but rather than having to pay start-up fees and taxes, the first year's registration and licensing could be linked to business support services, such as invitations to trainings and events at the Business Development Centers established in each of Rwanda's districts—places that many young Rwandans currently feel are beyond their reach in terms of social status and importance. Whatever tax revenue is lost through this change could surely be made up for in the increased number and effectiveness of the businesses that would be established, which would also begin paying taxes and fees once they actually start to earn a profit.

Another issue to examine in greater detail is the requirement of having a fixed and formal place of business. Mobile and roadside businesses can contribute to sanitation and traffic safety problems, and are perceived as unlikely to grow into formal enterprises (Mitullah, 2003). But it is equally true that many people who are willing to work, especially in a country like Rwanda, cannot afford to rent a place of business outside their homes. Rwanda has also recently instituted regulations in construction that have increased the costs of housing and business site rental across the board (Sommers, 2012). While the reasons for these regulations are good ones —making sure that people live and work in safe and durable buildings—it is important to consider and try to mitigate the perhaps unintended difficulties that these efforts have posed, especially for the poor. Furthermore, some of the new formally established market and other business locations are unsustainable for entrepreneurs because they are poorly sited for attracting a clientele. The Rwandan government could, therefore, study the possibility of encouraging home-based businesses, allowing registered mobile and roadside trading in certain areas with less intense traffic or under certain conditions in high-traffic zones, and making available some very small and low-rent spaces in busy commercial areas, and perhaps giving priority to certain disadvantaged groups such as youth heads of households, single mothers, and the disabled.

Rwanda's post-developmental goal of cultivating entrepreneurial self-reliance while keeping it under strict regulation and controls currently seems to be contradictory—at least for Rwanda's most disadvantaged youth. But this is not a foregone conclusion. It is possible to make policy adjustments with these challenges in mind, to help young entrepreneurs of all socioeconomic classes realize their goals.

Youth Livelihoods and the Post-Developmental State

Beyond Rwanda's particular entrepreneurship policies, this book represents an inquiry into the implications of the post-developmental style of governance for developing countries, broadly illustrating the internal tensions and paradoxes arising from the competing priorities of promoting creativity, credentials, and controls. To conclude this exploration, I would like to emphasize again what I consider the most significant paradox highlighted in this book:

post-developmental styles of governance can have unintended adverse effects on the most disadvantaged, despite their progressive developmental goals.

In her research on post-developmental states in East and Southeast Asia, Aihwa Ong (2006) called attention to the ways in which these governments were increasingly treating particular populations of their citizens differently, in accordance with their actual or potential connections to global circuits of capital. While the elite received special favors and freedom from the burden of certain regulations, low-skilled and disadvantaged populations were subject to much more extensive regimes of disciplinary and regulatory technologies. This differential treatment, Ong argued, effectively retained the poor in their lower socioeconomic positions.

Rwanda is not Singapore; it does not share the same developmental state history and its political and economic realities are unique. But as Rwanda and other developing countries experiment with applying post-developmental strategies to their own contexts, they must be prepared for the possibility of transferring both the beneficial and the harmful features of the post-developmental approach. In particular, this research has shown that post-developmental state strategies may result in increased inequalities not only through the application of differentiated regulations but also as a result of the way in which the same regulations, applied evenly across the board, can have differential effects on different populations. The very post-developmental regulations that are intended to promote economic growth and national self-sufficiency can actually block off a disadvantaged population's chances for advancement, by raising the cost of benefiting from low-capital economic opportunities. This risks creating ever-rising inequality, as fewer and fewer poor can find a way to break out of their inherited economic conditions.

In Rwanda's case, I do not believe that the government intends there to be differential treatment of particular populations, and certainly there is no wish for the poor to remain poor. Numerous ambitious policies and programs—universal schooling, scholarships for the disadvantaged, the Vision Umurenge program, and other examples—testify to the government's ambition that all Rwandans benefit from economic development.

Given these many positive efforts to improve the circumstances of disadvantaged youth in Rwanda, this research should serve as a helpful insight into the perspectives and experiences of young Rwandan entrepreneurs, and of the obstacles that stand in their way. Many young Rwandans in this study did not seem very entrepreneurial—they were content to just wait for the next year of school, as long as they had a reasonable assurance that they would be able to attend. But there were a number of disadvantaged students who had managed to advance their schooling from year to year, beyond their equally pressing concerns with basic survival, precisely because they put their entrepreneurial talents to use. What will happen to these sorts of Rwandan youth, as it becomes harder and harder to start an informal business with just a little capital? This is an opportune time for the Rwandan government to think about how to extend a partnership toward these young people—expecting them to abide by the regulations that are important to the Rwandan state but simultaneously making it truly possible for them to get a real working start in life. It is not just new knowledge and attitudes that these students need—they also need resources and the conditions that will make it possible for them to put those resources to use as they strive for a better future.

As Rwanda's entrepreneurship education policy enters its eighth year of implementation, further processes of complex social negotiation and learning, and the ongoing transformations of policy and practice they imply, are surely on the horizon. Like Rwanda's rich and varied topographic landscape, the sociocultural fields of education and livelihoods are intricately patterned and constantly evolving. Together, as policy makers, practitioners, teachers, and—not least—students and tomorrow's graduates plan for an ever-better future, education will continue serving as a context for questioning and improving social realities. The processes of social learning illuminated in this book, however unpredictable and unintended their outcomes may seem at the time, capture this generative quality and enduring hope, for Rwanda and beyond.

Notes

Chapter 1

1. From a focus group discussion with female Senior 3 students in School A, August 30, 2010. Students were divided by gender for all focus-group discussions to increase the likelihood that they would express themselves freely.

2. Some authors use the less-nuanced label "authoritarian state capitalism" (see, for example, Birdsall & Fukuyama, 2011a), or refer to a contemporary form of "authoritarian high modernism" (see, for example, C. Newbury, 2011).

3. With the more recent economic downturn in both of these countries, this story may yet change again; though of course China remains among the fastest-growing and largest economies in the world.

4. The outlook for Singapore is not uniformly positive (see, for example, Singapore at 50, 2015).

5. Some academics have disputed this "culture of obedience" (Collins, 1998).

6. This contrasting collection of adjectives comes from close observation of Rwandan public discourse and the conditions of social life; these are claims that I develop throughout this book. As I note here, however, one must keep in mind that public discourse is not the same in all settings, even in a single national society. The adjective *conforming*, for example, certainly does not apply to Rwandan public discourse regarding high-technology entrepreneurship, which is openly lauded as innovative and original. It may, however, apply to the subtle messages that lower-capital entrepreneurs, especially in rural areas and small towns, receive about what constitutes an appropriate and "real" business. I focus in greater depth on the socioeconomic class dimensions of post-developmental approaches to entrepreneurship in Part IV and the Conclusion of this book.

7. It should be noted that Rwanda's entrepreneurship curriculum was subsequently revised in 2014, as part of a national curriculum revision process for all subjects and all levels of education (see Honeyman & Rutiyomba, 2015).

8. At any given time during the year, classroom observations included up to 469 students, all of whom signed consent forms. The beginning-of-year questionnaire reached 429 students, most of whom participated in the midyear focus-group discussions, whereas only 388 took the end-of-year questionnaire, as a result of attendance fluctuations and school dropouts. To triangulate the ethnographic observations of students' attitudes and

practices that are the focus of this book, the questionnaire drew on methods used in both the psychological (see, for example, Athayde, 2009; Rasheed, 2000; Robinson, Stimpson, Huefner, & Hunt, 1991; Shariff & Saud, 2009) and sociological (see, for example, Davis, 2006; Levie & Autio, 2008; Organisation for Economic Cooperation and Development, OECD, 2009; Reynolds et al., 2005; Suddle, Beugelsdijk, & Wennekers, 2007) traditions of research on entrepreneurship, using Likert-type items with repeated measures. In this book, only a few of the statistical results have been explicitly provided, although the data informed and refined many of the qualitative interpretations given here.

9. At the end of the 2010 school year, 10 students were chosen at random from each classroom included in this research, for a total of 110 students. During the period between graduation and six months after graduation, we were able to contact 98 of these 110 students, including visiting two-thirds of them in their own homes (the other cases involved in-depth interviews by telephone only); all graduates were contacted two to three times each within the six-month period. For a follow-up study three years after graduation, we were able to contact 67 of these graduates, some of whom we had not been able to reach in the initial round. In total, 101 individuals were included in the tracer study.

10. A summary of research findings and policy recommendations was shared with the Ministry of Education; the Rwanda Education Board's Department of Curricula, Materials Production, and Distribution (formerly the National Curriculum Development Centre); the Ministry of Trade and Industry, and the City of Kigali's Vice-Mayor in charge of social affairs.

Chapter 2

1. From an interview available on YouTube (Fairbanks, 2007).

2. This was later reduced to six periods per week.

3. From a personal interview on July 30, 2008. As a general rule, names and identifying information are not cited in this book, except in the case of quotations from published documents.

4. *Jua kali* is another term for Kenya's informal enterprises, many of which work under the "fierce sun" (*jua kali*) rather than in established shops and factories. For more information, see King (1996).

5. From a personal interview on June 27, 2008.

6. From a personal interview with a UNIDO official on June 29, 2011.

7. Notably, the UN-funded Project for the Promotion of Rural Small and Micro Enterprises (PPPMER) and the Center for Support to Small and Medium Enterprises in Rwanda (CAPMER), the German government–supported Compétences Entrepreneuriales dans les Écoles Techniques (CEdET); and the World Bank's Competitiveness and Enterprise Development Project (CEDP).

8. The first phase of this research, in 2008, identified eight institutions as playing major roles in the promotion of entrepreneurship education in Rwanda: three internationally linked organizations: PPPMER, UNIDO, and the bilateral German Technical Cooperation Agency (GTZ); two Rwandan civil society institutions, CAPMER and Rwanda's

Private Sector Federation (PSF); and three Rwandan government institutions, the Ministry of Trade and Industry (MINICOM), the Ministry of Education (MINEDUC), and its semi-autonomous subagency, the National Curriculum Development Centre (NCDC). The discussion in this section is based on interviews with one or more representatives from each of these institutions.

9. From a personal interview at the Rwandan Private Sector Federation, June 18, 2008.

10. Colonial and church authorities were, however, strongly concerned by the 1950s about the "half-educated" youth who had completed only primary school. These had few formal job prospects, but they also "no longer adapt[ed] easily to traditional life" (Erny, 2001, p. 224).

11. This is my own summary of data from the recent national EICV3 study (Integrated Household Living Conditions Survey, or in the original French, Enquête Intégrale sur les Conditions de Vie des Ménages), drawn from a report focusing specifically on youth issues. This figure takes into account a recalculation due to an apparent error in the fifth line of the cited table, where it says that only 1 percent of this age group worked twenty-one to twenty five hours per week. Comparing this figure with the adjacent figures, which are all between 10 percent and 12 percent, and calculating the total for the column, which adds up to 90 percent, rather than 100 percent as it should, I assume that the figure in question is actually supposed to read 11 percent and not 1 percent, such that the total for the column is now 100 percent.

12. From a personal interview with a UNIDO official, June 29, 2011.

13. One case in point is that of Robert Nelson, a professor of business at the University of Illinois in the United States, who participated in the East-West Center's workshop in the Philippines. As a result of that workshop, Nelson went on to make a presentation on entrepreneurship education at an international conference on business development at which ILO representatives were present, and thereafter became a key consultant in the ILO's efforts to design entrepreneurship course materials for developing countries (Nelson, 1977, 1997). Specific details on these professional connections come from a personal email communication with Nelson on August 7, 2008.

14. There are, however, other human priorities, such as progress in moral capabilities, which do not fit easily within the metaphor of capital.

15. These terms ignored the fact that Rwanda has no "tribes" as such, and that the 1994 violence—far from being a spontaneous eruption of primitive warfare—was carefully organized and orchestrated by the then-governing regime.

16. Something that is like doxa, but is recognized enough to be open to questioning, may rather be called orthodoxy. Neoliberal tenets have taken the form of doxa in certain times and contexts, and orthodoxy in others. See the discussion of the multiplicity of social structures later in this chapter.

17. Individuals who belong to roughly the same constellation of social groups—often because of their association with a larger or more powerfully significant social grouping, such as socioeconomic class—may develop markedly similar dispositions (Bourdieu, 1972,

p. 85). However, there is always room for internal diversity and for an individual's different dispositional repertoires to be "played up" in distinct social settings, opening up new spaces for learning and negotiation among other members of the community of practice. Because individuals belong to multiple communities of practice simultaneously, some of which may emphasize conflicting presuppositions and dispositions, a person may not agree with the standards of every community he or she belongs to, and may even think or behave contrary to them. Individuals value their association with particular communities to different degrees, just as the dynamics of particular communities exercise different degrees of power to enforce conformity or compliance among their members. Individuals can perceive differences between the *doxa* and *dispositions* of one community they belong to and those of another, and may even deliberately provoke confrontation and/or interchange as a result. Even more common are the inevitable inadvertent crossovers of practice and perspective among different communities.

18. This model of negotiated social learning suggests that true *doxa*, in the strict sense of a completely pre-reflexive set of assumptions that is so hegemonic as to be effectively invisible, may be extremely rare or even nonexistent. Due to individuals' membership in multiple communities of practice, exposure to alternate points of view is a constant possibility. Whenever those social interactions open up a space for questioning certain fundamental assumptions, we are looking at a case of *orthodoxy* rather than *doxa*. However, whether certain presuppositions represent doxa or orthodoxy is an empirical question to be explored within specific social fields and communities of practice. For simplicity, I therefore use the term *doxa* throughout this book to refer to a range of deeply held commitments, some of them more available for conscious reflection to particular actors than others.

Chapter 3

1. From day 1 of the Training of Trainers event in the O-level entrepreneurship curriculum, Rwandan National Curriculum Development Centre, April 22, 2009. This presentation was in fact made during an evaluation, together with teachers, of the already-complete O-level curriculum. However, it highlights similar ideas regarding active pedagogy that were introduced to the O-level curriculum developers from the beginning of the process.

2. From an interview on July 18, 2008, at the NCDC offices.

3. From an interview on July 18, 2008, at the NCDC offices.

4. Centre d'Appui aux Petits et Moyens Entreprises au Rwanda (Center for Support to Small and Medium-Sized Enterprises in Rwanda), a Rwandan civil society organization that began as a joint effort of the Rwandan government, the UN Industrial Development Organization (UNIDO), and the Netherlands Development Organization (SNV).

5. From an interview on July 18, 2008, at the NCDC offices.

6. This particular quote is from an interview on January 18, 2012, at the NCDC offices in which I asked for clarification of an explanation that had originally been given to me on July 18, 2008. The information is the same, although I used this quote because it is a clearer explanation.

7. From observations during the O-level curriculum development seminar at the NCDC, July 18, 2008.

8. From observations during the O-level curriculum development seminar on July 24, 2008.

9. From observations during the O-level curriculum development seminar on July 31, 2008.

10. From a discussion about revising the O-level syllabus during the "Training of Trainers" seminar at the NCDC, April 22, 2009.

11. Although it is always possible that some had small-scale business activities on the side of their salaried professions, the fact that they did not mention these activities (if they held them) indicates that they may not have seen them as professionally relevant to the context.

12. Specifically, the Nyiginya kingdom encompassed most of central, western, and southern Rwanda, while eastern and northern Rwanda still retained some independence and difference in their social structures.

13. The plural is *amatorero*; for ease of understanding, I use only the singular form here.

14. For much of this discussion, I draw on the extensive sources cited by the French scholar Pierre Erny (2001, 2003, 2005) in a trilogy of books that represents the most comprehensive study currently available on the history of education in Rwanda. Erny is an emeritus professor of ethnology at the University Marc Bloch of Strasbourg, France.

15. During the period under German rule, from 1897 to World War I, only one small government school had been established (Erny, 2001, p. 17). During World War I, Belgium occupied the colony but did little to change its schooling system, only executing some modest plans that had been laid by the Germans for establishing a few more small schools for the sons of chiefs. By the time Belgium's rule was officially sanctioned by a 1923 League of Nations mandate, there were fewer than one thousand students enrolled in all government-sponsored primary and secondary schools in the territories of Rwanda and Urundi combined (Jesse Jones, 1923, pp. 290–291). These minor institutions were focused on training the existing elite and did not impose uniformity of structure or methods on the hundreds of mission schools that continued to serve the general population.

16. Many other considerations of ethnic, regional, and personal favoritism also apparently entered into the decision making; however, these were less under the control of students than their performance on examinations, which as a result were given great importance—no matter to what degree they actually determined placement results.

17. The Rwandan government has very recently instituted a few key policies that are transforming this route to higher education—these are discussed in greater detail in the Conclusion.

18. Except for the visit of two NCDC staff to Uganda mentioned in the previous chapter, which included a brief review of Uganda's curriculum.

19. The Rwandan and KAB syllabi include recommendations as to the amount of time to be spent on each topic. For the Ugandan curriculum, I counted each subtopic as representing roughly the same amount of course time, an assumption that was backed up with reference to the detailed content and activities in the Ugandan *Instructional Manuals*. Because the Rwandan O-level curriculum was originally conceived of as a complete course (i.e., there were originally no government plans to teach entrepreneurship at any other level of education, so the NCDC attempted to cover all the topics it considered relevant within these three years), here I compare the O-level syllabus to the full curriculum of each of the other programs mentioned (which are themselves of varying duration). The conclusions of this analysis would be quite different if the A-level course, which was only decided on at a later time, were included here, a point that I return to in Chapter 4.

20. One class period is equal to forty minutes.

21. Creativity is mentioned in numerous lessons in the KAB curriculum, where it is sometimes an explicit focus of attention. Here I count those KAB lessons in which creativity is most prominently featured—nineteen hours of KAB's course, which is shorter overall than Rwanda's. There are other lessons, however, in which it is also likely to be mentioned as part of the discussion prompted by related topics.

22. From a copy of the Francophone examination for the first term, 2010, shown to me in a Kicukiro District school, Kigali.

Chapter 4

1. From a discussion about revising the O-level syllabus during a Training of Trainers seminar at the NCDC, April 22, 2009.

2. A Training of Trainers in the O-level entrepreneurship curriculum, at the Rwandan National Curriculum Development Centre, beginning on April 22, 2009. For the NCDC, this training had a dual purpose—to help the participants become "expert" enough in the O-level entrepreneurship course to become trainers of other teachers at some unspecified future date and to provide the NCDC with some suggested improvements to the course.

3. From Day 1 of the Training of Trainers in the O-level entrepreneurship curriculum, Rwandan National Curriculum Development Centre, April 22, 2009. The speakers are numbered here to indicate that the comments come from different individuals.

4. From "Hodder Education: Market Leading Publisher for Schools and Colleges," http://www.hoddereducation.co.uk/About-Us.aspx.

5. From a photocopy of the textbook evaluation "Training Plan" and materials for June 3–5, 2009, provided by an NCDC participant in the training.

6. From a discussion in the NCDC offices, June 7, 2009.

7. Many have cited the move as partly politically motivated, signaling a shift away from France during a time of diplomatic crisis and a move toward Britain during Rwanda's application to become a member of the Commonwealth (McGreal, 2008). Some criticized the rapid transition (Steflja, 2012), while others have pointed out the numerous potential benefits, including the widespread business use of English in the region (Ntagungira, 2011).

8. Although Rwanda has been officially trilingual (Kinyarwanda, French, English) since the 1994 genocide, and the National University of Rwanda required students to speak both English and French, in practice most of those who had been educated primarily in Rwanda spoke French and were less confident in English.

9. From a personal interview with a UNIDO official in downtown Kigali, June 29, 2011.

10. From Day 2 of the Training of Trainers in the O-level entrepreneurship curriculum, Rwandan National Curriculum Development Centre, April 23, 2009.

11. From Day 3 of the Training of Trainers in the O-level entrepreneurship curriculum, Rwandan National Curriculum Development Centre, April 24, 2009.

12. From Day 3 of the Training of Trainers in the O-level entrepreneurship curriculum, Rwandan National Curriculum Development Centre, April 24, 2009.

13. Many of these requirements have since changed or been streamlined. See Chapter 8 for a discussion of current Rwandan business regulations.

14. From Day 3 of the Training of Trainers in the O-level entrepreneurship curriculum, Rwandan National Curriculum Development Centre, April 24, 2009.

15. The speakers are numbered here to indicate that the comments come from different individuals.

16. From Day 4 of the Training of Trainers in the O-level entrepreneurship curriculum, Rwandan National Curriculum Development Centre, April 25, 2009.

17. From Day 4 of the Training of Trainers in the O-level entrepreneurship curriculum, Rwandan National Curriculum Development Centre, April 25, 2009.

18. From an email communication to the NCDC staff, May 20, 2009.

19. From the A-level curriculum development seminar notes, August 10, 2009.

20. From the A-level curriculum development seminar notes, August 10, 2009. Later in the morning on that first day, the NCDC leader introduced me as an external researcher presumably with some expertise in entrepreneurship and curriculum (though I had claimed neither), to make a presentation on how to educate "someone who is able to start an enterprise [rather than] someone who can just work within one." In my presentation, I encouraged discussion on the issue of whether entrepreneurship education should be focused only on individual self-benefit or take the perspective of the surrounding community into account. I also tried to help participants draw a distinction between passive mastery of information and the development of the more complex capabilities that entrepreneurs might need to put into practice. I described some pedagogical alternatives to simply delivering notes for memorization and provided Internet links to six other entrepreneurship programs used in other countries. In this way, I became yet another one of the new members of the community of practice, bringing my own distinctive background and presuppositions to the conversation. A number of the questions I raised, in turn, became part of the group's process of negotiating a new way of thinking about the entrepreneurship curriculum. Later in this chapter I provide more information about a different aspect of the A-level curriculum development process I was more centrally involved in.

21. From the A-level curriculum development seminar notes, August 12, 2009.

22. From the A-level curriculum development seminar notes, August 12, 2009.

23. One class period is equal to forty minutes.

24. From the A-level curriculum development seminar notes, August 13, 2009.

25. These were not always consecutive days, since when the academic calendar began most of the consultants (teachers and professors) could not be available for weeklong meetings. The syllabus was thus developed over a series of meetings, from August to November 2009.

26. This excerpt comes from a draft document generated on Day 12 of the curriculum development seminar, in September 2009.

27. From a meeting at the NCDC offices, October 28, 2009.

28. From a suggested draft I developed October 28, 2009 and presented on November 1, 2009.

29. As mentioned, this suggestion was matched by the interest—though unconnected—of a team of Harvard MBA students in developing case studies.

30. From the A-level curriculum development seminar notes, November 1, 2009.

31. From the A-level curriculum development seminar notes, November 5, 2009.

32. From the A-level curriculum development seminar notes, November 4, 2009.

33. From Senior 4, Theme 2: Identification and generation of business ideas and opportunities.

34. From Senior 4, Theme 3: Business organization and management.

35. From Senior 6, Theme 2: Entrepreneurship and Socioeconomic development.

36. Including the International Labour Organization's materials *Know About Business*, as well as the entrepreneurship curricula from Uganda and Angola.

37. Such an educationally class-based outcome in Rwanda, if it came about, might be entirely consistent with post-developmental approaches to governance. Writing in the context of East and Southeast Asia, Ong (2006) has argued that differential treatment of subpopulations is in fact a signal strategy of post-developmental states, as "market-driven logic induces the coordination of political policies with the corporate interests, so that developmental decisions favor the fragmentation of the national space into various non-contiguous zones, and promote the differential regulation of populations who can be connected to or disconnected from global circuits of capital" (p. 77). Among other examples of this dynamic, "the middle-class citizenry whose credentials, skills, and overall well-being have been so critical to attracting foreign capital" may receive special training and treatment (Baildon, 2009, p. 66). It is A-level and university graduates, one might claim, who are the middle-class citizens most crucially targeted by Rwanda's vision of attracting international investment in the context of state-led development. In contrast, the state might prefer to maintain those who do not go on to A-levels in a state of obedient, and not necessarily creatively-aspiring, self-reliance. Under this interpretation, the outcome of Rwanda's entrepreneurship curriculum could be described as a "successful failure" (Kendall, 2007; Varenne & McDermott, 1998), in which the result of a policy—though not what

was explicitly intended—nonetheless reflects the underlying interests of powerful actors. However, and as I note in the main body of the chapter, the Rwandan government quickly implemented some changes to the education system—in particular, a principle of universal access to twelve years of basic schooling—that will arguably prevent such a nakedly class-based outcome from coming about.

38. Not all students studying in the 12-year basic education system will be oriented to A-levels; a significant percentage will instead go to technical and vocational education and training (TVET) institutions for upper secondary school. However, entrepreneurship education is also included in the TVET institutions, and arguably in an even more purely neoliberal-influenced form.

Chapter 5

1. From one of the first classroom observations at School A (Classroom A01), March 9, 2010.

2. A copy of the O-level syllabus was available in English on the National Curriculum Development Centre's website by January 2009, but judging from the stream of teachers who visited the NCDC offices to ask for a copy in person, a significant number of teachers were not aware of that fact or did not have the means to access it. The more detailed teachers' guides and student textbooks would not be distributed to schools until about midway through the year.

3. At the time of this research, the academic year in Rwanda ran approximately from January to October of each calendar year, although school sometimes started closer to February.

4. The sample included only Senior 3 and Senior 6 classrooms because of the interest in following students after graduation from a major cycle of schooling (O-level and A-level, respectively). Part IV of the book presents the results of that graduate tracer study.

5. According to 2008 examinations data provided to me by the Rwandan National Examinations Council.

6. Rwanda has a long tradition of public (state-supported) boarding schools, especially at the secondary level, in which students could be sent anywhere in the country for secondary studies on the basis of their examination scores in Primary 6 and Senior 3. Students may also be sent to stay with members of their extended family in order to be nearer the school their parents wish them to attend.

7. This data was gathered through a survey of participating students.

8. There were 473 students in these eleven classrooms, 469 of whom agreed to participate in the research. 58 percent of these participants were male, 42 percent female; with an average age of 17 in Senior 3 and 20 in Senior 6. Because this was still a period of transition for Rwanda's new language of instruction policy, roughly half of the classrooms were still studying in French, while the other half used primarily English.

9. The Senior 6 auto mechanics class in School C did not study the same entrepreneurship curriculum as was taught in the ordinary academic sections. Although we attempted

to observe their course Organization of Enterprises, which is mainly concerned with how to organize and operate a mechanics workshop, the teacher was never present during any of our visits to the classroom.

10. Schools have been assigned letter designations for this book.

11. All names given in this book are pseudonyms.

12. In all classroom vignettes, *T* signifies an entrepreneurship teacher, in this case Jacques from School A. *SS* signifies many students speaking at once. See the Technical Notes for more information on the abbreviations used in vignettes.

13. English and French are, of course, not the first languages of most teachers or students in Rwanda. Here, I reproduce whenever possible what was actually said in the classroom, even if there were errors. At other times, teachers and students switched to Kinyarwanda, in which case I have translated their comments back into English. To make reading easier, I do not always indicate which language was originally spoken.

14. Some of the gendered references in teachers' speech and notes come from the translation into English, which among other things does not have a gender-neutral pronoun like *on* in French. However, in other cases, the curricular materials and the teachers definitely represented certain kinds of work as more feminine or masculine than others. Though this is not a focus of my research, it could be taken up as a topic for further examination in reference to the entrepreneurship course and other youth employment policies. In general, however, and as Stambach (2000) has also described in the Tanzanian context, teaching in Rwanda seems, at least outwardly, quite gender neutral—teachers do not noticeably favor calling on girls or boys, and I never saw a girl's gender used in any way to belittle her capacity.

15. This vignette is from a class on Monday, March 15, 2010, in Classroom A02.

16. Schools certainly had textbooks—often a fine collection of them. However, they were stored in school stockrooms or libraries and virtually never made an appearance inside classrooms.

17. S(m) indicates a male student; S(f) a female student.

18. This vignette is from a class on Thursday, May 20, 2010, in Classroom B03.

19. In this and other places, I attempt to give a sense of the kinds of language and pronunciation errors students were making in French, since this seemed to be an important issue for the teacher.

20. This vignette is from a class on Friday, May 7, 2010, in Classroom E10.

21. MINEDUC had provided every public school with a set of about twenty-five entrepreneurship textbooks for each year in O-level, plus the teachers' guides. For A-level, teachers had only the syllabus and whatever supplementary materials they or their schools had been able to find, often books published in Uganda. Teachers constantly complained about the lack of materials, but even those who had access to them did not use them in class (this was true across the academic curriculum, not only in entrepreneurship). They seemed to feel that "enough" books meant one book per student, to take home for later examination review. They simply did not see textbooks as tools for use during class time,

as sources of reference reading, or as guides on the types of independent assignments and activities they could give to students.

22. Indeed, the same general observations I have recorded here, about entrepreneurship teacher practice in Rwandan schools, have been confirmed in two other recent Rwandan studies, in this case in the areas of information and communications technology (ICT) and mathematics teaching (Rubagiza et al., 2011; Uworwabayeho, 2009).

23. It is important to recall that even by the 2010 school year, teachers and students were still not extensively aware of the changes proposed in the national examinations approach, for three reasons. First, teachers tended to use old examinations papers to guide their teaching and may not have yet bothered to look for copies from 2008, the first year the reforms were implemented on a national level. Second, the entrepreneurship course itself, of course, had not been examined yet, so teachers had to base their assumptions about how it would be examined on their experiences from other courses. Third, the district-level examinations that students did take in entrepreneurship each trimester were in effect still quite focused on terminology and definitions.

24. Actual questions from the second trimester exam for Senior 3 entrepreneurship, as copied during observations at one of the schools in this research.

Chapter 6

1. As previously noted, excerpts of classroom dialogue employ the following short hand references: T refers to the entrepreneurship teacher in the featured school or classroom. $S(f)$ refers to a female student, $S(m)$ to a male student, and SS to a number of students speaking together.

2. From an observation in Classroom A01, Thursday, September 2, 2010.

3. According to data from the Global Entrepreneurship Monitor, an international study that also asks about intended business start-up within a three-year time frame (Global Entrepreneurship Research Association, 2009). This reported global average is based on my own analysis of the GEM 2008 individual-level data (the most recent year available at time of writing) in relation to the 16–25 age group (chosen to match the major age range of the students in this study). This survey covered a total of 1,003,910 people from the following countries: Angola, Argentina, Australia, Austria, Belgium, Bolivia, Bosnia and Herzegovina, Brazil, Canada, Chile, China, Colombia, Croatia, Czech Republic, Denmark, Ecuador, Egypt, Finland, France, Germany, Greece, Hong Kong, Hungary, Iceland, India, Indonesia, Iran, Ireland, Israel, Italy, Jamaica, Japan, Jordan, Kazakhstan, Korea, Latvia, Macedonia, Malaysia, Mexico, Netherlands, New Zealand, Norway, Peru, Philippines, Poland, Portugal, Puerto Rico, Romania, Russia, Serbia, Singapore, Slovenia, South Africa, Spain, Sweden, Switzerland, Taiwan, Thailand, Turkey, Uganda, United Kingdom, United Arab Emirates, United States, Uruguay, and Venezuela. The data is available at the following website: http://www.gemconsortium.org/data/sets.

4. The National Curriculum Development Centre had originally recommended that the new entrepreneurship course be examined in a progressive fashion, with each year's

graduates being examined only on the number of years of content that they had been exposed to. However, as a semiautonomous body, the National Examinations Council had the power to change that decision, reasoning that it only made sense to examine students when they had studied the full contents of the course (i.e., those who were in Senior 1 in 2009 and would be in Senior 3 in 2011, or those who were in Senior 4 in 2010 and would be in Senior 6 in 2012).

5. Even Classrooms D09 and E11, the least disciplined in this study, showed significantly more respect to the teachers of some of their more traditional academic subjects.

6. From observations in Classroom E10 on Friday, June 18, 2010.

7. From an observation in Classroom C05 on March 11, 2010.

8. There were two different entrepreneurship teachers in School C.

9. This lesson was originally intended for Senior 4, but as this was the first year these students were studying the course, they began with the Senior 4 material.

10. From an observation in Classroom C05 on March 18, 2010.

11. In most Rwandan schools, the students in each classroom choose or elect a head boy or head girl, formerly known as the *chef de classe* to represent them.

12. From an individual interview on August 25, 2010.

13. Now called the College of Education, part of the consolidated University of Rwanda.

14. From an individual interview on August 25, 2010.

15. From an observation in Classroom B03 on March 4, 2010.

16. From a personal discussion on July 8, 2010.

17. Rwanda's policy of Twelve Years Basic Education had not yet been announced this school year.

18. From an observation in Classroom D09 on March 16, 2010.

19. These data were calculated by taking the number of entrepreneurship classes Flora and I observed being taught in each given week and dividing by the number of entrepreneurship classes we had expected to see (according to each school's schedule). When only part of the time scheduled for entrepreneurship was given to another course, it is counted here as one lesson actually taught out of two possible. Periods of examinations and vacations (when no classes were taught) have been removed, as indicated by the longer lines in April and July where there are no registered data points.

20. We also carried out observations in an eleventh classroom, a Senior 6 auto mechanics class, for purposes of comparison—although no entrepreneurship course was implemented there.

21. These are pseudonyms, unique first names used in Rwanda that were assigned to each student quoted in this book. In this case, Adolphe was from School B, while Charity was from School E.

22. For a discussion of this social dynamic in Willis's (1977) study *Learning to Labor* (1977), see McGrew (2011).

Chapter 7

1. From a meeting with Senior 3 graduates at School B, in November 2010.

2. The Rwandan Labour Law of 2001 changed the minimum working age from eighteen to sixteen, specifying that a "less than sixteen years old child is not allowed to contract for employment in any company, even for apprenticeship" (Rwanda, 2001, art. 65).

3. Specifically, I employed stratified random sampling from within the eleven classrooms of students already selected for the study. Using the beginning-of-year questionnaire to differentiate between the students who stated they were interested in going into business in the short term and those who were not, I chose a proportional number of male and female students from each subgroup. The resulting sample was 43 percent female and 57 percent male, with 58 percent of the total saying they had plans to start a business within three years. All of the selected students gave their informed consent to participate in this last phase of the research.

4. Of the 110 students we originally selected, we were eventually able to reach 101 of them during the three-year period between graduation and the writing of this book. We conducted in-depth interviews (in person or by telephone) with ninety-six of these students by four months after graduation, and again made contact for two shorter updates with eighty three of them leading up to the end of the initial research period, at six months after graduation. Three years after graduation, we were able to reach sixty-seven of the original sample (including five whom we had not reached in the initial round of interviews) to produce an update for this book. The nine selected students we were never able to contact did not have valid phone numbers and their peers did not know where they lived or how to reach them after they left school.

5. The line defining entrepreneurial activity is blurry around self-employment and short-term jobs. Here, for example, I do not count as entrepreneurship one common form of short-term employment or self-employment—working as a mason's aid on a construction site for day wages.

6. Some, indeed, had started their entrepreneurial efforts long before, as part of an effort to pay for their school fees—this trend is addressed in detail later in the chapter.

7. The feeling that work is incompatible with their studies has a certain foundation in logistical facts. Under Rwanda's system of education, up until very recently most secondary school students studied in public boarding schools far from their homes, where their daily activities were extensively regulated. Even daytime-only students faced similar time constraints, often going to school in places far from their homes and walking or traveling by bus from one to three hours each way. This situation is now changing because of the national effort to expand access to schooling at institutions close to students' homes. Nevertheless, the notion of work being incompatible with studies seems to persist.

8. At the beginning and end of the year, students completed a full questionnaire including numerous questions about attitudes, activities, and plans. In the middle of the year, students were simply asked to write down their name and whether they were currently engaged in any kind of work.

9. See, for example, the Rwandan Office of the Ombudsman, in charge of anti-corruption activities in Rwanda (http://www.ombudsman.gov.rw) and the 2003 anti-corruption law, article 22, which states: "Any official of a private institution or his or her representative whose mission is connected with public interest, who will have taken a decision based on favoritism, nepotism or enmity shown with regard to a person seeking service, shall be sentenced to a term of imprisonment of between 2 and 5 years and a fine ranging from 50,000 Rwf to 1,000,000 Rwf" (Rwanda, 2003).

10. This is a very good starting salary for a Senior 6 graduate. All currency conversions given here are approximate, based on an exchange rate of 600 Rwandan francs (Rwf) to the US dollar, which was the rate in 2011 during the research. I have not given exact figures, but rather rounded to the nearest whole dollar, except in cases of very small amounts.

11. From an interview on March 1, 2011.

12. Other students, particularly girls, may have been involved in more perilous efforts to search for sponsorships through cross-generational sexual relationships. Rwanda's public health campaign *Sinigurisha!* ("I don't sell myself!") targets these widespread "sugar daddy" and "sugar mommy" relationships, which appear to widely spread gifts and school fees, as well as HIV and early pregnancy (Population Services International, PSI, 2010). Though the peculiarly entrepreneurial strategy of such a relationship did not figure in any of our interviews with graduates, many other unexpected forms of entrepreneurial "creativity" did emerge as central to students' efforts to earn a diploma.

13. See Chapter 5 for more details about the schools included in this research.

14. Despite Rwanda's strong progress in this area, a number of barriers still prevent Rwandan girls from achieving gender parity in education and the economy (A. Huggins & Randell, 2007). The gender dynamic was not a primary focus of this study, although there are a number of aspects of the collected data that could be further explored from this important perspective.

15. These categories are ideal types, obviously simplified from a more complex reality. Somewhere in a less determinate social location, for example, were the students with only a rural social network but better economic conditions than the rural majority, and the poor students who had guaranteed scholarships to finance their studies.

Chapter 8

1. From a follow-up interview with one of the original Senior 6 graduates from School E in December 2013, three years after graduation.

2. It is often argued that Rwanda's population groups of Hutu, Tutsi, and Twa do not strictly meet the definition of ethnicities.

3. From a personal interview at the Ministry of Education, July 30, 2008.

4. This study included a questionnaire administered to students at the beginning and end of the 2010 school year, drawing on methods used in both the psychological (see, e.g., Athayde, 2009; Rasheed, 2000; Robinson, Stimpson, Huefner, & Hunt, 1991; Shariff & Saud, 2009) and the sociological (see, e.g., Davis, 2006; Levie & Autio, 2008; Organisation for Eco-

nomic Co-operation and Development, 2009; Reynolds et al., 2005; Suddle, Beugelsdijk, & Wennekers, 2007) traditions of research on entrepreneurship, using Likert-type items with repeated measures. In addition, the questionnaire also included some open-ended and multiple-choice items specifically related to the Rwandan context. Finally, the questionnaire also provided certain demographic data regarding the gender, age, and socioeconomic distribution of the participating students. The results of these questionnaires have been summarized in a policy briefing paper distributed to Rwandan government agencies. In this book, only a few of the statistical results have been explicitly provided, although the data informed and refined many of the qualitative interpretations given here and in earlier chapters.

5. As there was little difference in students' answers from the beginning to the end of the year, here I use only the data from the end-of-year questionnaires as representative of their attitudes after completing a full year of the course.

6. Using analysis of variance (ANOVA) tests of differences between group means and a statistical significance threshold of 0.10. Interestingly, socioeconomic status was not a statistically significant factor in determining attitudes about taxation (nor were sex, age, or school level, also measured here). Only those students with friends who had their own business activities were statistically more likely to think that taxes made it difficult for new businesses to survive.

7. From a focus group discussion with Senior 6 boys at School C, May 26, 2010.

8. Fee setting has been decentralized, within certain limits, and actual rates vary from place to place (Bumbakare, 2009, as cited in Abbott, 2010).

9. Again, in this context, I define entrepreneurship as any activity in which the graduate was directly responsible for investing capital and attracting a clientele to earn an income. From school time through to six months after graduation, the rates of entrepreneurship experience were 15 percent for Senior 3 graduates and 19 percent for Senior 6 graduates. For the time period from six months after graduation to three years after graduation, the entrepreneurship rates of these two groups of graduates were 19 percent and 31 percent, respectively. Overall, 19 percent of Senior 3 graduates and 36 percent of Senior 6 graduates had initiated at least one entrepreneurial activity, from the time when they were still students up to three years after graduation. These figures include some data extrapolations for sixteen individuals who had continued to be full-time students up to the end of this study, and for whom we were unable to collect a complete update at three years after graduation because they were still in school or traveling. To avoid skewing the overall percentages, I applied to them the same rates of entrepreneurial activity as their same-age peers who had also continued their studies.

10. An *umudugudu* is an administrative unit of about fifty to two hundred households that is often translated as "village" in English but can also be equivalent to a "neighborhood" depending on the setting. I have been unable to determine whether what Didier's father was referring to is actually a national policy requirement or simply a decision made by local leaders. However, it echoes a number of similar initiatives, including the One Vil-

lage One Product scheme, which encourages each village to "develop and market a sin-gular product in a single village" (Rwanda, 2011), and the Crop Intensification Program, which requires farmers to consolidate a portion of their lands to intensify production of one staple food crop that is most suited to local growing conditions (Ministry of Agricul-ture and Animal Resources, 2012).

11. This business name, like all of the others in this research, is a pseudonym.

12. A workforce-readiness training program sponsored by the US Agency for Interna-tional Development and run by the Education Development Center through numerous local partners.

13. With respect to corruption, students often talked about having to pay some money to get a job, or not even being able to get a foot in the door without a relative or friend already inside to put in a word for them. Some also mentioned bosses who hired attractive girls in exchange for an ongoing relationship of sexual favors.

14. From a focus group discussion in 2010.

15. From a focus group discussion in 2010.

16. From follow-up interviews at the end of 2013.

17. From follow-up interviews at the end of 2013.

18. Though there were students in every school who made this argument, it was more common among Senior 6 than Senior 3 students. Senior 3 students also often asked for financial assistance from the government—but in their case, it was most often so that they could complete their secondary studies, again confirming the argument made in Chapter 7.

Conclusion

1. Now the Curriculum and Materials Production and Distribution Department, part of the Rwanda Education Board.

2. A summary of research findings and policy recommendations (Honeyman, 2013) was also shared with the Ministry of Education; the Rwanda Education Board's Depart-ment of Curricula, Materials Production, and Distribution; the Ministry of Trade and Industry, and the City of Kigali Vice-Mayor in charge of social affairs. Recipients of the research summary were provided with several copies and invited to share the document with any other interested individuals and institutions.

3. To my knowledge, with the exception of Rosen (2001), Freedman, Weinsten, Mur-phy, and Longman (2008), and Anderson-Levitt and Ntal-I'Mbirwa (2001), most ethno-graphic studies on curriculum development processes are unpublished presentations or dissertations (see, e.g., Arjona-Tseng, 1990; Janesick, 1980; Meaney, 2000; D. Meyer & Carlsen, 2001; Toepper, 1978).

4. This point has been amply argued in analyses of final curricular products (Anyon, 1980; Apple, 2004; Dreeben, 1968; Gatto, 2005; Giroux & Purpel, 1983; Jackson, 1968; Mar-golis, 2001; Snyder, 1971), but its dynamics have rarely if ever been demonstrated in the process of curriculum production itself, the focus of Part II of this book.

5. And now that the Ministry of Education has shifted toward a privatized model in which textbook production is outsourced to external consultants and companies, perhaps the Rwandan government should consider deliberately including people with such social histories on the review boards that will determine minimum quality standards.

6. From a personal email communication with a participant in the process, May 29, 2015.

7. However, the national examinations do continue to govern which students will be sent to the public and semipublic boarding schools around the country, institutions that are widely perceived to be of higher academic quality than the newly expanded local schools offering the cycle of basic education to those with lower scores. As a result, the Primary 6 and Senior 3 (O-level) examinations continue to be seen as crucial gatekeepers determining access to a quality education, especially for the Rwandan poor and middle class.

Technical Notes

Certain technical conventions are used throughout the book, as follows:

Rwf, franc	Rwandan franc: All currency conversions given here are approximate, based on an exchange rate of 600 Rwf to the US dollar ($), which was the rate in 2011 during the initial tracer study research.
O-level	Ordinary level of Rwanda's secondary education system, corresponding to Senior 1–3 (U.S. grades 7–9)
A-level	Advanced level of Rwanda's secondary education system, corresponding to Senior 4–6 (U.S. grades 10–12)
T	Teacher
S(f)	Female student
S(m)	Male student
SS	Multiple students speaking simultaneously
[*italicized text*]	Nonverbal actions that add meaning to the verbal quotation
[text]	Text in brackets has been substituted or introduced into the quotation
[...]	Certain text has been omitted from within a quotation. All cases of substitution or omission have been made with the objective of increasing the clarity of the quotation; I have been careful to retain the original meaning in every case.
...	A natural pause in speech
text—	Indicates that the speaker was interrupted or broke off midsentence.
Names	All personal and business names given in the main text of the book are pseudonyms.
Translations	All translations of spoken text and written materials originally in French or Kinyarwanda are the author's.

English to Kinyarwanda Translations

English	Kinyarwanda
controls, regulations	*umubwiriza*
creativity (lit. "to know how to create what is new")	*kumenya kurema gushya*
credential/diploma	*impamyabumenyi*
disorderly	*akajagari*
entrepreneur	*rwiyemezamirimo*
entrepreneurship (lit. "to create their own jobs")	*kwihangira imirimo*
government, the state (often used interchangeably)	*guverinoma, leta*
orderly (lit. "in line")	*ku murongo*

Kinyarwanda to English Translations

Kinyarwanda	English
abakarani (sing: *umukarani*)	market porters
akazi	job (stable connotation)
Akazi Kanoze	work readiness program (lit. "A Job Well Done")
amakuru; amakuru yawe?	news; what is your news?
birakomeye	difficult, hard
Hanga Umurimo	small business funding program (lit. "Create a Job")
ikarito	carton used to vend goods on the street
ikimina	a group savings and loan system, a tontine
ikiraka	job (temporary, irregular)
imihigo	government performance contracts
itorero (pl: *amatorero*)	education system (precolonial)
kwikura ubukene	to take yourself out of poverty
rwiyemezamirimo	entrepreneur
shebuya (also: *sebuja*)	patron, boss, employer
Sinigurisha	public health campaign (lit. "I Don't Sell Myself")
ubugabire	one basic form of patron-client relationship
umudugudu	administrative unit of approximately one hundred houses
umukomisiyoneri	a broker arranging sales between two parties
umurenge	sector, a larger administrative unit
umusaza	old man
umushoramari	investor, entrepreneur
Umushyikirano	National Dialogue

References

Abbink, J., & Kessel, I. V. (Eds.). (2005). *Vanguard or vandals: Youth, politics and conflict in Africa*. Leiden, Netherlands: Brill

Abbott, P. (2010). *Rwanda country study: Raising productivity and reducing the risk of household enterprise: Final diagnostic report*. Kigali, Rwanda: IPAR-Rwanda.

Abbott, P., & Rwirahira, J. (2010). *Millennium development goals progress report: Rwanda country report 2010*. Kigali, Rwanda: UNDP.

African Economic Outlook. (2012). *Promoting youth employment in Africa*. Retrieved from http://www.africaneconomicoutlook.org/en/theme/youth_employment/.

Anderson-Levitt, K. M. (Ed.). (2003). *Local meanings, global schooling: Anthropology and world culture theory*. New York, NY: Palgrave Macmillan.

Anderson-Levitt, K. M., & Ntal-I'Mbirwa, A. (2001). Are pedagogical ideals embraced or imposed? The case of reading instruction in the Republic of Guinea. In M. Sutton & B. A. Levinson (Eds.), *Policy as practice: Toward a comparative sociocultural analysis of educational policy* (pp. 25–58). London, UK: Ablex.

Anyon, J. (1980). Social class and the hidden curriculum of work. *Journal of Education, 162*(1), 67–92.

Apple, M. (2004). *Ideology and curriculum* (3rd ed.). New York, NY: RoutledgeFalmer.

Arjona-Tseng, E. M. (1990). *Curriculum policy-making of an emerging profession: The structure, process, and outcome of creating a graduate institute for translation and interpretation studies in the Republic of China of Taiwan* (Unpublished doctoral dissertation). Stanford University, Stanford, CA.

Athayde, R. (2009). Measuring enterprise potential in young people. *Entrepreneurship Theory and Practice, 33*(2), 481–500.

Baildon, M. (2009). "Being rooted and living globally": Singapore's educational reform as post-developmental governance. In R. Ismail, B. Shaw, & G. L. Ooi (Eds.), *Southeast Asian Culture and Heritage in a Globalising World: Diverging Identities in a Dynamic Region* (pp. 59–78). Surrey, UK: Ashgate.

Baker, T., & Nelson, R. (2005). Creating something from nothing: Resource construction through entrepreneurial bricolage. *Administrative Science Quarterly, 50*(3), 329–366.

Bale, J. (2002). *Imagined Olympians: Body culture and colonial representation in Rwanda*. Minneapolis, MN: University of Minnesota Press.

Ball, S. J. (1994). *Education reform: A critical and post-structural approach*. Bristol, PA: Open University Press.

Banerjee, A. (2011). *Poor economics: A radical rethinking of the way to fight global poverty*. New York, NY: PublicAffairs.

Barber, K. (2007). *The anthropology of texts, persons and publics*. Cambridge, UK: Cambridge University Press.

Barrett, A. M. (2007). Beyond the polarization of pedagogy: Models of classroom practice in Tanzanian primary schools. *Comparative Education, 43*(2), 273–294.

Bash, L., & Green, A. (Eds.). (1995). *Youth, education and work*. London, UK: Kogan Page.

Berry, F. S., & Berry, W. D. (1999). Innovation and diffusion models in policy research. In P. Sabatier (Ed.), *Theories of the policy process* (pp. 307–362). Boulder, CO: Westview Press.

Birdsall, N. (2011). Development's next top "model": China? India? Rwanda? Ghana? *Voices from the Center*. Retrieved from http://blogs.cgdev.org/globaldevelopment/2011/04/development%E2%80%99s-next-top-%E2%80%9Cmodel%E2%80%9D-china-india-rwanda-ghana.php.

Birdsall, N., & Fukuyama, F. (2011a). *New ideas on development after the financial crisis*. Baltimore, MD: Johns Hopkins University Press.

Birdsall, N., & Fukuyama, F. (2011b, February 23). The post–Washington Consensus: Development after the crisis. *Foreign Affairs*.

Booth, D., & Golooba-Mutebi, F. (2012). Developmental patrimonialism? The case of Rwanda. *African Affairs, 111*(444), 379–403.

Bourdieu, P. (1972). *Outline of a theory of practice*. Cambridge, UK: Cambridge University Press.

Bourdieu, P. (1977). Structures and the habitus. In H. Moore & T. Sanders (Eds.), *Anthropology in theory: Issues in epistemology* (pp. 407–416). Oxford, UK: Blackwell.

Bourdieu, P. (1986). The forms of capital. In J. E. Richardson (Ed.), *Handbook of theory of research for the sociology of education* (pp. 241–258). New York, NY: Greenwood Press.

Bourdieu, P. (1990). *The logic of practice*. Stanford, CA: Stanford University.

Bourdieu, P. (1993). *The field of cultural production*. Oxford, UK: Polity.

Bourdieu, P. (1999). The social conditions of the international circulation of ideas. In R. Shusterman (Ed.), *Bourdieu: A critical reader*. Oxford, UK: Blackwell.

Bourdieu, P., & Passeron, J.-C. (1990). *Reproduction in education, society and culture* (2nd ed.). London, UK: Sage.

Brand, U., & Sekler, N. (2009). Postneoliberalism: Catch-all word or valuable analytical and political concept?—Aims of a beginning debate. *Development Dialogue* (51), 5–14.

Bröckling, U., Krasmann, S., & Lemke, T. (Eds.). (2011). *Governmentality: Current issues and future challenges*. New York, NY: Routledge.

Bucyensenge, J. P. (2013, October 7). Hanga Umurimo inspiring innovation, says Kanimba. *New Times*. Retrieved from http://www.newtimes.co.rw/section/Email/2013-10-07/69743/.

Bumbakare, P. C. (2009) *Local taxes as impediment for SME formalisation: What is being done*. Kigali, Rwanda: Rwanda Revenue Authority.

Callick, R. (2008, May 27). The Singapore model: The city-state of Singapore may have a fix for America's healthcare woes. *The American*. Retrieved from https://www.aei.org/publication/the-singapore-model/.

Campioni, M., & Noack, P. (Eds.). (2012). *Rwanda fast forward: Social, economic, military and reconciliation prospects*. Basingstoke, UK: Palgrave Macmillan.

Chemouni, B. (2014). Explaining the design of the Rwandan decentralisation: Elite vulnerability and the territorial repartition of power. *Journal of East African Studies, 8*(2), 246–262.

Chen, S. (2011, October 21). Can the Singapore model solve US unemployment crisis? *Asian Correspondent*. Retrieved from https://asiancorrespondent.com/2011/10/can-a-singapore-model-solve-the-u-s-unemployment-crisis/.

Cheney, K. (2007). *Pillars of the nation: Child citizens and Ugandan national development*. Chicago, IL: University of Chicago.

Codere, H. (1973). *The biography of an African society: Rwanda 1900–1960, based on forty-eight Rwandan autobiographies*. Tervuren, Belgium: Musée Royale de l'Afrique Centrale.

Collins, B. (1998). *Obedience in Rwanda: A critical question*. Sheffield, UK: Sheffield Hallam University.

Crisafulli, P., & Redmond, A. (2012). *Rwanda, Inc.: How a devastated nation became an economic model for the developing world*. New York, NY: Palgrave Macmillan.

Dallaire, R. (2004). *Shake hands with the devil: The failure of humanity in Rwanda*. London, UK: Arrow.

Davis, T. (2006). *Understanding entrepreneurship: Developing indicators for international comparisons and assessments*. Paris, France: Organisation for Economic Co-operation and Development and Statistics Directorate Committee on Statistics. Retrieved from http://www.oecd.org/officialdocuments/publicdisplaydocumentpdf/?doclanguage=en&cote=STD/CSTAT(2006)9.

Deacon, R. (2006). Michel Foucault on education: A preliminary theoretical overview. *South African Journal of Education, 26*(2), 177–187.

Dean, M. (2010). *Governmentality: Power and rule in modern society*. London, UK: Sage.

Denby, N., & Hamman, D. (2009). *AQA business for GCSE: Setting up a business*. London, UK: Hodder Education.

Des Forges, A. L. (1999). *"Leave none to tell the story": Genocide in Rwanda*. New York, NY: Human Rights Watch.

D'Hooge, I. (2008). Into high gear: China's public diplomacy. *Hague Journal of Diplomacy, 3*(1), 37–61.

Dolowitz, D., & Marsh, D. (2000). Learning from abroad: The role of policy transfer in contemporary policy-making. *Governance: An International Journal of Policy, Administration, and Institutions, 13*(1), 5–24.

Dreeben, R. (1968). *On what is learned in school.* Reading, MA: Addison-Wesley.

Easterly, W. (2001). *The elusive quest for growth: Economists' adventures and misadventures in the tropics.* Cambridge, MA: MIT Press.

Education Development Center. (2009). *Rwanda youth employment assessment report.* Newton, MA: Education Development Center.

Education Development Center. (2013). *The youth perspective on entrepreneurship in Rwanda* (Unpublished policy briefing paper). Kigali, Rwanda: Education Development Center—Akazi Kanoze.

Elyachar, J. (2005). *Markets of Dispossession: NGOs, economic development, and the state in Cairo.* Durham, NC: Duke University Press.

Erny, P. (2001). *L'école coloniale au Rwanda, 1900–1962.* Paris, France: Harmattan.

Erny, P. (2003). *L'enseignement au Rwanda après l'Independance.* Paris, France: Harmattan.

Erny, P. (2005). *L'education au Rwanda au temps des Rois.* Paris, France: Harmattan.

Esiara, K. (2014, May 3). *Lack of funds threatens Hanga Umurimo project.* Kigali: Rwanda Today. Retrieved from http://www.theeastafrican.co.ke/Rwanda/Business/Lack-of -funds-threatens-Hanga-Umurimo-project-/-/1433224/2302124/-/gttme6z/-/index .html.

Esping-Anderson, G. (1990). *The three worlds of welfare capitalism.* Princeton, NJ: Princeton University.

Fairbanks, M. (Producer). (2007, July). *The entrepreneur president.* Retrieved from http:// www.youtube.com/watch?v=hS8ltTR6WYU.

Fanon, F. (1967). *Black skin, white masks.* London, UK: Pluto.

Fishlow, A. (1994). *Miracle or design? Lessons from the East Asian experience.* Washington, DC: Overseas Development Council.

Foster, P. (1965). The vocational school fallacy in development planning. In A. A. Anderson & M. J. Bowman (Eds.), *Education and economic development* (pp. 142–166). Chicago, IL: Aldine.

Foucault, M. (1975). *Discipline and punish: The birth of the prison.* Paris, France: Éditions Gallimard.

Foucault, M. (1982). The subject and power. *Critical Inquiry, 8*(4), 777–795.

Foucault, M. (1988). Technologies of the self. In L. H. Martin, H. Gutman, & P. H. Hutton (Eds.), *Technologies of the Self* (pp. 16–49). Boston, MA: University of Massachusetts.

Foucault, M. (1991). Governmentality. 1978. In G. Burchell, C. Gordon & P. Miller (Eds.), *The Foucault Effect: Studies in governmentality.* Chicago, IL: University of Chicago Press.

Foucault, M. (2016). *About the beginning of the hermeneutics of the self: Lectures at Dartmouth College, 1980* (G. Burchell, Trans.). Chicago, IL: University of Chicago Press.

Francomono, J., Lavitt, W., & Lavitt, D. (1988). *Junior achievement: A history.* Colorado Springs, CO: Junior Achievement.

Freedman, S. W., Weinstein, H. M., Murphy, K., & Longman, T. (2008). Teaching history after identity-based conflicts: The Rwanda experience. *Comparative Education Review, 52*(4), 663–690.

Friedman, A. (2012). Kagame's Rwanda: Can an authoritarian development model be squared with democracy and human rights? *Oregon Review of International Law, 253*, 253–277.

Fujii, L. A. (2009). *Killing neighbors: Webs of violence in Rwanda*. Ithaca, NY: Cornell University Press.

Fuller, B., & Snyder, C. W. (1991). Vocal teachers, silent pupils? Life in Botswana classrooms. *Comparative Education Review, 35*(2), 274–294.

Gahigana, I. (2008, 28 August). RNEC confident on exams reform. *New Times*. Retrieved from http://www.newtimes.co.rw/section/article/2008-08-27/4978/.

Gahigana, I., & Kagame, G. (2008, February 26). Education ministry reforms exam system. *New Times*. Retrieved from http://www.newtimes.co.rw/news/index.php?i=13452&a=4437.

Gatto, J. T. (2005). *Dumbing us down: The hidden curriculum of compulsory schooling*. Gabriola Island, BC: New Society.

Giroux, H. (2006). Dirty democracy and state terrorism: The politics of the new authoritarianism in the United States. *Comparative Studies of South Asia, Africa, and the Middle East, 26*(2), 163–177.

Giroux, H., & Purpel, D. (Eds.). (1983). *The hidden curriculum and moral education: Deception or discovery*. Berkeley, CA: McCutchan.

Gladwell, M. (2000). *The tipping point: How little things can make a big difference*. New York, NY: Little, Brown.

Global Entrepreneurship Research Association. (2009). *GEM 2009 APS global individual level data*. [Data file.] Retrieved from http://www.gemconsortium.org/data/sets.

Gordon, C. (1991). Governmental rationality: An introduction. In G. Burchell, C. Gordon, & P. Miller (Eds.), *The Foucault effect: Studies in governmentality* (pp. 1–52). Chicago, IL: University of Chicago Press.

Gourevitch, P. (1999). *We wish to inform you that tomorrow we will be killed with our families: Stories from Rwanda*. London, UK: Picador.

Government of Rwanda. (2001). *Law No. 51/2001 of 30/12/2001 Establishing the Labour Code*. Kigali, Rwanda: Author.

Government of Rwanda. (2003). *Law No. 23/2003 Related to the Punishment of Corruption and Related Offenses*. Kigali, Rwanda: Author.

Government of Rwanda. (2007). *Economic Development and Poverty Reduction Strategy, 2008–2012*. Kigali, Rwanda: Author.

Government of Rwanda. (2011). *MINICOM and JICA partners in "One Village One Product" program to revitalize SMEs*. Retrieved from http://www.gov.rw/MINICOMand-JICA-partners-in-One-Village-OneProduct-program-to-revitalize-SMEs.

Green, E. (2011). Patronage as institutional choice: Evidence from Rwanda and Uganda. *Comparative Politics, 43*(4), 421–438.

Hamann, E., & Rosen, L. (2011). What makes the anthropology of educational policy implementation "anthropological"? In B. A. U. Levinson & M. Pollock (Eds.), *A Companion to the Anthropology of Education* (pp. 461–477). Hoboken, NJ: Wiley-Blackwell.

Hamzeh, A. N. (2001). Clientelism, Lebanon: Roots and trends. *Middle Eastern Studies*, *37*(3), 167–178.

Harvey, D. (2005). *A brief history of neo-liberalism*. Oxford, UK: Oxford University.

Hayman, R. (2006). *The complexity of aid: Government strategies, donor agendas and the coordination of development assistance in Rwanda 1994–2004* (Doctoral dissertation). Retrieved from Edinburgh Research Archieve https://www.era.lib.ed.ac.uk/handle/1842/1766.

Hayman, R. (2007). Are the MDGs enough? Donor perspectives and recipient visions of education and poverty reduction in Rwanda. *International Journal of Educational Development, 27*, 371–382.

Heelas, P. (1991). Reforming the self: Enterprise and the characters of Thatcherism. In R. Keat & N. Abercrombi (Eds.), *Enterprise culture* (pp. 72–90). London, UK: Routledge.

Hennock, E. P. (2007). *The origin of the welfare state in England and Germany, 1850–1914: Social policies compared*. Cambridge, UK: Cambridge University.

Hill, M., & Hupe, P. (2009). *Implementing public policy*. London, UK: Sage .

Honeyman, C. (2013). *Entrepreneurship education in rwanda: A summary of research on curriculum, classrooms, and life after graduation*. Retrieved from https://www.academia.edu/11320317/Entrepreneurship_Education_in_Rwanda_A_Summary_of_Research_on_Curriculum_Classrooms_and_Life_after_Graduation.

Honeyman, C., & Rutiyomba, F. (2015). *"Why teach ubuntu? They should learn to make money, not give it away!": Incorporating social responsibility into Rwanda's entrepreneurship curriculum*. Manuscript submitted for publication.

Honig, M. (Ed.). (2006). *New directions in education policy implementation*. Albany, NY: State University of New York Press.

Honwana, A. M. (2012). *The time of youth: Work, social change, and politics in Africa*. West Hartford, CT: Kumarian Press.

Honwana, A. M., & de Boeck, F. (Eds.) (2005). *Makers and breakers: Children and youth in postcolonial Africa*. Lawrenceville, NJ: Africa World Press.

Hopma, A., & Sergeant, L. (2015). Planning education with and for youth. Paris, France: UNESCO International Institute for Educational Planning.

Hoppers, W. (2009). Participatory practices in policy-making: Negotiating democratic outcomes or manoeuvring for compliance? *International Journal of Educational Development, 29*(3), 250–259.

Huggins, A., & Randell, S. K. (2007). *Gender equality in education in Rwanda: What is happening to our girls?* Paper presented at the South African Association of Women Graduates Conference "Drop-outs from school and tertiary studies: What is happening to our girls?" Capetown, South Africa. Retrieved from http://afh-dc.org/files/FTP/project/Akilah/docs/Design%20Tools/Gender_Equality_in_Rwanda.pdf.

Huggins, C. (2013). *Seeing like a neoliberal state? Authoritarian high modernism, commercialization and governmentality in Rwanda's agricultural reform* (Doctoral dissertation). Retrieved from https://curve.carleton.ca/f042ba79-4f7f-47d6-85c4-150eb5b337e9.

Hyatt, S. B. (2011). What was neoliberalism and what comes next? The transformation of citizenship in the law-and-order state. In C. Shore, S. Wright & D. Peró (Eds.), *Policy Worlds: Anthropology and Analysis of Contemporary Power* (pp. 105–124). New York, NY: Berghahn Books.

Iliffe, J. (2005). *Honour in African history.* Cambridge, UK: Cambridge University.

Ingelaere, B. (2011). The ruler's drum and the people's shout: Accountability and representation on Rwanda's hills. In S. Straus & L. Waldorf (Eds.), *Remaking Rwanda: State building and human rights after mass violence* (pp. 67–78). Madison, WI: University of Wisconsin Press.

Inoue, K., di Gropello, E., Taylor, Y. S., & Gresham, J. (2015). *Out-of-school youth in Sub-Saharan Africa: A policy perspective.* Washington, DC: World Bank.

International Labour Organization. (2012). *History of Start and Improve Your Business.* Retrieved from http://www.ilo.org/empent/areas/start-and-improve-your-business/WCMS_159395/lang--en/index.htm.

Ismail, R., Shaw, B., & Ooi, G. L. (2009). *Southeast Asian culture and heritage in a globalising world: Diverging identities in a dynamic region.* Surrey, UK: Ashgate.

Jackson, P. W. (1968). *Life in classrooms.* New York, NY: Teachers College Press.

Jancsick, V. (1980, April 7–11). *The design of design: An ethnographic study of curriculum construction.* Paper presented at the American Educational Research Association, Boston, MA.

Jenkens, R. (2006). *Pierre Bourdieu.* London, UK: Routledge.

Jesse Jones, T. (1923). *Education in Africa: A study of West, South, and Equitorial Africa by the African Education Commission, under the auspices of the Phelps-Stokes Fund and Foreign Mission Societies of North America and Europe.* New York, NY: Phelps-Stokes Fund.

Johnson, C. (1982). *MITI and the Japanese miracle.* Berkeley, CA: University of California.

Jones, W., de Oliveira, R. S., & Verhoeven, H. (2013). *Africa's illiberal state builders* (Working Paper Series No. 89). Oxford, UK: Refugee Studies Center.

Junior Achievement. (2013). *Junior Achievement worldwide.* Retrieved from https://www.jaworldwide.org/inside-ja/Pages/Our-History.aspx.

Kagame meets for talks with Singapore Prime Minister. (2008, May 21). *New Times.* Retrieved from http://www.newtimes.co.rw/section/article/2008-05-22/3806/.

Kamugisha, J. (2008, March 19). Education loan recovery needs more streamlining. *New Times.* Retrieved from http://www.newtimes.co.rw/section/article/2008-03-19/99533/.

Karinganire, E. (2011, October 31). Rwanda still least corrupt among East African countries. *Rwanda Focus.*

Karinganire, E. (2013, January 20). Can Rwanda become like Singapore? *Rwanda Focus.* Retrieved from http://allafrica.com/stories/201301220066.html.

Kayizzi-Mugerwa, S. (2000). *Rwanda looking ahead: Reconciliation, reform and regional stability.* Stockholm, Sweden: Swedish International Development Cooperation Agency.

Kendall, N. (2007). Education for All meets political democratization: Free primary education and the neoliberalization of the Malawian school and state. *Comparative Education Review, 51*(3).

King, K. (1996). *Jua kali Kenya: Change and development in an informal economy*. Athens, OH: Ohio University Press.

Kinzer, S. (2008). *A thousand hills: Rwanda's rebirth and the man who dreamed it*. Chichester, UK: Wiley.

Kitschelt, H., & Wilkinson, S. (Eds.). (2007). *Patrons, clients and policies: Patterns of democratic accountability and political competition*. Cambridge, UK: Cambridge University Press.

Kössler, T. (2009). Towards a new understanding of the child: Catholic mobilisation and modern pedagogy in Spain, 1900–1936. *Contemporary European History, 18*(1), 1–24.

Kuremera should be premised on a sustainable approach [Editorial]. (2013, March 12). *New Times*. Retrieved from http://www.newtimes.co.rw/section/article/2013-04-26/65254/.

Kwizera, C. (2009, 30 July). Exam body introduces first practical exams. *New Times*. Retrieved from http://www.newtimes.co.rw/section/article/2009-07-30/47014/.

Kwizera, C. (2011, August 5). MINEDUC to promote learner-centred methodology. *New Times*. Retrieved from http://www.newtimes.co.rw/section/article/2011-08-05/33690/.

Lave, J., & Wenger, E. (1991). *Situated learning: Legitimate peripheral participation*. Cambridge, UK: Cambridge University.

Leftwich, A. (1995). Bringing politics back in: Towards a model of the development state. *Journal of Development Studies, 31*(3), 400.

Lemke, T. (2002). Foucault, governmentality and critique. *Rethinking Marxism, 14*(3), 49–64.

Leong, H. K. (2000). Citizen participation and policy making in Singapore: Conditions and predicaments. *Asian Survey, 40*(3), 436–455.

Levie, J., & Autio, E. (2008). A theoretical grounding and test of the GEM model. *Small Business Economics, 31*, 235–263.

Levinson, B. A., Foley, D., & Holland, D. (Eds.). (1996). *The cultural production of the educated person: Critical ethnographies of schooling and local practiced*. Albany, NY: State University of New York.

Lim, C. (2006, January 12). *Managing Political Dissent*. Paper presented at the Annual Seminar of the Institute of Policy Studies, Singapore.

Liow, E. D. (2011). The neoliberal-developmental state: Singapore as case study. *Critical Sociology, 38*(2), 241–264.

Lipsky, M. (1980). *Street-level bureaucracy: Dilemmas of the individual in public services*. New York, NY: Russell Sage Foundation.

Lugumba, S. M. E., & Ssekamwa, J. C. (1973). *A history of education in East Africa (1900–1973)*. Kampala, Uganda: Kampala Bookshop Pub. Dept.

Mains, D. (2013). *Hope is cut: Youth, unemployment, and the future in urban Ethiopia*. Philadelphia, PA: Temple University Press.

Mamdani, M. (2001). *When victims become killers: Colonialism, nativism, and the genocide in Rwanda*. Princeton, NJ: Princeton University Press.

Manu, G., Nelson, R., Thiongo, J., & Haftendorn, K. (2008). *Know about business: Training set*. Geneva, Switzerland: International Training Center of the International Labour Organization.

Maquet, J. (1954). *Le système des relations sociales dans le Rwanda ancien*. Tervuren, Belgium: Musée Royal du Congo Belge.

Margolis, E. (2001). *The hidden curriculum in higher education*. New York, NY: Routledge.

MasterCard Foundation. (2015). *Youth at work: Building economic opportunities for young people in Africa*. Retrieved from http://mastercardfdn.org/wp-content/uploads/2015/08/EOY-Thematic-Review-July-20151.pdf.

Mattee, A. Z. (1983). *The use of schools for socioeconomic transformation: A study of Tanzanian secondary school students' beliefs, attitudes and aspirations toward farming and rural life* (Unpublished doctoral dissertation). University of Wisconsin, Madison WI.

McClelland, D. (1961). *The achieving society*. Princeton, NJ: Van Norstrand.

McGreal, C. (2008). Rwanda to switch from French to English in Schools. *Guardian*. Retrieved from http://www.guardian.co.uk/world/2008/oct/14/rwanda-france.

McGrew, K. (2011). A Review of class-based theories of student resistance in education: Mapping the origins and influence of *Learning to Labor* by Paul Willis. *Review of Educational Research, 81*(2), 234–266.

McVeigh, B. (1998). Linking state and self: How the Japanese state bureaucratizes subjectivity through moral education. *Anthropological Quarterly, 71*(3), 125–137.

Meaney, T. (2000). *An ethnographic case study of a community negotiated mathematics curriculum development project* (Unpublished doctoral dissertation). University of Auckland, Auckland, New Zealand.

Meyer, D., & Carlsen, W. (2001, March 28). *Curriculum design and legitimate peripheral participation by preservice teachers*. Paper presented at the National Association for Research in Science Teaching, St. Louis, MO. Retrieved from http://ei.cornell.edu/pubs/Narst01.pdf.

Meyer, J. W., Boli, J., Thomas, G. M., & Ramirez, F. O. (1997). World society and the nation state. *American Journal of Sociology, 103*(1), 144–181.

Ministry of Agriculture and Animal Resources. (2012). *Crop intensification program (CIP)*. Retrieved from http://www.minagri.gov.rw/index.php?option=com_content&view=category&layout=blog&id=177&Itemid=38&lang=en.

Ministry of Education. (2013). *Innovation for education*. Retrieved from http://www.mineduc.gov.rw/spip.php?rubrique33.

Ministry of Education. (2014). *Backward-looking joint education sector review 2013–2014: Narrative report draft*. Kigali, Rwanda: Author.

Ministry of Education. (2015). *2014 education statistics*. Kigali, Rwanda: Author.

Ministry of Finance and Economic Planning. (2000). *Rwanda vision 2020*. Kigali, Rwanda: Government of Rwanda.

Ministry of Local Government. (2001). *National decentralization policy*. Kigali, Rwanda: Republic of Rwanda.

Ministry of Local Government. (2004). *Rwanda five-year decentralization implementation programme: Poverty reduction and empowerment through entrenchment of democratic centralisation*. Kigali, Rwanda: Author.

Ministry of Local Government. (2009). *Vision 2020 umurenge program (VUP)*. Kigali, Rwanda: Government of Rwanda.

Ministry of Public Service and Labour. (2013). *Kuremera programme will speed up job creation in Rwanda*. Retrieved from http://www.mifotra.gov.rw/index.php?id=79& L=0&tx_ttnews%5Btt_news%5D=109&cHash=87ce52f3fb7a1669bf321590eaof4f29.

Ministry of Trade and Industry. (2009). *Ministerial order N° 02/09/MINICOM of 08/05/2009*. Kigali, Rwanda: Government of Rwanda.

Ministry of Trade and Industry. (2011). *Hanga Umurimo project: Opportunities are all around you*. Kigali, Rwanda: Government of Rwanda.

Ministry of Trade and Industry. (2012, June 20). *Hanga Umurimo program: Entrepreneurs with the best business plans to be selected this week, Ministry of Trade and Industry*. Retrieved from http://41.74.172.18/t3_apps/minicom/index.php?id=77&tx_ttnews[tt_ne ws]=134&cHash=6322ed286a795c6abb26b5e36d05895e.

Mitullah, W. (2003). *Street vending in African cities: A synthesis of empirical findings from Kenya, Cote d'Ivoire, Ghana, Zimbabwe, Uganda, and South Africa* (Background paper for the 2005 World Development Report: Produced for the World Bank). Retrieved from   http://documents.worldbank.org/curated/en/2003/08/5573494/street-vending -african-cities-synthesis-empirical-findings-kenya-cote-divoire-ghana-zimbabwe -uganda-south-africa.

Moon, S. (2005). *Militarized modernity and gendered citizenship in South Korea*. Durham, NC: Duke University Press.

Morris, P. (1991). Freeing the spirit of enterprise: The genesis and development of the concept of enterprise culture. In R. Keat & N. Abercrombi (Eds.), *Enterprise culture* (pp. 21–37). London, UK: Routledge.

Mosko, M., & Damon, F. (2005). *On the order of chaos: Social anthropology and the science of chaos*. New York, NY: Berghahn Books.

Mulindahabi, C. (2015). *Obedience troubled? Exploring meanings of obedience in the post-genocide Rwanda* (Doctoral dissertation). Retrieved from Gothenburg University Library: https://gupea.ub.gu.se/handle/2077/40099.

Mwiria, K. (1990). Kenya's harambee secondary school movement: The contradictions of public policy. *Comparative Education Review, 34*(3), 350–368.

Mwiria, K. (1991). Education for subordination: African education in colonial Kenya. *History of Education, 20*(3), 261–273.

Nakayima, L. (2011, June 22). Rice trade guidelines set. *New Times*. Retrieved from http:// www.newtimes.co.rw/section/article/2011-06-22/32336/.

Napier, D. (2003). Transformations in South Africa: Policies and practices from ministry to classroom. In K. Anderson-Levitt (Ed.), *Local meanings, global schooling: Anthropology and world culture theory* (pp. 51–74). New York, NY: Palgrave Macmillan.

National Bank of Rwanda. (2010, January 12). *The Governor, National Bank of Rwanda, mobilizes citizens towards Umurenge SACCO.* Retrieved from http://www.bnr.rw/press release.aspx?id=17.

National Curriculum Development Centre. (2005). *Rapport de mission effectuée à Kampala du 24 a 29 Octobre 2005.* Kigali, Rwanda: Author.

National Curriculum Development Centre. (2008). *Introduction to entrepreneurship curriculum for ordinary level.* Kigali, Rwanda: Ministry of Education.

National Curriculum Development Centre. (2009). *Entrepreneurship education curriculum for advanced secondary level.* Kigali, Rwanda: Ministry of Education.

National Curriculum Development Centre. (2010). *Reform of the procurement and provision of learning and teaching materials for primary and secondary schools in Rwanda.* Kigali, Rwanda: Ministry of Education. Retrieved from http://www.ncdc.gov.rw/summary%20of%20textbook%20procurement%20reform.pdf.

National Curriculum Development Centre. (2008, August). *Programme d'initiation à l'entreprenariat au tronc comun.* Kigali, Rwanda: Ministry of Education.

National Curriculum Development Centre Uganda. (2000a). *Uganda advanced certificate of education entrepreneurship syllabus.* Kampala, Uganda: Author.

National Curriculum Development Centre Uganda. (2000b). *Uganda certificate of education (O Level) entrepreneurship syllabus.* Kampala, Uganda: Author.

National Institute of Statistics Rwanda. (2012). *EICV3 thematic report: Youth.* Kigali, Rwanda: Government of Rwanda.

Nelson, R. (1977). Entrepreneurship education in developing countries. *Asian Survey, 17*(9), 880–885.

Nelson, R. (1997). Entrepreneurship education as a strategic approach to economic growth in Kenya. *Journal of Industrial Teacher Education, 35*(1), 7–21.

Newbury, C. (2011). High modernism at the ground level: The imidugudu policy in Rwanda. In In S. Straus & L. Waldorf (Eds.), *Remaking Rwanda: State building and human rights after mass violence* (pp. 223–239). Madison, WI: University of Wisconsin Press.

Newbury, D. (2009). *The land beyond the mists: Essays on identity and authority in precolonial congo and Rwanda.* Athens, OH: Ohio University Press.

Newbury, D. (2011). The historian as human rights activist. In S. Straus & L. Waldorf (Eds.), *Remaking Rwanda: State building and human rights after mass violence* (pp. xxvii–xvii). Madison, WI: University of Wisconsin Press.

Ngarambe, A. (2012, February 29). SMEs pinned on tax evasion. *New Times.* Retrieved from http://www.newtimes.co.rw/section/article/2012-02-28/49991/.

Noakes, D. J. (1997). 3D work: Downsizing, de-hired and de-jobbed. *Canadian Vocational Journal, 32*(2), 6–8.

Nsanzimana, J.-C. (2012, July 30). Rwanda: Crop intensification—better communication required. *Rwanda Focus*. Retrieved from http://allafrica.com/stories/201207300794 .html.

Ntagungira, G. (2011, January 14). Why Rwanda adopted English. *New Times*. Retrieved from http://www.newtimes.co.rw/section/article/2011-01-14/96498/.

Nyesiga, D. (2012, November 14). Hanga Umurimo creates 1200 jobs. *New Times*. Retrieved from http://www.newtimes.co.rw/section/article/2012-11-14/59697/.

Ojulu, E. (2012, October 15). With a fair tax regime, RRA can help SMEs grow. *Rwanda Focus*. Retrieved from http://allafrica.com/stories/201210150085.html.

Ong, A. (2006). *Neoliberalism as exception: mutations in citizenship and sovereignty*. Durham, NC: Duke University Press.

Ooi, G. L., & Limin, H. (2002). Public space and the developmental state in Singapore. *International Development Planning Review, 24*(4), 433–447.

Organisation for Economic Co-operation and Development. (2009). *Measuring entrepreneurship: A collection of indicators*. Retrieved from http://papers.ssrn.com/sol3/ papers.cfm?abstract_id=1581491.

O'Sullivan, M. (2004). The reconceptualisation of learner-centered approaches. *International Journal of Educational Development, 24*, 585–602.

Oz, A. (2007). *Kigali conceptual master plan*. Kigali, Rwanda: OZ Architecture.

Park, I. (2007). The labour market, skill formation and training in the "post-developmental" state: The example of South Korea. *Journal of Education and Work, 20*(5), 417–435.

Paul, S., Ickis, J., & Levitsky, J. (1988). *Educating Managers for Business and Government: A Review of International Experience*. Retrieved from http://documents.worldbank .org/curated/en/1989/06/440543/educating-managers-business-government-review -international-experience.

Peck, D. (1970). Review of A. Coupez and Th. Kamanzi (ed. and tr.) *Littérature de cour au Rwanda*. *Bulletin of the School of Oriental and African Studies, 33*(3), 681–682.

Pells, K., Pontalti, K., & Williams, T. P. (2014). Promising developments? Children, youth and post-genocide reconstruction under the Rwandan Patriotic Front (RPF). *Journal of Eastern African Studies, 8*(2), 294–310.

Piattoni, S. (2001). *Clientelism, interests, and democratic representation*. Cambridge, UK: Cambridge University.

Pottier, J. (2002). *Re-imagining Rwanda: Conflict, survival and disinformation in the late twentieth century*. Cambridge, UK: Cambridge University Press.

Power, E. J. (1991). *A legacy of learning: A history of Western education*. Albany, NY: State University of New York Press.

Prunier, G. (1995). *The Rwanda crisis: History of a genocide*. New York, NY: Columbia University Press.

PSF. (2014). *Business plan competitions*. Retrieved from http://www.psf.org.rw/about-us/ services/business-plan-competions.

PSI. (2010, June). *Press releases: Rwandan cross-fenerational sex campaign enters new phase.* Retrieved from http://www.psi.org/news/press-releases/2010/06/rwandan-cross-generational-sex-campaign-enters-new-phase.

Purdékova, A. (2011). "Even if I am not here, There are so many eyes": Surveillance and state reach in Rwanda. *Journal of Modern African Studies, 49*(3), 475–497.

Purdékova, A. (2013, November). Rendering Rwanda governable: Order, containment and cleansing in the rationality of post-genocide rule. *L'Afrique des Grands Lacs: Annuaire, 2012–2013,* 355–378.

Rasheed, H. (2000). *Developing entrepreneurial potential in youth: The effects of entrepreneurial education and venture creation.* Tampa, FL: University of South Florida.

Reynolds, P., Bosma, N., Autio, E., Hunt, S., De Bono, N., Servais, I., Lopez-Garcia, P., Chin, N. (2005). Global Entrepreneurship Monitor: Data collection design and implementation 1998–2003. *Small Business Economics, 24,* 205–231.

Reyntjens, F. (2013). *Political governance in post-genocide Rwanda.* Cambridge, UK: Cambridge University Press.

Rizvi, F., & Lingard, B. (2010). *Globalizing education policy.* New York, NY: Routledge.

Robinson, P. B., Stimpson, D. V., Huefner, J. C., & Hunt, H. K. (1991). An attitude approach to the prediction of entrepreneurship. *Entrepreneurship: Theory & Practice, 15*(4), 13–31.

Rogers, E. M. (2003). *Diffusion of innovations* (5th ed.). New York, NY: Free Press.

Rollason, W. (2013). Performance, poverty and urban development: Kigali's motari and the spectacle city. *Afrika Focus, 26*(2), 9–29.

Roniger, L., & Günes-Ayata, A. (Eds.). (1994). *Democracy, clientelism, and civil society.* Boulder, CO: Lynne Rienner.

Rose, N., & Miller, P. (1992). Political power beyond the state: Problematics of government. *British Journal of Sociology, 43*(2), 173–205.

Rosen, L. (2001). Myth making and moral order in a debate on mathematics education policy. In M. Sutton & B. A. Levinson (Eds.), *Policy as practice: Toward a comparative sociocultural analysis of educational policy.* Westport, CT: Ablex.

Rubagiza, J., Were, E., & Sutherland, R. (2011). Introducing ICT into schools in Rwanda: Educational challenges and opportunities. *International Journal of Educational Development, 31*(1), 37–43.

Rwanda Development Board. (2012). *RDB launches new campaign to promote good customer service.* Retrieved from http://www.gov.rw/RDB-launches-new-campaign-to-promote-good-customer-service.

Rwanda Education Board. (2015a). *Entrepreneurship syllabus for advanced secondary level.* Kigali, Rwanda: Author.

Rwanda Education Board. (2015b). *Entrepreneurship syllabus for ordinary secondary level.* Kigali, Rwanda: Author.

Rwanda has negligible corruption—Transparency International. (2010, July 22). *BBC News Africa.* Retrieved from http://www.bbc.co.uk/news/world africa-10726324.

Rwanda National Examinations Council. (2012). *Rwanda National Examinations Council: Historical background*. Retrieved from http://www.rnec.ac.rw/page.php?His.

Rwanda Revenue Authority. (2012). *SMEs cautioned against tax evasion*. Retrieved from http://www.rra.gov.rw/rra_article947.html.

Rwirahira, R. (2012, January 23). 12-year basic education program to start in February. *Rwanda Focus*. Retrieved from http://focus.rw/wp/2012/01/12-year-basic-education -program-to-start-in-february/.

Salzano, C., Bahri, S., & Haftendorn, K. (2006). *Towards an entrepreneurial culture for the twenty-first century: Stimulating entrepreneurial spirit through entrepreneurship education in secondary schools*. Geneva, Switzerland: International Labour Organization and UNESCO.

SCE. (2011). *About us: Our story*. Retrieved from http://www.sce.gov.sg/aboutUs.asp.

Schweisfurth, M. (2006). Global and cross-national influences on education in post-genocide Rwanda. *Oxford Review of Education, 32*(5), 697–709.

Sewell, W. (2005). *Logics of history: social theory and social transformation*. Chicago, IL: University of Chicago Press.

Shariff, M. N. M., & Saud, M. (2009). An attitude approach to the prediction of entrepreneurship on students at institution of higher learning in Malaysia. *International Journal of Business Management, 4*(4), 129–135.

Shore, C., & Wright, S. (1997). *Anthropology of policy: Critical perspectives on governance and power*. New York, NY: Routledge.

Shore, C., & Wright, S. (2011). Conceptualising policy: Technologies of governance and the politics of visibility. In C. Shore & S. Wright (Eds.), *Policy worlds: Anthropology and analysis of contemporary power* (pp. 1–25). New York, NY: Berghahn Books.

Shore, C., Wright, S., & Peró, D. (2011). *Policy worlds: Anthropology and analysis of contemporary power*. New York, NY: Berghahn Books.

Shorter, A. (2006). *Cross and flag in Africa—The White Fathers during the colonial scramble (1882–1914)*. New York, NY: Orbis Books.

Singapore at 50 needs to relax a little [Editorial]. (2015, August 6). *Bloomberg View*. Retrieved from   http://www.bloombergview.com/articles/2015-08-06/singapore-at-50-needs-to -relax-a-little.

Smith, S. (2011). Youth in Africa: Rebels without a cause but not without effect. *SAIS Review of International Affairs, 31*(2), 97–110.

Snyder, B. (1971). *The hidden curriculum*. New York, NY: Knopf.

Sommers, M. (2012). *Stuck: Rwandan youth and the struggle for adulthood*. Athens, GA: University of Georgia Press.

Ssekamwa, J. C. (1997). *History and development of education in Uganda*. Kampala, Uganda: Fountain.

Ssekamwa, J. C., & Lugumba, S. M. E. (2002). *History of education in East Africa*. East Lansing, MI: Michigan State University Press.

Stambach, A. (1994). "Here in Africa, we teach; students listen": Lessons about culture from Tanzania. *Journal of Curriculum and Supervision, 9*(4), 368–385.

Stambach, A. (2000). *Lessons from Mount Kilimanjaro: Schooling, community, and gender in East Africa*. New York, NY: Routledge.

Steflja, I. (2012, May). The high costs and consequences of Rwanda's shift in language policy from French to English. *Backgrounder, 30*. Retrieved from https://www.afri caportal.org/dspace/articles/high-costs-and-consequences-rwandas-shift-language -policy-reform-french-english.

Stone, D. (2002). *Policy paradox: The art of political decision making*. New York, NY: Norton.

Straus, S. (2006). *The order of genocide: Race, power, and war in Rwanda*. Ithaca, NY: Cornell University Press.

Straus, S., & Waldorf, L. (Eds.) (2011). *Remaking Rwanda: State building and human rights after mass violence*. Madison, WI: University of Wisconsin.

Suddle, K., Beugelsdijk, S., & Wennekers, S. (2007). *Entrepreneurial culture and its effect on the rate of nascent entrepreneurship SCALES (Scientific Analysis of Entrepreneurship and SMEs)*. Zoetermeer, Netherlands: Netherlands Ministry of Economic Affairs.

Sundberg, M. (2014). *Training for model citizenship: An ethnography of civic education and state-making in Rwanda* (Unpublished doctoral dissertation). Uppsala University, Uppsala, Sweden.

Sung, J. (2006). *Explaining the economic success of Singapore: The developmental worker as the missing link*. Cheltenham, UK: Elgar.

Sutton, M., & Levinson, B. A. U. (Eds.). (2001). *Policy as practice: Toward a comparative sociocultural analysis of educational policy*. Stamford, CT: Ablex.

Tabulawa, R. (2003). International aid agencies, learner-centred pedagogy and political democratisation: A critique. *Comparative Education, 39*(1), 7–26.

Teo, M. (2008, July 15). The Singapore model: Liberal democracy works for the West—but in South-East Asia, we have different views. *Guardian*. Retrieved from http://www.the guardian.com/commentisfree/2008/jul/15/1.

Tey, T. H. (2008). Confining the freedom of the press in Singapore: A "pragmatic" press for "nation-building"? *Human Rights Quarterly, 30*(4), 876–905.

Toepper, R. M. (1978). *An ethnographic case study of the initial phases of a curriculum development effort* (Unpublished doctoral dissertation). Washington University, St. Louis, MO.

Tong, G. C. (1997). *Speech by Prime Minister Goh Chok Tong at the opening of the 7th international conference on thinking: Shaping our future—Thinking schools, learning nation*. Singapore: Ministry of Education. Retrieved from http://www.moe.gov.sg/media/ speeches/1997/020697.htm.

Triki, T., & Faye, I. (Eds.). (2013). *Financial inclusion in Africa*. Tunis, Tunisia: African Development Bank.

Trocki, C. A. (2006). *Singapore: Wealth, power and the culture of control*. New York, NY: Routledge.

UNESCO. (1999). *Second International Congress on Technical and Vocational Education: Final Report*. Seoul, Republic of Korea: Author.

UNESCO & International Labour Organization. (2002). *Technical and vocational education and training for the twenty-first century: UNESCO and ILO recommendations*. Retrieved from http://unesdoc.unesco.org/images/0012/001260/126050e.pdf.

Unsworth, S., & Uvin, P. (2002). *A new look at civil society support in Rwanda?* Unpublished paper.

Uvin, P. (1998). *Aiding violence: The development enterprise in Rwanda*. West Hartford, CT: Kumarian Press.

Uwanziga, A. (2016, January 21). *Ministiri Kanimba yanenze abashinzwe gahunda za Hanga Umurimo*. Kigali, Rwanda: Izuba Rirashe. Retrieved from http://izubarirashe .rw/2016/01/minisitiri-kanimba-yanenze-abashinzwe-gahunda-za-hanga-umurimo/.

Uworwabayeho, A. (2009). Teachers' innovative change within countrywide reform: A case study in Rwanda. *Journal of Math Teacher Education, 12*, 315–324.

van Hoyweghen, S. (2000). From human(itarian) disaster to development success? The case of Rwanda. Leeds, UK: Centre for development studies, University of Leeds.

Vansina, J. (2004). *Antecedents to modern Rwanda: The Nyiginya kingdom*. Madison, WI: University of Wisconsin Press.

Varenne, H., & McDermott, R. (1998). *Successful failure: The school America builds*. Boulder, CO: Westview Press.

Vavrus, F. (2003). *Desire and decline: Schooling amid crisis in Tanzania*. New York, NY: Peter Lang.

Vavrus, F. (2009). The cultural politics of constructivist pedagogies: Teacher education reform in the United Republic of Tanzania. *International Journal of Educational Development, 29*(3), 303–311.

Vavrus, F., & Bartlett, L. (Eds.). (2013). *Teaching in tension: International pedagogies, national policies, and teachers' practices in Tanzania*. Rotterdam, Netherlands: Sense.

Waldorf, L. (2007). Ordinariness and orders: Explaining popular participation in the Rwandan genocide. *Genocide Studies and Prevention: An International Journal, 2*(3), 267–270.

Walford, G. (2003). Introduction: Investigating education policy. In G. Walford (Ed.), *Investigating Educational Policy through Ethnography* (pp. 231–250). Oxford, UK: Elsevier Science.

Weber, M. (1978). *Economy and society*. Berkeley, CA: University of California Press.

Wharton, C. R. (1994, April 9). The nightmare in Central Africa. *New York Times*.

Wiggins, G. (1989). Teaching to the (authentic) test. *Educational Leadership, 46*(7), 41–47.

Willey, P., de Cointet, P., & Morgan, B. (2008). *The catechism of the Catholic Church and the craft of catechesis*. San Francisco, CA: Ignatius Press.

Williams, T. P. (2013). *At what cost? The untoward costs of children's schooling in Rwanda: An in-depth case study*. Kigali, Rwanda: Plan Rwanda.

Williams, T. P., Abbott, P., & Mupenzi, A. (2014). "Education at our school is not free": The hidden costs of fee-free schooling in Rwanda. *Compare: A Journal of Comparative and International Education, 45*(6).

Willis, P. (1977). *Learning to labor: How working class kids get working class jobs*. New York, NY: Columbia University.

World Bank. (2011). *Promoting entrepreneurship in Botswana: Constraints to micro business development*. Washington, DC: World Bank. Retrieved from http://docu ments.worldbank.org/curated/en/2011/03/16396993/promoting-entrepreneurship -botswana-constraints-micro-businessbrdevelopment.

World Bank. (2015). *Doing business: Measuring business regulations*. Retrieved from http:// www.doingbusiness.org.

World Bank & Singapore. (2010, November 10). *World Bank Group President Robert Zoel- lick and Singapore Minister for Finance Tharman Shanmugaratnam launch a regional infrastructure finance center of excellence*. Retrieved from http://www.worldbank.org/ en/news/2010/11/10/world-bank-group-president-robert-zoellick-singapore-minister -finance-tharman-shanmugaratnam-launch-regional-infrastructure-finance-center -excellence.

World Economic Forum. (2015). *The global competitiveness report 2014–2015*. Geneva, Swit- zerland: Author.

Wright, S. (2011). Studying policy: Methods, paradigms, perspectives. In C. Shore, S. Wright, & D. Peró (Eds.), *Policy worlds: Anthropology and the analysis of contemporary power* (pp. 27–31). New York, NY: Berghahn Books.

Yoemans, D. (2008). *Constructing vocational education: From TVEI to GNVQ*. Retrieved from http://www.leeds.ac.uk/educol/documents/00002214.htm.

Index

Page numbers followed by "f" or "t" indicate material in figures or tables.

Anthropology of Policy

Cris Shore and Susan Wright, editors

ADVISORY BOARD

Donald Brenneis

Janine Wedel

Dvora Yanow

SERIES DESCRIPTION

The Anthropology of Policy series promotes innovative methodological and theoretical approaches to the study of policy. The series challenges the assumption that policy is a top-down, linear and rational process, and a field of study primarily for policy professionals. Books in the series analyze the contradictory nature and effects of policy, including the intricate ways in which people engage with policy, the meanings it holds for different local, regional, national, and internationally-based actors and the complex relationships and social worlds that it produces.

Coercive Concern: Nationalism, Liberalism, and the Schooling of Muslim Youth
Reva Jaffe-Walter
2016

Fragile Elite: The Dilemmas of China's Top University Students
Susanne Bregnbæk
2016

Navigating Austerity: Currents of Debt along a South Asian River
Laura Bear
2015

Drugs, Thugs, and Diplomats: U.S. Policymaking in Colombia
Winifred Tate
2015